D0969504

How Did That Old Fart Get into My Mirror?

How Did That Old Fart Get into My Mirror?

• • •

A Reminiscence of My 56-Year Marriage to Mimi
and
Some of the Bumps along the way
or
Mrs. Korsakov, Can Rimsky Come out and Play?

Bob Schwarz

Copyright © 2016 Bob Schwarz
All rights reserved.

ISBN-13: 9781533018908
ISBN-10: 1533018901

For
Mimi, my wife
and
Marc, my brother

Acknowledgments

I THANK NANCY Smith who convinced me that what I was writing was worth reading, and encouraged me to keep on writing.

I also mention Mary Croghan who cried with me and put me on to Stacey Donovan, the amazing editor of my book.

Stacey made suggestions (many of which I took), but she never tried to alter my "voice."

"It's your book, Bob."

I am especially grateful for the "HaHaHa's" she managed to find space to insert between the myriad spelling and grammatical errors she pointed out in the crowded mark-up column.

I thank and embrace Cindy and Brad Loewen who shepherded me through desperate times.

There are others, too, too numerous to mention, so I won't mention them.

Springs, New York – April, 2016

Una buena risa es casi tan satisfactorio como un buen movimento intestinal.
"A good laugh is almost as satisfying as a good bowel movement."

—Anonymous

Table of Contents

Acknowledgments vii
Preface, Foreword, Introduction,
Apology and Caveats xiii

Chapter 1   It All Depends on Depends 1
Chapter 2   The Gravity of the Situation 30
Chapter 3   It's the Pressure, Darling. 39
Chapter 4   A Change of Pace 50
Chapter 5   The Heart of the Matter 62
Chapter 6   Please Pass the Trousers 76
Chapter 7   Don't be Still My Heart . . . Please! 90
Chapter 8   About Me 103
Chapter 9   Words, Word, Words 117
Chapter 10   When I Was a Lad 134
Chapter 11   Memory 148
Chapter 12   Say What? 164
Chapter 13   We return to those thrilling days
             of Yesteryear 178
Chapter 14   Moving on 198
Chapter 15   I'm Not an Old Fart yet 216
Chapter 16   Eye-Eye-Eye! 225

Chapter 17 Where there's a Will 247
Chapter 18 Don't Touch that Dial! 252
Chapter 19 The Gorilla in the Room 275
Chapter 20 The Days Are Getting Shorter now 293

Preface, Foreword, Introduction, Apology and Caveats

THE TITLE OF this book announced itself one morning a few years ago when I looked up from the washbasin into the mirror and saw an Old Fart squinting at me.

I was astonished.

We both touched the baggies under our eyes at the same time.

We both slipped our glasses on, and leaned in for a closer look.

There was no doubt about it, it was me all right.

I felt as if I had been ambushed.

I was no longer a gentleman "of a certain age."

The tipping point had been tipped.

I was an Old Fart.

Where was I while this was happening?

A few moments of further reflection, made me realize I shouldn't have been surprised.

The wear and tear of more than eighty years is enough to put an Old Fart into anybody's mirror, and you might as well go with the flow.

So with the flow I go.

Then and there I made a decision.

I told a friend that I was going to write a book about how Mimi and I got to be old.

He said, "Write fast."

The book's title suggests a less than academically rigorous approach, and although, most of the time, I've tried to keep a light touch, I do not treat my topics lightly.

I have expended considerable effort translating the descriptions of medical procedures from the original "doctorese" into a less intimidating style; sweetening the material with a bit of humor, to make the medicine easier to swallow.

However, all my descriptions have been vetted by medical professionals; the historical references have been vetted by people versed in those areas.

That is not meant to imply that students should include parts of this text in their doctorial theses, and cite them as unimpeachable.

I am not a linear thinker.

A linear thinker starts at the beginning and plods unswervingly forward following a logical plan, step-by-step, never distracted until he or she arrives at the conclusion.

I am a horizontal thinker; I jump around.

When I start a project, I may begin in the middle and then work in either direction, or skip back and forth as the whim strikes me.

So, as you read, you will be taken on a great number of side trips along with reminiscences of moments that Mimi and I shared because, as my mind picks up an echo of something, off I go.

My wife and I have not fallen victim to every disease possible as we have aged, but we've met up with a good number of them.

My descriptions of these events are as accurate as memory allows.

However, as many of you are aware, what you remember and what actually happened are sometimes not exactly the same.

Mark Twain once remarked that, unlike other older folks, his memory improved with age.

He said that as he grew older he could even remember things that never happened.

I'm sure it's the same with me.

I have also made extensive use of Wikipedia, and articles I've found on Google; if I have included any errors – and I'm sure I have – I claim them as my own.

They say that if you are going to write something, write about what you know.

I'm 84 now, and I know about getting old.

• • •

CHAPTER 1

It All Depends on Depends . . .

BEING OLD IS a lot like being young, except almost everything hurts, and what doesn't hurt, leaks.

This is the time of your life most politicians refer to as the Golden Years.

They call it that because they pander to us and they haven't arrived here yet.

To see what's waiting for them, all they have to do is look at the commercials you see on TV featuring a handsome couple strolling along a woodland trail, demonstrating how healthy and happy you'll be after swallowing their pill, or sipping their elixir, or sniffing their inhaler for only a few weeks.

Meanwhile, the announcer is rattling off a list of possible side effects that sounds as if he's reciting the index of the Merck Manual: "May cause death or diarrhea, or both."

There is no doubt that our bodies, both Mimi's and mine, which we took for granted during those run-up, ski-down decades, are not so subtly reminding us that the cogs and gears which run the machine each of us calls "me" are like any parts of any machine: subject to wear and tear.

Stairs seem to be steeper: hold on to the rail. The floor seems to be farther away, and slipperier.

Regaining your feet after having gone to your hands and knees in order to retrieve a nut that has rolled to the back wall under the workbench, can be an exercise in the opportunistic use of the environment.

I remember standing in a furniture showroom, not too long ago, watching a toddler crawl along the floor to get to a cocktail table in front of a couch. She reached up and with grim determination pulled herself to her knees; finally, passing through a moment of suspenseful teetering, she rose in triumph to a none too steady standing position.

I turned to her mother. "That's how I do it."

Regaining my feet wasn't always such an arduous task.

● ● ●

In 1956 I was in the army stationed in Munich, Germany. I was twenty-five years old, in great shape and ready for anything – well, almost anything.

I came out of the PX one wintry day, and happened to run into a former classmate I hadn't seen since high school.

After getting over the coincidence of running into each like that, we chatted for a few minutes. Before leaving, he invited me to a party he was giving for a girl he'd recently met.

As I walked through the door that evening, I immediately noticed an exceedingly beautiful woman sitting on a sofa with her legs crossed.

I couldn't help approaching her and telling her that she had a beautiful leg.

"Two of them," she said.

Of course, she was Mimi. That was the first time we spoke, and neither of us have ever forgotten that moment.

You've probably guessed that she was the one my high school friend was giving the party for.

I got a couple of drinks and Mimi and I hit it off right away.

Although Mimi was German, she spoke English beautifully, with practically no accent. I told her I was an announcer at A.F.N. (American Forces Network), and I learned that she was secretary to the Director of the Haus der Kunst; a huge museum-like structure where art exhibits were held. She liked skiing and tennis, the theatre and jazz, and before we knew it, it was late and the party was breaking up. Some people had volunteered to give Mimi a ride home so, after exchanging phone numbers, I left a little early.

The radio studios were not far from where Mimi worked and as I walked home, I had to pass the Haus der Kunst on Prinzregentenstrasse.

It was an Olympic year and even though the games were being held in Melbourne that summer, they had hoisted long Olympic banners on poles all along the front of the building.

I must have downed a few more tots of John Jamison than were good for me, or perhaps it was because I had just met Mimi; maybe a combination of both, because I was suddenly overcome with an irresistible desire to possess one of those Olympic banners.

Whoever tied them off obviously had to stand on a ladder.

Here I was, at two o'clock on an icy cold morning shinnying up the pole reaching for the cleat when behind me a car horn blared. I looked toward the street to see a VW Beetle speeding along on Prinzregentenstrasse loaded with party revelers (I recognized Mimi among them), leaning out the windows hooting and tooting and applauding.

How I got the banner down, I'll never know, but I finally had it rolled around the batten and carried it over my shoulder back to the A.F.N. studio where I was able to secret it behind a sofa in the basement.

The next morning, having put the banner business out of my mind, and not wanting Mimi to forget me, I phoned the Haus der Kunst.

I was put through, and I recognized her voice at once. "Guten tag, Buero der Direktor."

"Hi, Mimi, this is Bob. We met at the party last night."

There was a pause at her end; then in an official voice, "I'm sorry, sir, it is impossible to disturb the Direktor at the moment. One of our Olympic flags was stolen last night, and he is discussing the matter with the police."

There was a somewhat longer pause at my end, then in as calm a voice as I could muster I said, "Well, I'm terribly sorry about that, but do you think you might have dinner with me tonight? I'll be at the Wilhelm Tell at eight."

"Certainly, I'll see that he gets the message."

At a few minutes after eight, when she walked through the door, she looked even more beautiful than I remembered. She was tall and slim and very well dressed; short dark hair and eyes so blue I could tell their color from across the room.

She gave me a little wave and, as she crossed in I suddenly panicked at the thought that she must be at least six inches taller than I was, but as we shook hands I discovered thankfully, that at six feet, I was just a little taller.

We ordered and, getting directly to the point she said, "The police think it was a political act."

"Oh, no. I've got to get that flag back somehow."

"Where is it"?

"At the studio behind a sofa."

"I have an idea."

"Tell me please."

"We can carry the flag to the parking lot in back of the Haus der Kunst and leave it. There is no one there late at night and I think the watchman sleeps."

"Mimi, how am I going to carry that thing around in the streets without anybody noticing?"

She spread her hands as if the answer was obvious. "Under your overcoat."

It was awkward getting down the steps of the studio building.

We took one step at a time because a five foot baton with an Olympic flag wrapped around it was hidden under my coat and I couldn't bend my right leg.

Mimi clutched my arm, acting as if we were simply a loving couple out for a walk. I rocked along, walking as if my right leg was in a full cast. I'm sure I resembled a Rockette imitating a wooden soldier at the Radio City Christmas Show.

Whenever a car passed, Mimi would turn toward me and adjust my collar in order to cover the fact that a gilded wooden finial was sticking out up to me ear.

Luckily, the Englischer Garten, a park directly behind the Haus der Kunst, was not far away, and a few minutes later I limped awkwardly across the street into its welcoming darkness.

When we got to the parking lot, I huddled behind a tree; Mimi stepped out onto the pavement.

She tried to give the impression that she was evaluating the quality of the architectural integration of the parking lot vis-a-vis the rear of the building. Upon completing her appraisal she gave me an all clear sign.

I darted out from behind the tree – well, I didn't exactly dart, I more or less lurched forward, because I was frantically trying to unbelt the damned coat, and as it loosened the rolled-up flag started to drop out onto the parking lot.

I hobbled toward the building as quickly as I could, unbuttoning my coat and praying that the watchman was snoring away inside.

In a trice (or maybe a trice-and-a-half) I had leaned the flag against one of the doors and, with her hand in mine, Mimi and I walked casually, but briskly, toward the safety of the park.

Once out of danger, we both breathed a huge sigh of relief, had a good laugh and folded into an absolutely spectacular kiss.

• • •

That was more than half a Century ago; and neither Mimi nor I are in the fettle we were in then.

Over the fifty odd years together we've taken spills, had multiple coronary problems, broken bones, survived cancers, acquired hearing aids, suffered depression, and underwent angioplasty; the list could go on.

We've also had a hellova lot of good times on the way.

Along with the good times, I'll describe some of what happens to us as we grow old and why our aging bodies act the way they do because, even though we seem to be at the mercy of so many inevitable age-related indispositions, many of us don't know a lot about them.

A few years ago, when I went to Wikipedia to inform myself about the genesis of a certain embarrassing problem, I was amazed at how little I knew about its causes, and how difficult it was to untangle the process so that I finally felt I understood it.

So, it is in the spirit of sharing what I've learned that I have written this.

• • •

Many older folks are subject to more security leaks than the federal government.

I have never been to Olduvai Gorge. "Professor Leaky" is not my idea of a cute nickname.

Therefore, I have a personal interest in sphincters; yes sphincters, the muscles that control the flow of liquid through our bodies. Their actions dictate how far we venture from home. Their vagaries create a scrupulous balance between urge and opportunity. Their limitations dictate the amount of beverage consumption during an outing.

I am attempting to formulate an algebraic expression that will help calculate the velocity at which I must drive in order for us to arrive home from the party not high, but dry.

It will go something like: "Speed equals Need since the last time I Peed."

It needs some refining.

● ● ●

Sphincters 101

"Sphincter = a ring-like band of muscle that surrounds a bodily opening constricting and relaxing as required for normal physi-ological functioning" per Wiktionary.

I was astonished to discover that the body has over fifty dif-ferent kinds of sphincters, some of which are microscopically small. The numbers of *precapillary sphincters*, which control the flow of blood through the body, run into the billions – yes, billions.mal

The action of sphincters is observed very clearly during a celebratory occasion such as an anniversary or birthday when I present Mimi with a pretty ring or a diamond pin.

The *orbicularis oris*, the muscles that act like a sphincter around her mouth, relax allowing a large aperture to form from which the ejaculation "Wow!" issues forth. It is almost instantly followed by a constricting of *orbicularis oris* around her lips to form a sweet Cupid's bow which is pressed firmly and warmly against my constricted *orbicularis oris*.

That's amore!

Sphincters are everywhere in our bodies, and a lot of them are involved in getting what we eat and drink to where it ought to go.

There is the *upper esophageal sphincter* in the throat; it relaxes to let you swallow the grilled cheese you are eating, allowing it to enter the esophagus.

The sound of burping, *eruction,* is caused by the vibration of the *upper esophageal sphincter.*

If that muscle performed no other function, the very fact that it allows the thoroughly satisfying "buuuuuurp" that follows the ingestion of a tall cool one on a hot summer's day would be enough to praise it.

But there's more, much more.

While researching sphincters, I became fascinated with the whole process of swallowing.

Yes, swallowing, which we all do so many times a day without thinking, is an amazingly complicated cascade of muscular sequences.

You realize, of course, that there are two pipes leading down from the throat.

One is the *esophagus,* the food and drink pipe, which leads toward the stomach; the other is the *trachea* or windpipe which leads to the lungs.

You obviously want the food you swallow to go down the food pipe and you want the air you breathe to go down the windpipe.

You actually do swallow air down your *esophagus* when you eat. It doesn't do much harm. It will end up in your stomach where it will eventually be burped up or farted out. It may cause some uncomfortable bloating in the meantime, but ultimately you and possibly others, will notice its exit.

However, if the grilled cheese you swallow goes into your *trachea,* you are in for a bad fit of coughing, or maybe a Heimlich.

So, this is how nature has rigged the system to avoid the mix-ups.

Let's go back to that grilled cheese.

The digestive process begins in your mouth; chomp, chomp, chomp.

Chewing takes that bite-size piece of food, and breaks it down into more manageable bits. You chew and chew, listening as your boring luncheon companion goes on and on describing a humorous but edifying book he is writing about a long marriage and becoming old.

You've chewed that bite long enough, breaking it down, soaking it with saliva.

Without too much thought, you begin to swallow.

All hands on deck!

Your tongue moves the *bolus* (that's the mushy wad of sandwich) to the back of your mouth, aided by a group of muscles with household names like *genioglossus, styloglossus* and *hyoglossus*.

Before the chunk-a-cheese gets to the throat, the *orbicularis oris* (remember? that's the sphincter-like band of muscles around the lips) draws the lips together. Have you ever noticed how hard it is to swallow with your mouth open?

The swallowing process proceeds apace and the bolus is passed into the *pharynx*.

The pharynx is the fleshy wall at the back of the throat. It covers the empty space that extends upwards into the nasal cavity above the roof of the mouth and downwards behind the tongue. It has muscles which propel the food toward the *esophagus*.

Once the bolus arrives in the pharynx, it's "Over the teeth and past the gums, look out stomach, here it comes."

The *uvula*, that little dangly thing at the back of the soft palate, slaps up against the pharynx to prevent the bolus from going up into your nasal cavity. Very unsettling if that happens.

Next, a flap, the *epiglottis,* cleverly placed opposite the base of the tongue, slams down covering the windpipe (you can't breathe while you swallow), allowing the esophagus to remain open.

Waves of muscular contractions, *peristalsis,* conduct your blob-wich down the approximately ten-inch esophagus to the *lower esophageal sphincter* which guards the upper end of the stomach; the sphincter obligingly relaxes opening the way.

Kerplunk, or maybe splish.

The reason I've made this simplified sketch of how swallowing works is to describe the brilliantly choreographed ballet of muscular relaxations, contractions, blockings and openings that shepherd what we eat and drink to our stomach.

Something we might not think about as we pop a pill or tip down the last sip of a delightful Montrachet.

There is a sphincter at the top of the stomach which has two functions; it is supposed to relax and open up to receive sustenance from above, and once it has, it is supposed to contract and remain closed to prevent the acid and other nasty stuff in the stomach from rising back up into the esophagus.

Sometimes it doesn't remain closed, and the result can be acid reflux – the most common digestive complaint in the country. Lord knows we've all seen enough TV commercials describing it.

They say that each year Americans spend around $13 billion on liquids, capsules, caplets, pills and chewables to ease the burning burps of this affliction; the Little Purple Pill and all that.

Acid reflux may be a symptom of esophageal disease, so it's prudent to consult your practitioner if you suffer from it often.

The acid in the stomach is really strong. It is *hydrochloric* acid. Industrial strength hydrochloric acid is used to remove rust from iron or steel for processing.

The strength of the acid produced by cells in your tummy is not industrial strength, but it is strong enough to cause serious problems if your stomach walls were exposed to it.

So, coincidently, while the acid and the enzymes are working at dissolving the cheese sandwich/bolus into mush, one group of cells is producing mucus to protect the stomach walls while other cells are producing *bicarbonate of soda*; the antacid that's in Alka-Seltzer, Bromo Seltzer, and Seidlitz powders.

Bicarbonate of soda is the same thing as baking soda (not baking powder); you know, the stuff in the yellow package with the Arm & Hammer logo; a teaspoon of it in a glass of water is an old-time remedy used to neutralize the acid in acid reflux.

Because of the acidic conditions in the stomach, the lining is continuously being replaced; it is completely relined about every three days.

• • •

So far, on our journey south, we've investigated only half of the digestion process.

Won't you join me as we continue this sketchy voyage through the alimentary canal to its end?

Welcome aboard.

We learn that once the bolus is in the stomach it is broken down by acids and enzymes into a mushy liquid – *chyme* (pronounced "kime," rhymes with crime or slime). This process takes anywhere from 40 minutes to a few hours.

Then, by the good offices of the *pyloric sphincter* at the bottom end of the stomach, the chyme is transferred bit by bit to the small intestine.

The small intestine is about one inch in diameter and over 20 feet long; yes, 20 feet long.

It begins with a section about ten inches in length called the *duodenum* – pronounced "do-a-DEEN-um"; it rhymes with "you ain't SEEN-em."

There, almost all of the chemical digestion process is completed with the help of acids and enzymes secreted by the nearby "chemical industrial complex" that includes the liver, the pancreas and the gall bladder.

Most of the nutrients from the food you eat are absorbed into the bloodstream through the wall of the small intestine as the chyme is moved along by peristaltic action into the large intestine.

It's called the large intestine because it's about twice the diameter of the small intestine even though it's only about five feet long as compared to the small intestine's twenty plus feet.

Do you believe there's over twenty-five feet of plumbing curled up in your belly?

Side trip . . .

Not only do the intestines act as a conduit for the chyme, but they are also home sweet home to a group of microorganisms (bacteria) referred to as "gut flora."

If you haven't heard of gut flora, you should know that it plays a major role in the normal functioning of the body; such a major role, that many experts nowadays consider it an "organ." However, it is an "acquired" organ. Babies are born sterile. Gut flora is acquired as the baby passes through the birth canal. It makes its way into the infant's intestine, and increases as the child grows.

Gut flora works to our benefit in several ways. It helps the body to digest certain foods that the stomach and small intestine have not been able to. It helps with the production of some vitamins (B and K). It inhibits the growth of malicious bacteria, is helpful to the immune system, and there is some evidence now that gut flora influences the way the brain works.

If that isn't enough, two studies at the National Cancer Institute suggest that gut flora may increase the effectiveness of certain types of cancer treatments.

If you have ever taken antibiotics and notice changes in your toilet habits, you learn that while the medicine destroys the bad bacteria, it also destroys the good gut flora that aid in digestion; and when you consider that almost half of the solids in your stool are gut flora, it's no wonder that the loss of these bacteria result in rumbles in your belly and *mal-de-toilette*.

When I was having problems caused by taking antibiotics, my doctor recommended taking acidophilus, which is an over-the-counter form of gut flora.

It helped.

So, these little buggers are good to have around and it's gratifying to know that, according to Wikipedia, there are about 100 trillion of them residing in our intestines at any given time; more than ten times the number of cells in the rest of your body.

I tried to count them once, but I only got up to ninety-seven trillion, three hundred and fifty billion before the doorbell rang and I lost count, so you're going to have to trust Wikipedia.

Back to the intestines . . .

The large intestine connects with the small intestine on the right side of your body just above the groin. It rises almost to your ribs and takes a sharp turn across to the left side of your body, all the while absorbing water and any leftover food matter from the chyme and transferring it to the blood stream. Then it plunges down and back until it terminates in the sigmoid colon, the rectum and the anus.

The dehydrated chyme, now more or less fecal matter, moves from the large intestine to the sigmoid colon and the rectum; its final stop in the body before passing through the anus which controls its launch into outer space.

It takes twenty-four hours or more for the stool to arrive there.

The anus has two sphincters; *ani internus* and *ani externus*. One is inside the other, sort of like a shirt cuff inside a sweater cuff. Not exactly like that, but you get the picture.

Just as the vibration of the *upper esophageal sphincter* is responsible for the sonorous belch during the expulsion of gas from the stomach through the throat, so it is the vibration of the *ani internus* sphincter that upon the release of gas pressure in the colon, produces that unmistakable, and often snicker-producing "BLAAAT" of a fart.

Side trip . . .

Your typical fart is composed mainly of nitrogen and hydrogen; nearly ten percent carbon dioxide, about seven percent methane and four percent oxygen – all odorless gases.

It is hydrogen sulfide that imparts to farts their di-*stink*-tive odor, and it was with more than passing interest, and deep gratitude, I learned that hydrogen sulfide gas makes up only about one percent of the package.

Cattle and other ruminants produce most of their methane by burping, not by farting.

All creatures, great and small, with stomachs fart. This factoid puts a gastric interpretation to Cole Porter's:

> "Birds do it, bees do it,
> Even educated fleas do it . . ."

Vegans fart more than meat eaters.

Women fart as often as men; they just don't brag about it.

A "petard" which is what is meant in the famous quote from Hamlet: "hoist with his own petar." It is the French word for (you guessed it) fart.

A petard was a small explosive device used during the 16th Century to blow down doors. It was dangerous to use and was wont to explode prematurely with a flatulistic resonance, hoisting the petardier.

There is a beignet type of pastry called a Nun's Fart. It is described as "light, tender and heavenly," and if you want a chuckle, google "Farting Nun Organ."

Why nuns take farting on the chin, so to speak, is a mystery to me.

In the early 20th Century, a Frenchman, Joseph Pojul, enjoyed the "sweet?" smell of success as a professional farter. He was billed as a "Petomain" (fartomaniac), or more genteelly as a Flatulist or a Farteur or (the one I like best) a Fartiste. He exercised a preternatural and inexplicable control of his anal sphincters.

He appeared at the Moulin Rouge where the management presented him with an open-ended contract to perform his toot suite before such luminaries as Edward, Prince of Wales; King Leopold II and Sigmund Freud.

He played tunes, imitated all sorts of farm animals and musical instruments, cannonades and thunderstorms.

He could blow out a candle at twenty paces.

Back to sphincters . . .

Sphincters manage to perform their designated functions fairly well under normal conditions.

Some of us have discovered though, that certain medications, among other things, can combine to cause an urgent situation which tests their resoluteness.

On a regular visit to our gastroenterologist, Mimi complained that she had very irregular bowel habits, sometimes too fast and sometimes too slow.

What was the cause?

He looked at her list of over a dozen medications. He shook his head, shrugged and said that with all the interactions it was impossible to say what the exact cause was.

Constipation is what sends most patients to the gastroenterologist.

There are over 700 laxative and enema products being sold across the United States and over a billion dollars being spent on preparations that promote pooping and probably as much to promote the preparations that promote pooping.

It affects women more often than men and, although it is not automatic with age, there are a bunch of things that occur as you grow older; some of those may affect your toilet habits and it's likely to get worse as you age.

Thirty four percent of women and twenty-six percent of men over sixty-five complain of constipation; when they reach their mid-eighties the percentages go up.

There are many possible causes of the problem. They can involve everything from physical changes in your body, to lack of exercise, to dietary changes, to medications, even the way you breathe when you sit on the toilet.

Mimi is mostly wheelchair bound, and since she has recently returned home after a nearly three-month stay in hospitals and a rehab center, bowel habits have changed.

So, arriving at the current "Goldie Locks" amount of poop-aid (not too sticky, not too icky) can be tricky. It requires keen judgment, a fair amount of patience, a dependable washer/dryer and an outlook on life that encompasses the philosophical proposition that a little bit of shit never hurt anybody.

• • •

Kidneys are involved in the production of urine. You've got two kidneys about the size of your fist; one on each side of your body near the bottom of your rib cage. They are shaped something like a kidney bean which is shaped something like a kidney.

Every twenty-four hours your kidneys process about 200 quarts of blood and, among other tasks, they sift about two quarts of waste products and extra water. The waste and extra water become urine, which flows down to the bladder through tubes called *ureters*. There it remains until you feel the urge.

Exit from the bladder is controlled by, what else, a sphincter, the *urethral sphincter*. It, and the muscles around the bladder (*detrusor muscles*) are in charge.

In the best of worlds, when you're taking a pee, the sphincter should relax and the muscles around the bladder should contract simultaneously, forcing the bladder to empty. But, sometimes, things don't coordinate properly and the sphincter closes before the bladder is completely voided.

Then it fills up faster than ordinarily and you're off to the races.

TV commercials depict men answering an urgent call by dashing to the small room, even at the most exciting moment in the ball game; female relatives, rush unwillingly from the fitting room, missing the final adjustments to their niece's wedding dress.

Tant pis.

Slight digression . . .

Interruptions at sporting events may be avoidable, however, if you avail yourself of a *"Stadium Pal."*

"Stadium Pal?" you ask.

"Yes, Stadium Pal," I respond.

It is a jim-dandy gadget that is actually an external catheter attached to a plastic bag taped onto your calf.

According to the description, the catheter is similar to a condom. It comes in assorted widths and must be cut to the appropriate length.

It goes without saying that the condom is to be cut to length before it is slipped on.

The plastic bag holds slightly more than a quart of liquid, which should easily get you through the first few innings.

Don't feel neglected, ladies; you will be pleased to learn, there is an *aide-de-pipi* designed with you in mind.

Stadium Gal is on the market, appropriately modified to accommodate the female form, operating on much the same principal as the aforementioned Stadium Pal.

Back to the bladder . . .

The bladder can hold almost two cups of liquid, but a variety of factors determine how quickly your drink prompts the urge.

If you have just exercised and your body is dehydrated you will hold liquids longer because you are replacing the liquids that were lost perspiring.

But the average amount of time that elapses between the time you take a good slug of Snapple, or empty a cup of Darjeeling Second Flush, is about forty-five minutes.

Bladder problems can cause one to have to "go" several times during the night. If the urge is urgent and it causes you to rush, you are putting yourself in danger of falling.

An effective precaution is to have a commode next to your bed. A commode is a potty chair, quite stable and easy to use. You place it half a step from your bedside and all you do is roll out of bed, turn, sit and do your business. Men can sit too!

• • •

As long as we're on the toilet . . .

Toilet-like devices were being sat upon in the Indus Valley Civilization as early as 3000 BCE. They were benches situated above simple flowing-water sewage systems.

Convenience devices of this sort were in use in Greek and Roman times.

If you didn't have running water the receptacle of choice was a pot or a hole in the ground, or simply the ground.

The commode is an old and well-established device for self-relievation. (My word.)

The name "commode" comes from the French word "conve-nient," and believe you me, it applies.

It is named for the low cabinet or chest of drawers that was introduced in France in the early 1700s.

Eventually this cabinet or commode proved to be a conve-nient place to stow the chamber pot.

When society wasn't so ipsy-pipsy about bodily functions, commodes were secreted behind screens in drawing rooms so that guests could perform their necessities and not miss out on the gossip.

During the Victorian period, chamber pots were commonly presented as a wedding gift. They were often inscribed with whimsical verses:

This pot it is a present sent.
Some mirth to make is only meant.

We hope the same you'll not refuse,
But keep it safe and oft it use.
When in it you want to piss
Remember them who brought you this.

I had an aunt who would send a case of toilet paper as a wedding gift.

The word "toilet," when applied to that ubiquitous porcelain convenience of which we avail ourselves, has evolved in a round-about way from its root meaning. Its genesis is from Greek and Latin words that mean textile; it came into the French with the word "*toile*"— cloth, used to cover the table where, in the morning, madams and doubtless many monsieurs, made their faces ready to face the world.

By extension, "toilette" came to describe the event itself, where all the ointments, unguents, emollients, powders, combs, brushes, mirrors and the rest of the impedimenta involved in prettying up came into play.

After toilette became synonymous with the event, by another extension the toilette became the chamber in which one performed all the activities described above, including washing.

Because of the presence of flowing water the aforementioned porcelain convenience was established there; thence the name of the room became attached to the convenience itself.

A flush toilet had been invented in England by John Harrington in 1596. He made two of them; one for himself and the other for his godmother, Queen Elizabeth.

His invention must have been a glorified commode with a valve that released water to wash it out.

In any event, it surely provided the first Royal Flush.

Apparently, the queen preferred her other thrones, since the noise of the water rushing through the valves was so loud that it announced her every movement to one and all; so only two of these were made.

Until the middle of the 19th Century, the commode or something like it, remained the seat of power.

Folks used the chamber pot – the "thunder mug" – at night, and would either take it out themselves in the morning or have the "chambermaid," who took care of things in the bedchamber, do the emptying.

But in large cities like London, by the 1850s, the amount of waste that was dumped into open cesspits and barrels on the streets, or simply being tossed out the window ("look out below") finally caused the "Great Stink" of the summer of 1858, not to mention the cholera epidemics.

The government prohibited getting rid of waste by tossing in into the streets.

Parliament appropriated three million pounds (over a quarter of a billion pounds in today's money) to have Joseph Bazalgette, a civil engineer, remedy London's problem by designing and supervising the construction of 550 miles of sewers (more or less, depending on what you read), which he finished in 1870.

They are still in use today.

A hundred years previously in 1775, Alexander Cummings was the first to patent a design for the flush toilet. His great contribution was to apply an S-shaped trap at the bottom of the toilet; after flushing, the trap filled with water and prevented the cesspit odors from returning into the small room.

Fundamentally, however, things hadn't changed; flush toilets weren't in general use until the sewer system was finished.

That happy moment coincided with the arrival of a plumbing entrepreneur with a name that still echoes down the hallowed corridors of sanitary engineering.

One can almost hear the trumpets sounding when Thomas Crapper arrived upon the scene.

He didn't invent the flush toilet; he was a manufacturer of sanitary equipment, and what he manufactured was top quality.

Better yet for him, he knew how to promote himself.

He caused a sensation by displaying his toilets behind large plate glass windows at street level.

Victorian ladies would faint away.

But, as they say, there is no such thing as bad publicity.

His superior product was ordered by none other than HRH the Prince of Wales (later Edward VII) for Sandringham, his new country residence.

You couldn't have a better advertisement than to have your toilets sat upon by His Royal Highness's royal hiney.

Because of connections like that, Mr. Crapper sold a lot of toilets and he made a lot of money.

It may surprise you to learn that Mr. Crapper's name was not the source of the word "crap."

Apparently, "crap" was in use long before Thomas Crapper was born; it is of Middle English origin and it means . . . well . . . crap.

It is simply a coincidence that Thomas Crapper's name and his plumbing supply business arrived on the scene at that particular moment.

Installed with most of his devices were large plaques proclaiming that the manufacturer was Thomas Crapper & Co.

"Crapper," as a euphemism for toilet, was not in use in America until around the time of the First World War when many US service personnel had the opportunity to visit the small rooms across the pond.

Although, "crap" did not derive from Mr. Crapper's name, there is little doubt in my mind that "crapper" did.

Some men and women are born to have their names associated with enduring historical monuments: Constantine to Constantinople, Marie Curie to Curium, Pope Sixtus to the Sistine Chapel.

Then there is Thomas Crapper.

Nick Valéry writes in *The Economist*: "More even than the miracle of antibiotics, the flush toilet has done most to rid us of infectious disease. Without plumbed sanitation within the home to dispose of human waste, we would still be living in a brutal age of cholera, dysentery, typhus and typhoid fever—to say nothing of bubonic plague."

That's all well and good but currently over forty percent of the world's population doesn't have access to a toilet; they poop alfresco or otherwise lack adequate sanitation facilities.

Even in urban areas where household and communal toilets are more available, many of them are connected to septic tanks that are not safely emptied or use systems that discharge raw sewage into open drains or surface waters. Poor sanitation contributes to about 700,000 child deaths from diarrhea every year.

So, over 500 years after the proto flush toilet was invented, getting rid of human waste is still a major problem in much of the world.

• • •

Toilet paper; whence?

In 6th Century China we find the first documentation of the use of "TP", or rather the non-use of it.

Yan Xhitui, a Chinese scholar, calligrapher, painter, musician, and government official wrote: "Paper on which there are quotations or commentaries from the *Five Classics* or the names of sages, I dare not use for toilet purposes."

I should say not!

Millions of sheets of toilet paper were manufactured in China in the 14th Century.

During the Ming Dynasty, over 700,000 sheets were manufactured for the imperial court alone; each sheet of paper was two by three feet.

Your guess is as good as mine.

Records show that some of the paper was especially soft and perfumed.

Paper was expensive, though, and if you weren't a Chinese courtier, you probably had to resort to other methods for the next few hundred years.

The list of cleansing aids that were pressed into service is long: fabrics, furs, foliage, feathers, scrapers and scoops; even corncobs – I shudder.

In the early 1850s, Rabelais' character Gargantua, after investigating many possibilities, decided that the best option is "the well downed neck of a goose".

A hundred and fifty years later, in the late 1850s, toilet paper rolled up on the shores of the new world.

It was manufactured by Joseph Gayetty, who is said to be the "father" of modern commercially-produced toilet paper in the US.

He sold his product in packs of 500; it was scented and adorned with his name watermarked on each and every sheet.

People were so sensitive about human waste by then that he had to sell the tissue as a nostrum that prevented hemorrhoids.

Apparently hemorrhoids weren't as sensitive a subject as toilet paper.

But the product was very expensive, so the majority of Americans lived with their hemorrhoids and had to make do-do with the Sears Roebuck catalogue, the *Farmer's Almanac*, newspapers, or whatever else they could lay their hands on.

In 1890, the Scott brothers presented America with toilet paper on a roll – "hold the mayo . . . Please!"

More and more flush toilets were put into use as time went on and the methods of producing TP improved accordingly.

It must have shaken the tweezers industry to its very pincers when, in 1930, Northern Toilet Paper announced the introduction of a "splinter-free" product.

You can just imagine the outcry when, in the 1930s, Sears Roebuck and Co., not wanting to be behind *The Times*, changed over to glossy paper.

In 1964, Mr. Whipple became the face of Charmin TP. He squeezed the rolls for more than twenty years and, in 1978, according to one poll, he was the third best known man in the United States after Richard Nixon and Billy Graham. Draw your own conclusions.

Just in time for Mr. Whipple to do his squeezing, the fluffy puffy, double quilted, velvety stuff began to appear.

People love it and it has become the roll of choice among the toilet seat elite.

It has a drawback, however: it can't be made with recycled paper; more live trees have to be harvested in order to produce it.

This has caused Greenpeace and other environmental groups to mount a campaign to promote the use of recycled TP.

Marcal produces a TP that they claim is made from 100 percent recycled paper. It is slightly grayer than other brands because they don't use bleach in the manufacturing process.

It's probably not as soft as a goose's neck, but my bottom line is that if it helps the environment, even a little, use it.

As globalization continues, there will be more and more Sheratons, and Hiltons, and Holiday Inns built, each with many, many flush toilets that use toilet paper.

That will only add to the huge amount of human waste that has to be reckoned with.

A paperless toilet has been introduced in Japan. It washes, rinses, blow dries and even has a heating element for those shivery cold days; just be thankful it doesn't iron out the wrinkles.

Seventy percent of households in Tokyo have one of these devices installed and, according to the prospectus, it is not only paperless, it uses less water per flush than our porcelain pots.

It, or something like it, could solve the TP problem, but at over $2,500 a crack, it doesn't seem that's going to happen soon.

Currently, however, toilet paper is a necessity; we spend about six billion dollars a year on it, and it isn't going to get the bum's rush anytime soon.

The average person visits the toilet over five times a day, almost 2,000 times a year; during a lifetime of eighty years at five minutes or so per pot-squat, he or she will pass between one and a half and three years there, depending on how long it takes to do the puzzle.

They will use over 400 million miles of TP each year (Mr. Whipple, wherever you are, take note).

Poll after poll indicates that the majority of users prefer to have their toilet paper come off the top of the roll, not the bottom.

A humiliating statistic is that about one in five people who use cell phones in the bathroom drop them down the toilet . . . "Oh, shit!"

Mark your calendar, gang, November 19th is "World Toilet Day."

During the festivities, Elton "John" has been invited to perform, and in "loo" of another venue, the celebration will be held in Queens at Flushing Meadow.

Back to the bladder . . .

Pee problems are not an inevitable part of becoming an Old Fart, but the majority of older people do suffer them. The Urology Care Foundation estimates that "up to fifty percent of women and thirty percent of men will have bladder control problems (BCP) during their lifetime."

Why didn't mother ever tell me?

The strains related to bearing children may contribute to the predominance of BCP among women, but seeing that more than a quarter of those with BCP are men, that can't be the only reason.

As far as I know, not many men have the equipment to bear children, but they do have a prostate gland which surrounds the *urethra*, the canal through which urine passes out of the body.

The prostate can enlarge, squeezing the urethra, causing a reduction in the flow of urine.

This irritates the bladder, causing it to contract even when it ordinarily wouldn't need to.

Over the years I have become an authority on urgent trips to the small room.

If I were ever asked to sift through history and list the greatest boons ever granted to humankind, fire and the wheel might have to give way to Wet Ones and disposable diapers.

● ● ●

After "The Olympic Banner Affair," Mimi and I began seeing each other regularly.

I bought a used VW beetle so Mimi and I could travel together.

Mimi asked me if I could ski.

When I was a kid I had skied on a golf course near where we lived, so I said, "Sure."

We made a reservation at a pension near Kitzbuhel in Austria.

I had no idea what I was letting myself in for. My golf course was nothing more than a series of gentle slopes; these were Alps!

As we approached the cable-car station, and I looked up to see the towering mountain of white soaring toward the heavens, a feeling of apprehension began to assert itself.

In the gondola, as I watched the village recede until it became nearly undistinguishable, apprehension was replaced by foreboding.

When I stepped out of the cabin, it was as if the only part of my skis that touched the mountain top were the three inches under my arches. Skiers next to me pushed off and disappeared over the edge in a fraction of a second.

At that point, forboding vanished completely – replaced by dread.

"Come on, let's go." And off she went.

As I slid over the edge, my dread blossomed into terror.

I feel proud of the fact that I made two turns before I went ass-over-teakettle sliding on my kisser.

When I looked up out of the snow, there was Mimi sidestepping on her skis back up toward me.

When we finally got me to my feet and I looked around, I saw that I was standing on a pitch so steep I was amazed people could actually stick to it.

Nevertheless, bit by bit and traverse by traverse, we slowly descended the slope.

We had started late and by the time we were halfway down the sun passed behind the mountain and a chill set in.

The snow started to freeze.

By then I was doing a brilliant snowplow and Mimi was guiding me, skiing down the slope in front of me – backwards.

I skied like an ass, I felt like an ass, and half the time I was sliding on my ass.

When we finally reached the bottom, the lights in the village were twinkling in the dusk and we were teeth-chattering cold.

We made our way to our pension and opened the door to our room where it felt as if it were 100 degrees below zero inside, because the maid had left the window open to air out the featherbed which was still lying over the sill.

Luckily we had brought along a bottle of raspberry brandy which we disposed of as we snuggled; warming up the featherbed and each other.

CHAPTER 2

• • •

The gravity of the situation . . .

In 1957, when I was discharged from the army, I wore a 44 long jacket and my slacks measured 32 inches at the waist. I was in terrific shape. At the ripe old age of 84 my chest measurement isn't what it used to be, and my girth is now nearly 40 inches around.

I'm not trying to suggest that this state of affairs was all caused by gravity. I readily admit that I have tucked away a great many hearty meals since 1957. I have enjoyed plenty of wine and lately I have not indulged overmuch in exercise.

That said, I still feel strongly that if gravity had not tugged at me all these years, my pear shape would not have become as distorted as those wax figures in Madame Tussauds' museum when Vincent Price sets the place on fire.

So, I decided to find out what I could about gravity. What is it?

The circumference of the earth is about 24,000 miles, so simple math tells you that if you are standing on the earth's equator, the earth would spin you through space at more than 1,000 miles per hour in order to get you back to the same spot nearly twenty-four hours later.

Of course, you wouldn't be in the same spot because the earth has moved in relation to the sun, and the sun has moved in relation to the Milky Way, and the Milky Way has moved in relation to the universe, and if – as some astrophysicists, and some half-astrophysicists postulate – there are an infinite number of universes, then where are you standing, I ask you?

I don't know how we got to this point (string theory and all that), but what I was trying to say is that the earth is spinning pretty fast. So fast, in fact, that skeptics pooh-poohed the idea of rapid rotation, saying that if the earth was spinning that fast, people on the equator would be flung off into space; it would be raining up, and so forth.

But the folks who live in Ecuador are not clinging upside down to the treetops. Donkeys are not fitted with magnetic donkey shoes to stay grounded.

How can that be?

Gravity, that's how.

Please don't ask me to explain what gravity is. Even Sir Isaac Newton and Albert Einstein couldn't explain what gravity is, though Sir Isaac did figure out how gravity works.

He came up with mathematical formulae which allow physicists to determine how much gravitational attraction an egg has on the earth as contrasted to how much gravitational attraction the Earth has on an egg.

Splat!

The Earth has more.

Neptune is more than two and three quarter billion miles from the sun, yet mutual gravitational attraction keeps it in its orbit.

Mutual gravitational attraction is universal; and this titanic force that makes galaxies rotate, keeps planets in their orbits and causes tides to ebb and flow on the Earth's oceans, do you know what else it does?

It makes baggies under my eyes.

Do you believe it?

At this very moment while the Horsehead Nebula is hurtling toward the edge of the Universe my baggies are getting dragged down. Black Holes suck stars into them, and my baggies sag a little. Meteors are drawn into our orbit and explode cataclysmi-cally, and my pouches sag just a little more.

Each moment Big G is a'pullin' on yer: pullin' on yer baggies, pullin' on yer boobs, pullin' on your belly, pullin' on yer buns – ever part-a-you.

No place to hide.

Gravity drags on your upper body and makes you walk slumped over.

I have to remind myself to stand up straight; stop dragging my feet.

Then I am able to walk like any other normal human being. My gait is regular and my stride confident. My head is high, and there is purposefulness about me.

When I forget to remind myself to stand up straight, which is most of the time, I walk bent forward from the waist as if I'm trudging into the face of a Category 5 hurricane.

I shuffle a bit and rock from side to side.

Yesterday, I was walking up to a store where I was going to shop for dinner. As I approached the glass door, I saw my reflection. There I was rocking, rolling and shuffling as I moved along.

I reminded myself of something. It took me a few seconds to realize what it was.

Suddenly, it came to me, and I said to myself, "I'm walking like a ghat damn penguin!"

I was rocking back and forth, taking funny little steps with my arms stiff out to the side. All I needed was a white jumpsuit and a black bellhop jacket to look as if I had just popped out of McMurdo Sound onto the sidewalk.

It's the Old Age Shuffle, which is a sub-section (under Ramifications) of Old Fart Syndrome.

I'm simply not that high steppin' dude I used to be.

Old Age Shuffle can be caused by lack of muscle tone, a loss of coordination between the brain and the muscles; other things too, but gravity has something to do with it.

If you see an elderly gentleman stumble slightly and reach out to balance himself when he steps up onto the curb, you may be witnessing the effects of arthritis, or failing vision, or neuropathy, or balance problems, or the interactions of medications, or the wrong shoes, or it may be that he had been distracted by the cute behind behind the cute brunette he's walking behind.

Of course, it's also possible that the old coot is crocked.

Shuffling when you walk can lead to tripping over things: curbs, area rugs, toys, wires on the floor, your cat; things like that. Tripping can lead to falling, and falling can lead to hitting the ground hard; hitting the ground hard can lead to severe damage.

If you fall once, the chances are that you will fall again within half a year, and as the old saying goes: "If the brick hits the pot or the pot hits the brick, it's going to be bad for the pot."

As you get older, the risk of falling increases.

Katie Hafner, in a 2014 *New York Times* article, reports that according to the Centers for Disease Control and Prevention almost 24,000 deaths in the United States were related to falls in 2012 alone; nearly double the amount that occurred just ten years previously.

From 2002 to 2012 more than 200,000 people over sixty-five died after falls.

The percentage of old-timers that die from falls is increasing. No one is quite sure why, but it's a sad fact that that a quarter of seniors who suffer a hip fracture will die within six months.

I've been very lax in doing something about my posture.

Although there could be medical reasons for it, I'm convinced that in my case it's because I've been too lazy to get off my duff and exercise properly; and since I am the caregiver and homemaker for Mimi and me, I figure that I should try to stay as healthy as I can.

I know that there are many exercises I can do at home that would be good for me. I've tried Tai Chi at home and yoga at home, and various other training routines that I got off the Internet.

I would do each one in the morning for a day or two.

Then, instead of exercising in the morning, I would put it off until the afternoon; only to make some excuse that would defer it until the next day.

I'd soon realize guiltily that I hadn't done any exercise for a week. Ultimately, that particular regimen would drift into the past like flotsam floating down the river passing out of sight over a waterfall.

It's different if you get professional help at a gym. You'll have set aside a definite time, you're away from home and you have someone directing you, "Do that fifteen times – three reps." You're not concerned with shopping or answering the phone or other quotidian activities.

So, starting next week I'm going to go to a trainer and begin a strengthening and stretching routine.

I am!

Since I made that declaration, I've begun to attend a physical therapy session twice a week along with Mimi.

It has made a huge difference, especially in my ability to transfer Mimi out of her wheelchair.

Side trip . . .

Mimi developed Type 2 diabetes after a fall in 1985. There is some discussion as to whether trauma causes diabetes in adults, or simply unmasks the latent disease. At any rate, the diabetes has caused neuropathy in her Mimi's feet. She has little feeling in the bottom of her feet and has trouble balancing. She used a cane, but she took another bad spill a couple of years ago, and broke her right arm and injured the area around her hip. After a stay in the hospital, she was in rehab for three weeks, but they were never able to get her back to where she could walk securely. She now uses a walker, and sometimes a wheelchair.

In a way I'm glad, because when she used the cane she walked like those tightrope walkers who you are constantly afraid will slip off the cable and go kerplunk.

The tightrope walkers don't usually go kerplunk.

Mimi kerplunked.

Now she is much more stable on her walker, and her chances of falling are greatly reduced.

Back . . .

A lot of old people don't want to use canes or walkers. They don't want people to think they're old.

A month or two ago I was taking a stroll, (or what passes for a stroll as I trudge along) and happened to pass the home where an acquaintance lives. She had just closed the gate and started to hobble toward her car door. She reached out like a trapeze artist who had just let go of the swinging bar, hoping against hope that her partner would be somewhere out there to grab on to.

I helped her to her car and asked, "Sylvia why aren't you using a cane?"

"If I use a cane, they'll all think I'm old."

I looked her directly in the eye. "My dear, you *are* old. You don't want to be falling down."

She said I was right and that she'd think about it.

I don't know if she ever started using a cane. I only bring it up to point out that vanity can get in the way of good sense.

I see it all the time; Old Farts, who look as if they're doing the breaststroke, swan along, their arms swimming through the air as if parting the waters.

What is it about aging that affects your balance?

Overseeing balance is the primary function of the *vestibular system*.

The what?

I'd never heard of it either, but as it turns out, we rely on it every time we turn our head, get up out of a chair or walk across the room.

The vestibular system is a group of organic gyroscopes and accelerometers in our inner ears that sense our body's motion, balance and spatial orientation at any given moment.

This system is constantly updating this information and sending instructions to the eyes and muscles to help us navigate.

When the system is working as it should, it provides us with a remarkable ability to sense the direction and speed at which we are moving and still maintain balance, even when it would seem as if our spatial orientation should be totally screwed up.

Think of a cheerleader doing backflips, or a skater spinning triple toe loops.

If you are in your eighties you are not liable to be performing triple toe loops unless you are totally out of control sliding down an icy slope.

Growing old can cause a few glitches to develop in the vestibular area: spatial disorientation, vertigo and dizziness.

So if you fall, negligence might not be the only reason; it could also be that your balance equipment is rusty.

Those little gyroscopes and accelerometers are probably not working as well as they did when they were fresh out of the box.

Try standing on one foot for one minute – maybe thirty seconds – twenty seconds? – try ten seconds, or even five.

You'll most likely be surprised at how difficult it is.

By the way, if you're intending to stand on one foot for any length of time be sure to have a sturdy chair within easy reach.

They say exercise may help improve your balance, especially Tai Chi; but how many of us have the gumption to begin, or the stick-to-itiveness to keep it up?

Recently I've discovered "pickle ball". You may know about it, but not a lot of folks around here do. I have to explain it to almost everybody. It's a badminton/ping-pong/tennis-like game that's played indoors or outdoors over a low net on a badminton-sized court with wooden paddles and a Wiffle ball.

It can be played at any level, and it is ideal for older people like the dozen of us who show up and play an easygoing friendly game suited to our abilities.

You move around and get a lot of exercise. My vestibular system is getting a workout.

In this country, as many as thirty-five percent of adults aged forty or over — nearly seventy million people — have experienced some form of vestibular problem; dizziness or vertigo or both.

No matter what the reason, at least thirty percent of people over sixty-five have difficulty walking three city blocks or climbing one flight of stairs, and around twenty percent need some sort of a mobility aid to get around.

"Hand me down my walkin' cane."

In one study, gait disorders were detected in about twenty-five percent of people seventy to seventy-four years old, and in nearly sixty percent in those eighty to eighty-four; it gets worse as you grow older.

The University of Mississippi has an extremely informative website filled with "Vestibular Exercises." If you suffer from dizziness or have trouble balancing you might want to investigate.

Or maybe google pickle ball and see if you can find a group in your area.

• • •

When Mimi's parents were alive, we used to travel to Munich to see them and we would almost always make our way to Venice. It was Mimi's favorite place.

When we landed at Marco Polo Airport, Mimi would head directly to the water taxis. No vaporetto for Mimi. We would climb aboard and off we would go into the twilight, speeding across the lagoon toward Venice sparkling in the distance.

It was magical.

Of course, we stayed at the Victoria Regina on the Grand Canal.

We breakfasted on our balcony across from the Santa Maria della Salute watching the traffic on the canal, barges delivering vegetables, or flowers, or piled with mysterious boxes and barrels; pleasure boats and gondolas and vaporettos; even an occasional brave kayaker.

A late morning stroll to buy yet another Venetian glass bottle (we have a couple dozen); lunch at a wine bar and coffee at Caffé Florian on Piazza San Marco – what a show!

Mimi loved it. I did too.

Once when we were crossing the Academy Bridge, I looked down into the canal and pointed to all the junk that was floating in it.

Mimi said, "In my memory it will be perfectly blue and crystal clear."

That's how she remembers it.

CHAPTER 3

— • • • —

It's the pressure, darling.

THE FIRST THING that happens when Mimi or I visit our caregiver is that our "vitals" are checked.

Vitals include your general appearance, what medications you are taking, pulse rate, blood oxygen level, weight, and your blood pressure – those sorts of things.

After all the questions have been asked and answered, I step on the scale. If you are like me, you wish you had worn a lighter pair of shoes, and left your wallet stuffed with credit cards locked in the trunk of the car.

I watch resignedly as the nurse coaxes the sliding weight to the right. At that moment I think I should have worn a thinner pair of trousers, and had not put on socks. The weight gets to the end of the bar, and the damned thing still hasn't tripped the balance.

Perhaps if I hadn't worn my wristwatch and wedding ring; removed my glasses, left the loose change on my dresser, clipped my toe nails . . .

By now the nurse has moved the fifty-pound indicator up a notch and a few coaxings later I read the bad news.

Ah, well.

After the temperature and the pulse, the nurse takes that black Velcro cuff off the wall and prepares to take my blood pressure.

Blood pressure (BP) is the pressure that blood puts on the walls of your arteries as it courses through your body; it is one of the most important vital signs.

If it is high (*hypertension*), it is putting extra pressure on your arteries and can eventually cause a whole series of bad things to happen including stroke and heart attack.

If it is low (*hypotension*), it can result in fainting and falling which is not what you want to happen when you are an Old Fart.

BP doesn't stay the same all the time. It lowers as you sleep and rises when you wake up; it also rises when you're excited, active or nervous and upset, as I was a while ago.

● ● ●

Side trip . . .

Most of the time I think I have myself under control; I don't think I get nervous.

I had noticed that Mimi had been spitting up bits of food for some time.

She would swallow and then cough it up.

Sometimes, something will go on for a while and you don't really notice it.

All of a sudden – wham!

I thought, "Good grief, why can't she swallow?"

Mimi is a two-time cancer survivor and here she is spitting up food.

I don't have to tell you where I was going.

I tossed and turned until 3:00 or 4:00 a.m. First thing the next day I called Ken Dodge.

Ken is a physician's assistant who had been a Navy medic in the Vietnam War. He's been taking care of us for the last forty years.

There are probably more than 10,000 registered PAs in New York; his PA registration number in New York State is 100, so he's been at it a long time.

That afternoon when I showed up at his office, I was sure I was going to have a calm and sensible chat with Ken.

While I was waiting for him the nurse gave me the obligatory exam. She read my BP and remarked that it was rather high.

I didn't make the connection.

Ken came in and I told him about Mimi not being able to swallow.

He immediately said that I should take Mimi to Dr. Georgeopolus. He is our very competent gastroenterologist. He is a nice guy and I refer to him as Dr. George-oscopy (but not to his face).

I said I didn't want to see Dr. George, because if he found something terrible, I don't know what I'd do, and if there was nothing wrong then there was no need to see him.

You can tell I didn't major in logic.

I went on like that for several minutes.

I was near tears when I finished. Ken said that it was entirely up to me, but that it was always best to know what the problem is and what your options are.

The way he said it made me realize that I was not the first jerk who had come to him with a similar story and mixed-up logic.

As an afterthought, I said that for some reason my blood pressure was a little high.

He waved his hand and said that he wasn't even going to look at my blood pressure.

Aha!

It all turned out OK.

I bit the bullet. There had been a cancellation and we got an appointment with Dr. George the next afternoon.

I was thinking upper endoscopy. That's where the doctor anesthetizes you and puts a scope down your throat and takes a gander at what's happening in your esophagus.

You can tell that I'm the kind of guy who always looks at the bright side.

In talking to Doctor George I remembered that Mimi had had many of her teeth removed and that chewing hard food was a problem, but she swallowed soft foods well.

He said he understood but that he'd still like to check. He'd order a less invasive procedure.

I like it when doctors say "less invasive."

He told us that he would order an "esophagram."

I immediately imagined answering a knock at our door and opening it to a lad in uniform who would hand me a yellow envelope and sing out "Esophagram for Missus Schwarz."

It wasn't like that.

An esophagram involves lying on an X-ray table, left side, right side, on the back, and having several X-rays taken in each position while you are swallowing mouthfuls of barium. They don't even flavor the damned stuff.

Very uncomfortable.

As it turned out there was no problem with Mimi's esophagus.

Dr. George's recommendation was "eat soft food."

Something for all of us to chew on.

But anxiety certainly can raise your blood pressure.

• • •

Back to blood pressure . . .

That nurse has been standing around doing nothing long enough.

We've all had our blood pressure taken dozens of times; but how does it work, what does it tell us and what do the numbers mean?

She takes the cuff of the *sphygmomanometer* – yes, sphygmomanometer – and places it around your arm.

Sphygmomanometer comes from the Greek *"sphygmos"* = pulse and *"manometer"* is a pressure meter.

It is a device to measure blood pressure that was invented in 1905 by Dr. Nikolai Korotkov.

Modern ones are composed of an inflatable cuff that is wrapped around the arm to restrict blood flow. The cuff is inflated by a squeeze bulb, which also has a valve to release the pressure. These two parts are connected to a mercury pressure gauge.

When she completes the procedure, I ask the nurse what my blood pressure is.

"It's 120 over 70, which is very good for someone your age."

[Actually, my BP is somewhat higher than that, and there is currently some discussion about the optimum blood pressure for someone in his eighties, so you should consult your physician.]

In younger folks a good BP is around 120 over 70, so that's what I'll use.

As the nurse begins putting the cuff away, I realize that I don't have a clear idea of what she means.

I ask her, "What does that mean; 120 what over 70 what?"

"It means that it takes the pressure from 120 millimeters of mercury to stop the blood from flowing through your arm at *systole*, and the blood doesn't start flowing again until the pressure of the mercury is down to 70 millimeters at *diastole*."

Ah, that explains it, or does it?

120 millimeters at systole? 70 millimeters at diastole?

A 120-millimeter column of mercury is a little over four and a half inches high; 70 millimeters of mercury is just over two and a half inches.

What the sphygmomanometer will tell us is how many millimeters tall a column of mercury has to be in order apply enough pressure to stop the blood from flowing through the artery in your arm.

When your BP is taken, the cuff is placed snugly around your upper arm and the squeeze bulb is exercised until the cuff is so tight that it constricts the artery, and the back-pressure has pushed the column of mercury up the gauge to about 150.

Most of the time a pressure of 150 will be enough to keep the artery constricted too tightly for the blood to get through, although, there have been cases of people with BP as high as 300. But you don't want to go there. I don't either.

Let's stick with "normal."

Now the nurse has the column of mercury at 150, and she places a stethoscope on the crook in the arm over the constricted artery where the elbow bends, below the inflated cuff.

She's doing that so she can hear when the blood starts forcing its way through the artery.

Slowly she opens the valve on the bulb and begins to deflate the cuff.

As the air pressure lowers in the cuff, the back-pressure lessens and the column of mercury begins to descend from 150.

If everything is normal, she won't hear anything until the mercury column arrives at the 120 mark, or close to it.

By then the artery will have relaxed enough so that the pressure of the blood from the heart has the power to force itself through.

The nurse will hear the turbulent sound of the first rush of blood being pushed through the artery by the contraction of the heart.

She is not listening for the heartbeat. She is listening for the noise of the blood rushing through the artery. She takes note of the reading on the height of the mercury column at the moment; let's say it's 120.

That is the *systole* number, "systole" meaning contraction, more or less; it is the top number of your BP reading.

Now let's get to the bottom half of the BP reading.

After the heart contracts, it rests for a brief time as it fills with blood. The blood pressure drops, so no blood is pushed through the artery which is still partially constricted. Then there is another contraction, and once again the nurse hears the spurting sound.

As the air is gradually let out of the cuff there is a time during which the nurse is hearing spurt . . . pause . . . spurt . . . pause . . .

As the artery relaxes and widens, the blood flows more freely, and the spurting noise becomes less audible until it can no longer be heard. Then the blood is running freely and minimum pressure is exerted on the artery.

The nurse takes note of that *diastole* (relaxing) moment.

If the column is at 70 when this happens, then the bottom number of the BP is 70, and the blood pressure is calculated to be 120/70.

That's the way it works.

If there are any questions, make a large donation to the Wounded Warriors Project. You might not get an answer, but it's a worthwhile charity.

After some research, I found out that a BP of 120/70 translates to a maximum pressure of somewhere around two pounds per square inch against the artery wall when the heart beats (at systole), and minimum pressure of about 1 pound per square inch between beats (at diastole).

Those numbers are the answer to the question I asked the nurse when she told me what my blood pressure was.

Do you happen to know that a column of one millimeter of mercury exerts 0.019336721269668 pounds of pressure per square inch at sea level?

If, at a crowded cocktail party, you loudly proclaim, "I am often comforted by the knowledge that at sea level, one millimeter of mercury exerts zero point zero one nine three three six seven two one two six nine six six eight pounds of pressure at sea level," it is sure to create plenty of room for you at the hors d'oeuvre table.

• • •

Years ago I had been diagnosed with hypertension and was put on a prescribed medication.

After a few years, I felt fine and I took myself off of it.

I have a friend who attends a VBC (Very Big Cardiologist) on Park Avenue in New York.

Just for the hell of it, I made an appointment with the VBC and in the course of the pre-examination it was noted that my BP was high.

When the VBC examined me, he asked if I had ever been on blood pressure medication.

I told him yes, but I don't like taking pills if I don't need them, so I stopped taking it.

The VBC noted that I had hypertension, and told me in no uncertain terms that there was no reason at all for me to have hypertension. He said that the medication I had been taking had no side effects that he knew of and that I should go back on it.

I did.

Since then, my BP has been normal for my age.

Except, I guess, when Mimi spits up bits of un-chewed food, and I get anxious about it.

• • •

I always feel an uneasy twinge whenever my gastroenterologist suggests a procedure that ends in "oscopy." All several billion of my sphincters contract involuntarily.

I am not going to indulge in cheap puns about a race to the bottom, or being glad that the ordeal is behind me. Butt (sic) there is the story about a man who accidentally swallowed his glass eye the night before he was to have a colonoscopy. Halfway through the procedure the doctor paused and said impatiently, "Mister Harrison, we have to learn to trust each other."

In truth, the way that colonoscopies are done today, there is little discomfort during the actual procedure.

You are sedated, and wake up not knowing that the poking and peeking has already been completed.

In colonoscopies the discomfort occurs during the day previous to the procedure when you have to take a laxative to clean out your colon.

I'll admit running back and forth to the small room for a few hours is not the most enjoyable way to get your exercise.

However, colon cancer is a lot less enjoyable.

I have always felt that the colonoscopy is *the* great social equalizer. Whether one is a hedge fund billionaire, a king or a superstar; a plumber or a panhandler, we are all the same from the point of view of the gastroenterologist: a bunch of assholes.

Mimi had never had a colonoscopy until she was seventy. Our physician at that time had not recommended she have one.

In 2001 she began having bowel problems. A colonoscopy was performed and it was discovered that she had colon cancer.

She underwent surgery, and a 23-inch section of her colon was removed.

It was like a deathwatch waiting to hear if the cancer had spread. It hadn't.

Mimi's brother, who is a physician, never mentioned that her father had had colon cancer, and that she was genetically at risk. The fact is, she should have had her first colon screening twenty years previously; at around age fifty.

But, you have to be your own advocate. If you are over fifty and your physician hasn't talked to you about a colonoscopy you should ask him or her for advice.

One day of slight discomfort is a small price to pay to ensure a healthy colon.

I said that you must your own advocate. That was never truer than when we discovered in 2007 that Mimi had breast cancer.

She had gone through an annual breast screening.

A week or so later I went to Ken Dodge for a checkup.

I happened to mention to him that Mimi had had a breast screening and that since we hadn't heard anything, I assumed everything was normal.

He shook his head and told me never to assume anything when it came to test results.

The next day I called the oncologist's office to check.

They discovered that "by golly" the X-ray folks had seen something they didn't like, and Mimi was supposed to have had a biopsy scheduled, but somehow the papers were misplaced.

Two weeks later she had a small cancer removed from her left breast.

You have to realize that people are fallible. Papers get lost. Computers crap out. Stuff happens.

It's your duty to check the results of every test you or a family member undergoes.

● ● ●

Mimi and I both love jazz and we made the rounds of all the clubs in Schwabing, which is Munich's equivalent of Greenwich Village. She was a regular there and it wasn't long before the two of us became fixtures.

American music was all over the place. The bands played songs the G.I.s had introduced during the war – Glenn Miller, and Tommy Dorsey tunes: "In the Mood", "Moonlight Serenade". There was touch dancing then; arms wrapped around each other in a barely moving two-step – more like swaying on the dance floor. Mimi's head would rest on my shoulder while I held her right hand low behind her back and pressed her against me (I saw it once in a movie) we danced close.

Sometimes, late at night, we'd take a bottle of champagne and go to the record library at the AFN studios. Each time we did I'd put on the same transcription, the one that played a dozen different versions of the waltz from Die Fledermaus. We would waltz until we were out of breath. Then we'd sit on the sofa, drink champagne, and smooch.

It was a great way to polish off a bottle of bubbly.

CHAPTER 4

• • •

A change of pace . . .

IN 2007, MIMI started having fainting spells. It was no fun when I'd be walking with her and she would suddenly take a nosedive with absolutely no warning.

Doctors thought that low blood pressure might be the problem, but support hose and standing up slowly, in order to equalize the pressure, didn't help.

Finally it was discovered that Mimi was suffering from *bradycardia* (abnormally slow heartbeat). The normal pulse rate is close to 65; her heart was beating at around 34 beats per minute; about half of what it should have been doing.

Her heart was simply not pumping enough blood to her brain.

Bradycardia can be caused by aging, by a combination of medications, physical disturbances in the heart, or even by diseases not related to the heart.

Well-conditioned athletes have slow pulse rates, but that's because they have more efficient heart function and better cardiovascular fitness than the rest of us. It's not unusual for them to have rates of 40 beats per minute or below.

But when you're nearly eighty years old and your pulse rate is in the mid-30s you have a problem.

Why this wasn't discovered earlier is a mystery to me. We were seeing many doctors at the time and Mimi had her blood pressure and heart rate taken during each visit.

But as I've learned over the years, conditions arise, and no one in the medical profession seems to be able to figure out where they came from or why they came from there.

There's a natural pacemaker in your heart. It sends out electrical impulses that make the chambers in your heart contract when they should, pushing the blood around your body.

Mimi's problem turned out to be AV (*Atrioventricular*) block. That's when the electrical connection between the heart's natural pacemaker and the heart's chambers breaks down.

To stop Mimi's fainting spells and generally improve her quality of life, she had a pacemaker implanted during an outpatient procedure.

A mechanical pacemaker helps the natural pacemaker send its signal to the heart as often as it should, or it can take over the job completely.

She recently received a new one and, when interrogated electronically, it indicated that it expected to be pulsing away for eleven years.

I don't know how much electrical power is used for each pulse, but if that battery can last eleven years, the amount of electricity required for each pulse must be nearly infinitesimal.

It is a remarkable device.

The modern pacemaker is about the size of a thick half dollar.

It gets around the AV block.

It has two parts, a generator and wire leads.

In what is usually an outpatient procedure, the surgeon cuts a shallow pocket into the chest, usually below the left shoulder.

That's where he imbeds the pacemaker (generator).

The leads are inserted into the heart through a vein in the neck, and then they are connected to the generator.

The leads carry electrical signals back and forth between the generator and the heart.

The generator is actually a computer that monitors the heart's electrical activity, and regulates it so that the heart beats at a rate that sends an adequate amount of blood through the body.

Modern pacemakers keep a diary of every heartbeat; they react to your activity, pacing up if you are more active; they check their own battery life, warning you when they are running low and perform many other computer driven regulatory functions.

● ● ●

It was not always thus . . .

In the early 1950s a Canadian made an external pacemaker using vacuum tube technology (you remember those glass tubes in radios that you used to peer into wondering how the symphony orchestra could fit in there). The machine was plugged into the AC, and since the wires went in through the chest wall there was the chance that you could be electrocuted at any time.

"Hello, Gertrude, it's me, Felix, I just wanted to –YOWWWW!"

Pacemakers were in use in Sweden in the early '50s too, but they looked like a beer cooler connected to the wall by an electric cord. They had the same sort of problems that the Canadians had.

In 1958 a Columbian team constructed an external pacemaker weighing ninety-nine pounds, powered by a 12-volt auto battery connected to electrodes attached to the heart.

Believe it or not, this device was used successfully to sustain the life of an elderly priest.

It probably fell out of favor because tennis pros had a difficult time finding ball boys who could push the battery cart around fast enough.

Which brings us to Sweden in 1958.

The big difference then was that silicone transistors were commercially available. That meant it was possible to make a pacemaker small enough to be implanted inside a human being.

We zoom into the *Karolinska Institutet* in Solna, Sweden. A fellow named Arne Larsson is lying there attached to one of those plug-into-the-wall pacemakers with wires sticking in his chest. He faints and has to be resuscitated twenty to forty times a day, plus he has a lung infection. His insurance broker is no longer returning his calls.

Larsson's wife reads in the *Daily Smorgasbord* that Larsson's doctor, Ake Senning, and a buddy of his, Rune Elmqvist, a doctor who is also an electrical engineer, have been fooling around with an implantable pacemaker. They miniaturized the device by using silicone transistors.

It is the size of a hockey puck.

Larsson's wife rushes to Dr. Senning and begs him to try the device on her hubby.

But the thing has never been tested on a human; Senning and Elmqvist are naturally reluctant.

Anne Larsson must have been a formidable persuader, because, in the end, Dr. Senning agrees.

Late at night, in order to avoid publicity, they attempt the implantation.

With apologies to Edward Bulwer-Lytton, Mary Shelley, Sir Walter Scott and Samuel Taylor Coleridge, I'll set the scene:

"It is a dark and stormy night." Lightning pierces the midnight sky and fierce blasts of thunder "resound up the rocky way," "through caverns measureless to man." A small group of men (and a woman) are gathered at an operating table wondering if they "might infuse a spark of being into the lifeless thing that lay at their feet. It is already one in the morning; the rain patters dismally against the panes."

One of the participants raises a flat cylindrical object above his head. It looks strangely like a hockey puck.

He slowly lowers his hands and reverently deposits the object into the lifeless body before him.

Moments pass.

Then, lub-dub.

Success!

Ake Senning embraces Rune Elmkvist.

Rune Elmkvist embraces Ake Senning.

Anne Larsson embraces them both.

Three hours later, the hockey puck crapped (past tense verb form of medieval word) out.

Darn!

But . . . those crafty Swedes have another one, just in case.

The hockey puck was primitive, but it worked well enough to keep Larsson alive until better models came on the market, and he was still alive forty years later, after having received twenty-two pacemakers.

He eventually outlived both men who invented that hockey puck and saved his life.

Lub-dub.

One of the problems of the early pacemakers was that the mercury-zinc and nickel-cadmium batteries didn't last terribly long. You'd be walking along the street and the "Game Over" signal would bring you to your knees.

The lithium battery that was developed in the early 1970s solved that problem.

A lithium battery may last for as long as ten or eleven years before it needs replacement, depending on the power and the duration of each pulse.

In most cases this replacement is an outpatient procedure.

Currently (2015) there are more than 3,000,000 pacemakers pulsing away around the world with about 600,000 more being implanted every year; over 100,000 in the United States alone. That makes lithium batteries a good investment.

According to a 2012 Reuters article, the out-of-pocket expense of adorning yourself with such a life-enhancing accoutrement, including the surgical and hospital services can run from $20,000 up to $80,000 – retail. I doubt that most insurance companies pay that amount.

When the battery runs low, the pacemaker must be replaced.

Maybe you're wondering why they don't just pop off the lid and stick in a new battery, rather than replace the whole expensive device.

Richard Frogos, a doctor, wrote a pretty complete answer to that. The fact is that they can't "just pop off the lid"; to open it is to destroy it.

Originally pacemakers were sealed with epoxy resin, but the seal couldn't stand up against the conditions to which it was exposed.

The inside of you is warm, wet and salty; not a hospitable place for things that don't belong there.

The modern pacemaker is made of titanium which is "biocompatible"; it is hermetically sealed to protect the inside of the device from the corrupting chemicals that are inside your body.

Titanium (named in honor of the Titans, the elder gods of Greek mythology) is as strong as steel and only half the weight. It has excellent resistance to seawater which may be why it can exist in the salty conditions inside us; it is also used in stealth bombers and salad dressings among a couple of thousand other things.

Titanium is going to outlast the battery.

Rechargeable batteries?

In the late 1950s they had a rechargeable battery that worked in pacemakers.

It wasn't very practical because you had to recharge it every few days, and of course, since you were probably a doddering Old Fart when you had the pacemaker implanted, you might have a problem.

"Let's see, now, I was supposed to take out the garbage, have the car inspected ... Oh, yeah, make sure the lawn mower has gas . . . I know there was something else . . ."

Uh-oh.

The lawyers for the pacemaker industry decided that even if it was the patient's fault that the battery wasn't recharged, there would probably be a ton of lawsuits. That and the advent of long-lasting lithium batteries made the rechargeable battery history.

Nevertheless, the pacemaker is an electrical device: it doesn't have moving parts but it can't last forever.

Pacemakers are designed so that the battery tells the interrogator how much life it has left. That way you have advance warning and the device can be replaced while it is still working.

You should know that there was a battery developed in the '60s and '70s that had the capability of lasting a long, long time.

It had a couple of drawbacks even though it could last for over a quarter-Century.

The battery I'm talking about was a battery powered by Plutonium-238. It was developed by the Los Alamos National Laboratory for the express purpose of providing (get this) radio-isotope thermoelectric generator power for batteries which were used in spacecraft.

They were also used in cardiac pacemakers.

You'll be happy to know that the amount of radiation released by those batteries in pacemakers was very low; they were deemed to be safe even for pregnant women.

Of course, the child would glow in the dark – only kidding.

Ten percent of the batteries were operative twenty-five years later. Whether the other ninety percent pooped out, or the people who wore the atomic pacemakers just wanted to get rid of the nuclear option is impossible to say.

In 2007, Reuters published an article quoting a surgeon who stated that a woman was still hale and hearty almost forty years after receiving a Plutonium-238 powered pacemaker.

Walking around with a nuclear furnace in your chest had some disadvantages, though.

There was a problem moving from state-to-state or country-to-country since you were transporting radioactive fuel.

You could also be a tempting target for terrorists who could use the plutonium for nefarious purposes. They might remove you first and then remove the radioactive material and pulverize it so that they could use the powder to poison things; a little bit of a radioactive isotope goes a long way.

And, when you died, if you had one of those atomic batteries, the pacemaker was supposed to be returned to Los Alamos to be decommissioned (buried in a concrete silo?). How they were supposed to keep track of everybody who had one of these contraptions inside is anybody's guess.

People ask if a pacemaker will keep them alive even when they are on their death-bed and they want to die.

The answer is no.

In a *CHI Health Blog*, Dr. Eric Van De Graaff explains that as the organs in the body fail, the blood becomes slightly acidic. This small change in blood chemistry renders the heart indifferent to the electrical pulse of the pacemaker.

The pacemaker keeps sending pulses, but nobody at the other end picks up the phone.

He goes on to say that, sometimes he is asked to decommission the pacemaker in a dying person.

After all, antibiotics, and IV fluids are being scaled back and artificial ventilation has been removed; why not do the same with the pacemaker?

Van De Graaff points out that disabling the pacemaker would probably not lead to quicker death, but might, instead, make the last days more fatiguing, and reduce whatever quality of life is left to the dying person.

It is the law in this country that pacemakers must be removed from the body if it is to be cremated.

The high temperature which must be reached for the cremation process may cause the titanium device to explode and wreck the furnace and quite possibly any bystanders.

Pacers are normally thrown away as medical waste.

Now, however, there are organizations like *Heartbeat International* which clean and sanitize pacemakers. They make any needed repairs, so the devices may be implanted in another person where such practices are allowed.

It is also my understanding that discarded pacemakers may be used by veterinarians (on their clients that is).

But many pacemakers are left *in situ* when a person is buried.

If you have had occasion to visit a cemetery recently, you are most likely unaware of the macabre fact that in many of the newer graves there are pacemakers pulsing away at 60 beats per minute, hour after hour, day after day, like that faithful dog sitting expectantly by the door waiting for his master to return.

This rather grotesque revelation can't help but remind us of Poe and his *The Fall of the House of Usher* and *The Tell-Tale Heart* and *Buried Alive*.

In Edgar Allen's time, cholera epidemics were not uncommon, and in a few cases when someone died of the dreaded disease there may have been a rush to punch his ticket before the train had actually left the station.

Reports appeared in the newspapers, supposedly written by doctors, of people who had been planted while they were only comatose.

The thought gave rise, among a segment of the population, to taphophobia –fear of graves; also to some unusual organizations and industries.

In 1896 a group of Americans founded the *Society for the Prevention of People Being Buried Alive.*

I probably would have joined.

The method they suggested to ensure that the deceased was truly dead was to let the corpse lie around for a few days until it started to stink.

The nose knows.

Safety Coffins were produced.

Some had features like bells, or flags or fireworks or speaking tubes that went to the surface and could be activated by the plantee if he or she awoke.

One of the more bizarre efforts was proposed by a German physician, Dr. Adolph Gutsmuth.

It came complete with "tomb service".

In 1822, in order to demonstrate its practical benefits, he had himself buried in one of his contraptions, during which time he had passed down to him through a feeding tube in the lid of the coffin, a meal of soup, bratwurst, sauerkraut, spaetzle and beer.

His hunger not satisfied, the good doctor then polished off a portion of prinzregententorte for desert.

It was not recorded if he finished with demitasse and Weinbrand.

Although there is little doubt that there were people who awakened to find themselves interred and in trouble, there is no record of anyone ever having been saved by Dr. Gutsmuth's Safety Coffin, or any other similar device.

• • •

The two of us would take auto trips into Italy, and as we drove along we would pass rivulets running along the side of the road.

There would always be a sign reading "Aqua non potable" warning us not to drink the water.

We would be driving along singing at the top of our lungs, "Aqua non potable" to the tune of "La done e mobile" from Rigoletto.

In Rome when we were on a tour bus every church seemed to have an epithet attached to its name. There was St. Paul within the walls, and St. Paul in Chains. Mimi pointed to a small church we were passing.

"That's St. Mary the Elastic . . . you give a little, you take a little."

After we ate at a trattoria the waiter wanted to know how we enjoyed the meal.

Mimi kissed her fingertips and gave it her highest accolade, "It was Mussolini!"

This sort of nutty humor tightened the bond between us.

Mimi had been brought up in the time of Hitler and everything had been extremely regimented.

She had to join the Girls Section of the German Youth and they would march out to a field in order to exercise in unison.

This was not a communal event that Mimi looked forward to.

Because she had a bicycle, she would march at the end of the column and when the head of the column made a right turn, she would turn left and ride off to play tennis.

Even then, she had a mind of her own.
That hadn't changed when I met her.
And believe me, it hasn't changed since.
The course of our marriage has been influenced by her style and taste, and I've been happy with the results.

- - - -

CHAPTER 5

The heart of the matter . . .

ON OUR JOURNEY Mimi and I have had some problems with our hearts. She was fitted for a pacemaker; I received a couple of cardiac stents a few years ago.

So you can understand why I became interested in learning a bit about how the heart functions.

I was astonished at what I learned about this miraculous pump and the blood it forces through our arteries.

The heart is located behind and slightly to the left of your breastbone; it is about the size of your fist and it weighs less than a pound. It beats around sixty times a minute or approximately 42,000,000 times a year. During a leap year it will have to beat a few thousand times more.

If you live to be eighty years old, which is not so terribly old nowadays, your heart will have lub-dubbed well over three billion times.

Blood is the juice your heart squirts around inside you through an incredibly vast network of blood vessels (arteries, veins and capillaries).

Slight side trip . . .

When I say incredibly vast, I'm not kidding. I'll include just three statistics. Some of the numbers fall into the astronomical range and seem impossible, but they are taken from websites that appear to be authoritative, so I'll show them to you and let you decide.

The *University of Minnesota Physiology Tutorial* tells us that if you counted just the capillaries, you would find that there are about ten billion in our bodies.

According to the *Human Heart* section of the *Franklin Institute* website, if all of the plumbing involved in the circulatory system was laid end to end, it would stretch for nearly 100,000 miles, or around four times to circumference of our planet.

This next statistic isn't about our arterial system, but the numbers are so staggering that I felt compelled to include it.

In 2012, Jennifer Walsh (a genetic counseling graduate student at Boston University) wrote in answer to a question on the *National Human Genome Research Institute* website " . . . if you were to [stretch out and] line up all of the DNA in every cell of a human body, it would reach from the earth to the sun 100 times."

That's what she wrote, folks.

Back to the heart . . .

There are about seven pints of blood in your body, and a lot of it moves through your circulatory system in about one minute; yes, once every minute.

Your heart will pump fifty million gallons of blood in an eighty-year span, give or take.

If that were gasoline at $4.00 per gallon, you'd spend $200 million on gas alone, and that doesn't include oil or wiper fluid.

A little more than half of your blood is made up of a watery liquid (plasma) that the cells float around in.

Most of the cells in the blood are red blood cells – red corpuscles. Under a microscope they look like little red life rafts; round with raised edges.

The red cells contain a protein called hemoglobin.

Hemoglobin contains iron which combines well with oxygen, so the cells are red – think rust (iron oxide).

Cells need oxygen to live; they are continually sitting down to a hearty dinner of roasted oxygen with all the trimmings; as they do, most of the oxygen is turned into waste products, among which are carbon dioxide and heat.

The heat, generated during the metabolic process, is what makes us warm-blooded.

The waste products are carried away by the plasma and the red blood cells.

Red blood cells make up about a quarter of the cells in your body – about twenty to thirty trillion. They are born in the bone marrow and after a week they are released into the bloodstream.

They have a life span of about three months before they expire and are sent to the junkyard by the spleen and the liver.

In fact, every second somewhere between two and three million of them die; and every second somewhere between two and three million new ones are produced in the bone marrow.

Side trip . . .

There is a lot of work going on in your body every minute.

Our skin cells change about every thirty-five days; most of the adult skeleton is replaced around every ten years.

Some researchers say that your heart replaces itself three or four times in 80 years.

Almost all the cells in your body have a limited life span; some for only a day, others for years.

If you bought a Buick, and over the years had all the parts including the chassis replaced, is it the same Buick?

Richard Dawkins, the evolutionary biologist, has a thought-provoking comment about this continual transformation. "Not a single atom that is in your body today was there [years ago].

Matter flows from place to place and momentarily comes together as you. Whatever you are, therefore, you are not the stuff of which you are made."

Back to blood . . .

Along with red blood cells, blood also contains white blood cells. They protect your body from infection. They amount to only about one percent of your blood, but they are very important.

The most common type of white blood cells are the "immediate response" cells. They are the first responders to infection or inflammation; they attack viruses and bacteria and other nasties that somehow manage to get into your system.

They live for less than a day, so your bone marrow has to work really hard to make enough of them.

Your blood also contains platelets. They aren't actually cells, but small fragments of cells. They gather at the site of a wound to help the clotting process by sticking to the injured blood vessel. That way the blood clots and you don't bleed to death.

Blood acts as a delivery system too, carrying vitamins, minerals, sugar, amino acids, and hormones to the cells.

None of this would be possible if the heart wasn't pumping away.

● ● ●

The heart is a pear-shaped muscle containing two sets of pumps side by side.

Each pump has two hollow chambers, an *atrium* on top and a *ventricle* below.

The atria receive the blood, pump it down to the ventricles, and the ventricles pump it out.

Each of the four chambers has a one-way valve at its exit.

When the chambers contract, the valves allow the blood to be forced out, and when the chambers relax the valves prevent backflow.

The heart pumps the blood in two stages.

First, the two atria (the top chambers) contract simultaneously, forcing their blood into the right and left ventricles below; then both ventricles contract.

The right ventricle pumps blood into the lungs to be replenished with oxygen and the left ventricle pumps blood out into the body.

The lub-dub that the doctor hears through the stethoscope is the sound of the two sets of valves slapping shut, one after the other before the heart muscle relaxes allowing each atrium to fill up once more.

The pump-and-fill sequence repeats itself all your life; it never stops, because you cannot live without fresh oxygen being supplied to the cells.

Which explains why stopping breathing for long periods of time is so dangerous to your health.

● ● ●

This is how the circulatory system works (more or less). The right side of the heart receives deoxygenated blood and forces it into the lungs to be refreshed.

The atrium on the left side receives the newly oxygenated blood from the lungs and pumps it down to the left ventricle, which contracts and forces the oxygen-rich blood out through the *aorta* where it begins its circulation through the arterial system.

The arteries branch off into narrower and narrower blood vessels until the arterioles connect to capillaries, the narrowest blood vessels in your body. Capillaries are five to ten microns in diameter. A micron is one millionth of a meter.

There are about ten billion capillaries in your body. They are so narrow that the red blood cells have to flow through in single file; capillary walls are only one cell thick, so thin that gasses can pass back and forth through them.

As the cells in the body use up oxygen, they produce a high concentration of carbon dioxide as a waste product. They need to absorb new oxygen and get rid of the carbon dioxide.

Conversely, and contrariwise, the red blood cells, refreshed by the air you have just inhaled, have a high concentration of oxygen and a low concentration of carbon dioxide; a situation that is just the opposite.

Nature has figured out a way to rectify this imbalance. It is called the *process of diffusion*.

Diffusion takes place when gas flows from a higher concentration to a lower concentration, the same as when you let the air out of a balloon.

In this case the diffusion of gasses occurs through the thin-walled capillary, and there are enough capillaries in your body so that every cell is near one.

As the red blood cells move through the capillary, their higher concentration of oxygen passes through the thin walls into the cells in the body.

At the same time the cells in the body pass excess carbon dioxide, back through the capillary wall into the red blood cells.

This transfer of gasses is happening all over your body continuously, and it occurs in a fraction of second.

So, outward bound, the oxygen-laden blood enters the capillary from the artery side and, having given up its oxygen, exits on the other side of the capillary into the venous system, loaded with carbon dioxide, heading homeward to the right side of the heart where, in the lungs, it gets rid of the carbon dioxide and is returned to its youthful vigor refreshed with oxygen.

This is how it happens.

The blood flows back to the heart through veins of ever-increasing diameter until it arrives at the two large veins next to the heart – the *venae cavae*; they empty the blood into the right atrium.

The right atrium pumps the blood down into the right ventricle, which contracts and forces the blood into the lungs.

Our lungs are located under the ribs on either side of the heart.

They are a pair of spongy organs about the size of pineapples; their job is to exchange carbon dioxide in the blood with oxygen in the air that you breathe.

They are really efficient at doing that too, because when you are breathing at rest, you use only about fifteen percent of your lung capacity.

When you breathe, the fresh air travels down your trachea and bronchial tubes into piping that gets narrower and narrower until, at the end of the bronchioles, it reaches tiny clusters of air sacks that look like bunches of grapes; they are called *alveoli*.

These tiny sacks have an elastic quality which allows them to expand and fill with air when you breathe in and then collapse to help expel the used air as you breathe out.

That's why it's important that a child starts to cry as soon as it's born: those alveoli have to start performing as soon as possible.

The alveoli are small, but there are 300 million of them, and if you had the patience to cut each one open and lay it flat, you would end up covering about half of a tennis court.

When the blood is forced through the lungs, it too travels through narrower and narrower veins until it enters the capillaries that surround the alveoli.

The fresh air you are breathing contains lots of oxygen and not so much carbon dioxide, so you would be right in assuming that everything is going to even itself out.

You'd be right because as the blood passes through the capillaries in the lungs, oxygen from the fresh air diffuses into the blood, and the carbon dioxide from the blood diffuses into the air and is carried off as you exhale.

This exchange of gasses happens in the few seconds during which you breathe in and out.

Now the newly oxygenated blood – bright red and rarin' to go – passes into the left atrium which pumps it down to the left ventricle.

The left ventricle contracts and forces the blood out through the *aorta* where it begins its commodious recirculation through the arterial system once again.

This is a continuing process perpetuated by every beat of your heart.

• • •

A side trip down various arteries . . .
The heart has a whole other life outside the body.

To ancient Egyptians, the heart was more than just a body part.

They believed that the heart, rather than the brain, was the source of human wisdom, as well as emotions; it reflected the quality of the person's life.

In the afterlife, the heart was weighed against a feather of the goddess Ma'at.

If the heart was light and pure, it was balanced by the feather and the individual was welcomed into paradise.

Anger, fear, joy and love all affected the rhythm of the heart, so it was only a hop, skip and a lub-dub to deduce that the emotions resided there.

There isn't any definitive papyrus trail, but it seems plausible.

This concept continued through the 4th Century BCE, promoted by no less a thinker than Aristotle. He identified the heart as the seat of intelligence, motion, and sensation.

Aristotle must also have been aware of the elevated coronary activity that occurs when one is emotionally enmeshed with a special partner.

He was very important and very smart, so what he thought mattered. He was a student of Plato, and the teacher of Alexander the Great. You can believe that when the slaves brought out the baklava, he got first dibs.

● ● ●

Nobody knows how the heart ended up looking like a red Van Dyke beard with Mickey Mouse ears; it didn't start out that way.

The first known depiction of the heart as a symbol of love is in a 13th Century manuscript.

A lover is handing his heart to a lady. It looks sort of like a pinecone. The lady has her hand raised as if to give him a slap up the side of his head. Tough love?

The shape of the base of the pinecone slowly evolved, until in the 15th Century, it came to look pretty much like the one the one we see now on Valentine's cards.

● ● ●

The origin of Valentine's Day itself is in some dispute, one scenario carries us all the way back to a pre-Roman festival called

Lupercalia. It was observed from February 13th to the 15th, so the dates are suggestive. It was supposed to cleanse the city and promote fertility.

Lupercalia replaced Februa, an earlier spring cleansing ritual. Februa (goddess of passion) gave her name to February.

Plutarch described Lupercalia like this: "At this time many of the noble youths . . . ran up and down through the city naked for sport and laughter striking those they met with shaggy thongs. And many women of rank purposely in their way . . . believed that the pregnant will thus be helped in delivery and the barren to pregnancy . . ."

Lupercalia was supposed to have ended with a lot of foolin' around to everyone's satisfaction.

So, festivals in the early spring, celebrating fertility have a long history – think bunny rabbits and Easter eggs.

● ● ●

Things went on like this until the late 5th Century when Pope Gelasius, not happy with a holiday that celebrated a pagan deity, abolished Lupercalia and replaced it with a Christian holiday devoted to the Virgin Mary.

How a Christian holiday dedicated to Mary ended up as Saint Valentine's Day is also rather vague. There were several Saint Valentines, one of whom was martyred and buried in Rome on February fourteenth.

Some historians dispute that Valentine's Day had its origins in Lupercalia, other authorities postulate (I like it when authorities postulate) that the connection was invented by Geoffrey Chaucer who, in 1381, was the first one to mention Valentine's Day in print, where he linked it to romance.

He wrote in his *Parliament of Fowls*:

"For this was on seynt Volantynys day
Whan euery bryd comyth there to chese his make."

I think you probably can translate the Middle English, but just in case:

"For this was on Saint Valentine's Day, when every bird cometh there to choose his mate."

After this, Saint Valentine's Day, as a romantic moment, was mentioned occasionally by authors including Shakespeare and Donne.

Around 1600, Shakespeare gave Ophelia a plaintive ditty about having lost her virginity to Hamlet on Saint Valentine's Day:

Tomorrow is Saint Valentine's day,
All in the morning betime,
And I a maid at your window,
To be your Valentine.
Then up he rose, and donned his clothes,
And dupped the chamber door.
Let in the maid that out a maid
Never departed more.

By the 17th Century the custom of sending handmade cards and exchanging gifts became popular in England and spread to the colonies (that's us).

In 1847, Esther Holland graduated from Mount Holyoke Female Seminary, near Worcester, Mass, where Valentine festivities had been banned as being too frivolous.

Soon after, Ms. Holland received an elaborate lacey valentine from one of her father's business associates in England.

She knew she could make a better lace valentine than that, so she created some samples. Her brother, who was a salesman for their family's stationery business, took them along to New York in the hope of drumming up a little business.

Wonder of wonders, he returned with $5,000 worth of orders. Esther was off and running.

Ms. Holland, whose hallmark was creating beautiful lacey valentines, also knew how to run a business.

She became known as "The Mother of the Valentine" and was grossing $100,000 a year when she sold her business in 1881.

● ● ●

The connection between Valentine's Day and romantic love may have originated with Chaucer, but the connection of Cupid and his arrows with romantic love goes far back; back to the Greek civilization.

Ovid wrote of Cupid (Eros):

"Then Cupid . . . opened
His quiver of all his thousand arrows
Selected one, the sharpest and the surest,
The arrow most obedient to the bow . . .
And shot the barbed shaft deep in Pluto's heart."

In early times, Eros was credited for the mating of Heaven and Earth; in fact, responsible for the hatching of the whole human race.

He was a power player in those days; he started out as a handsome winged youth before he became the chubby the little fellah that we all recognize today.

He was worshiped as a fertility god and an erratic one at that. Depending on his whim, his arrow was said to arouse desire or, if he felt like it, indifference. He was a dangerous dude to have around.

Ultimately his cult joined that of Aphrodite, where they were represented as mother and son, as were Venus and Cupid later in Roman times.

Everyone is pretty sure that Venus was Cupid's mother, but depending on which mythical gossip column you read, the father could have been Mercury, or Vulcan, or Mars.

After all, Venus did get around and there was no DNA testing in those days.

If it was Mercury, that could explain why Cupid has a set of wings, or maybe it's because lovers are apt to be flighty.

He is sometimes portrayed as blindfolded because . . . need I say it?

It is not surprising that Cupid, that cute little putto, would be thought of by Victorians as a harmless representation of light romance.

His phallic arrows that inflamed the heart with lust didn't seem to threaten their sensibilities.

Bloomberg reported in 2012 that during the two weeks surrounding Valentine's Day, "sales of Durex condoms jump about twenty percent, the equivalent of about 180,000 condoms."

The most home pregnancy tests are sold in March. What did they do with all those condoms?

Florists like Valentine's Day a lot. They sell around 200 million roses.

Card makers are happy too, since about a billion of them are sent worldwide.

Candy manufacturers aren't exactly complaining either. Candy is the most common gift on Valentine's Day; around fifty-eight million pounds of it is purchased costing over $350 million.

I don't know if that includes the eight billion "conversation hearts" (100,000 pounds of them) made by the NECCO candy company since 1902. You know what they are, they're those little pastel heart-shaped candies with two word, too cute semi-suggestive mottos: KISS ME, BE MINE, UP YOURS, GET LOST, FALL OVERBOARD, etc.

It's a big deal for the champagne industry too. In a 2009 article, Nielson reports that during the Valentine season over a million bottles of sparkling wine will be sipped, swigged, swilled, guzzled or gulped.

All of this is OK with me and I don't mind Valentine's Day as long as they don't try to commercialize it.

• • •

In the '70s and '80s, when we lived in Manhattan, Mimi would always throw a New Year's Eve party. Everybody had a swell time.

People were invited for 10:30 p.m. but the thing didn't really get rolling until nearly midnight.

By then Mimi and I would have had a few glasses of champagne and by time the ball dropped, it was almost a letdown.

This particular year, Mimi promised things would be different.

The evening arrived; the place was all decorated and the bathtub was filled with ice and champagne.

Mister Ellison had his white jacket on and was ready to pass the hors d'oeuvres.

It was 7:30 p.m. Everything was prepared for the party to begin later.

At that point Mimi produced two tickets to the Metropolitan Opera for a performance of Die Fledermaus *beginning at 8:00 p.m.*

We grabbed our coats and left.

We got back to the apartment just before midnight, and when we opened the door, we were greeted by applause and a splendid party in full swing.

CHAPTER 6

• • •

Please pass the trousers . . .

DURING MY *GRADUS ad* geezer-hood I'm putting on weight. It might be because I finish up a lot of Mimi's food, it might be gravity; maybe my mass is increasing in relation to that of the earth's; but whatever it is, when I went to Kmart to buy a new pair of blue jeans, I discovered that all the 38s were too damned tight.

At first I thought that they were making the 38s narrower in order to save fabric, and there was a time when, for vanity's sake, I'd buy the 38s anyway and suck my stomach in so that I could pull the fly together and zip up.

This created an unsightly stomach bulge in front and I'd have to wear a loose sweater in order to hide it.

I realized that I had had trouble buttoning my trousers for some time and rather than the manufacturer skimping on the fabric, my belly was encroaching.

At that point I began to wonder why men wore trousers in the first place. All over the world there are men who wear long robes which look very comfortable.

You've seen pictures of them and if you've traveled at all, you've seen the real thing in India, Africa, the Middle East and the Orient. Loose-fitting robes obviate the necessity to zip up at all, and eliminate the embarrassment of pulling your pants out of your crotch when you rise from a chair on a steamy summer's day.

During Biblical times, robes were all the rage.

Not once in any of his 969 years did Methuselah ever try to squeeze his *avoirdupois* into a size 38 robe when he was really a 40. Habakkuk didn't have to worry about his wife telling him that he had missed a belt loop. Obadiah or Jeramiah or Zachariah or Zephaniah never had to concern themselves about whether cuffs were in or out.

Another feature of robes and togas was that when you needed to go out of town you never had to call out to your wife, "Medea, where did you put my studs?" You'd simply toss half a dozen togas into a sack, hop onto your dragon and take off into the rosy-fingered dawn.

So it's not surprising that for a long time, long pants or leg coverings were not what most PLU were wearing.

In fact, they were considered barbaric, even laughable, and no self-respecting man would wear anything like them.

Did I hear someone ask, "How can that be?" No? Well, even if I didn't . . .

Believe it or not, it all came down to horses.

There is a great deal of speculation as to the exact time horses were domesticated, because there are a lot of opinions as to what constitutes actual domestication, but as near as I can place it, it was at 3:15 in the afternoon on June 4th, 3751 BCE by a bunch of yokels sitting around in ancient Kazakhstan.

Horses were smaller then and they weren't very practical to ride, but they could haul things and they tasted good.

As time went on, though, horses were bred to be larger and by 1700 BCE they were being used to pull chariots in battle.

For the next three hundred years, chariots were the dreaded weapon against which the foot soldier had little chance.

But horse breeders weren't asleep at the corral, and horses had finally become large enough to support cavalry.

Watch out!

Horse cavalry was nimble; could turn on a drachma. Horse cavalry could dart in and out among the chariots. Horse cavalry was good at attacking foot soldiers with spear and sword; bow and arrow, and then galloping away.

Horse cavalry was now *the* weapon.

After that you could buy all the war chariots you wanted . . . cheap.

In the flux and flow of time, about 750 BCE, Scythians, who were great cavalry- men (and women), swept out of the East and beat the bejeepers out of anybody who stood against them. They were able to do that pretty much because they were good at riding horses.

If you stood against them you wouldn't be standing long because they knew how to use their horses in battle against both infantry and the pitiful cavalry of their opponents.

Too, Scythians were armed with those nifty short recurved bows (Model M-3), and they were good at using them. They were reputed to be able to put a bird's eye out at fifty yards, and could shoot an arrow through a pickle while they rode past at break-neck speed.

All this was pretty amazing considering their saddles were rudimentary, and they didn't have stirrups which weren't invented until 10:00 a.m., Aug. 4th, 200 AD; almost half a century later.

If you discovered the Scythians were on the way, the best thing you could do was to get in touch with your real estate agent and tell her to accept that last offer . . . Fast!

The Scythians were fierce. They were tattooed, they drank their victim's blood, and they used their enemies' scalps to wipe their faces. Definitely not the kind of folks you'd want to invite to your barbie.

They were barbarians, but even barbarians have their weak-nesses, and their weakness was gold decoration. They, or those they employed, raised the art of goldsmithing to a very high level; one that set the standard for centuries to come.

They wore golden jewelry. They decorated their horses, their headgear, their jackets and (you guessed it), they even decorated their trousers with gold; not trousers exactly, more like padded leggings.

Yes, they wore long pants. They had to because wearing robes wasn't terribly helpful when riding horseback, and they couldn't ride all day with their bare legs rubbing against the coarse horsehides.

I'll bet nobody snickered at them when they swaggered in to the local bar with their glittery pants tucked into their boots and ordered "Blood for everybody!"

The same scenario was true for many groups of nomadic Eurasian cavalry that ravaged the area then.

They all wore leg coverings; some looser, some tighter, but they all covered their legs.

You'd think that somebody would have taken the hint. Pants were a very macho form of attire.

But no; nomadic barbarians might wear pants, but such a garment was not suitable for the elite (that's us).

No one wanted to emulate the barbarians because they were . . . well . . . barbarians.

To show just how difficult it was to overcome the cultural prejudice against pants, consider the plight of a 3rd Century BCE Chinese statesman, King Wuling. (He was obviously a member of the Wuling Class.)

He wondered if he should order his cavalry to switch to pants from the traditional robes. "It is not that I have any doubt about the advantages concerning the wearing of trousers," Wuling told an advisor. "I am afraid that everybody will laugh at me."

Nevertheless, after much opposition from traditionalists, he prevailed and created a cavalry that was trained in horse archery. Because of their new capability he added a good deal of territory to his kingdom.

In the west, as time went on, cavalries of various nations discarded robes because they had to in order to be competitive, but the upper classes just kept toga-ing along until Rome fell.

By the 8th Century Europe was controlled by a bunch of thugs who fought from horseback; they were called knights.

Everybody wants to look like a winner, so if the knights wore pants, then the upper class finally decided that leg coverings were manly after all.

Now, these "pants" weren't like the ones you order from L. L. Bean.

Workers and farmers wore a sort of loincloth cum diaper called *braies*; tied around the waist. Braies hung to the knees.

By the 1360s, two tubes of fabric (hose) were added and attached to the tops of the braies with cords; sort of a medieval garter belt.

Eventually the hose became joined in the rear and the front, but there was still a big split in the middle.

The split didn't matter much because this sartorial mishmash was completed with a doublet that hung down halfway to the knees.

As we all know, however, fluctuations of fashions are fickle and despite the obvious outcome, the length of the tunic kept receding upward toward the waist.

As the tunics became shorter, the split-crotch hose were bound to end up creating an eye-catching combo.

Imagine the sight when a fellow threw his leg up to mount his horse; talk about "southern exposure."

In the mid-1400s, the solution to the problem was to sew a triangular patch across the front of the hose; a patch that was buttoned or tied, or unbuttoned or untied should the urge require it.

The unintended consequence of this practical patch was to create an aberration in the development of trousers that lasted for over a century; that aberration was the codpiece.

A codpiece is not a fish fillet.

"Cod" is defined in the O.E.D. as "the integument enveloping the testicles." The Brits do have a way with words.

Stylish men wore doublets to the waist, with knicker-like britches that reached down to the knee.

It didn't take long for hopeful fellows to begin pointing out their virtues by padding their resumes, as it were.

What were formally mere bulges, morphed into conspicuous appurtenances projecting enthusiastically from the crotch. For a time, they became quite the rage among the fashionable set.

I'm reminded of the popular radio show of the 1940s, *The Make Believe Ballroom.*

The most famous codpieces of the era adorned the royal porker of King Henry VIII who ruled England during the first half of the 1500s.

He was one of the leaders of the "wad your cod" movement and had his portrait painted, in a particularly pugnacious pose, prominently parading a prodigious protuberance; his expression seeming to dare you to do something about it.

It's a fact that these bulges grew so large that the possessors sometimes used them for the storage of small weapons; mad money and the like.

Even suits of armor were adorned at the crotch with codpieces. Some had droll caricatures engraved on the tips.

The fashion was already starting to fade by 1588 when Henry died and his daughter Elizabeth became queen.

Not long after, the fever had passed, the swelling subsided, and wear (sic) houses were crammed with flaccid codpieces.

Oddly enough, the codpiece has enjoyed a resurrection among leather lovers and heavy metal rock bands, although it is doubtful that it will ever become the outstanding fashion statement it once was.

As long as we are investigating genital impedimenta, we mustn't neglect one that is currently in vogue with a certain segment of the bondage and sadomasochistic crowd. I refer, as you suspect, to the chastity belt.

To most people the chastity belt is inextricably associated with the Crusades and Medieval times.

In reality, if you lived in the 13th Century, it is not likely you would have seen a knight riding his charger across the castle moat on his way to the Holy Land being chased by a trusted retainer brandishing a small metal object shouting, "Wrong key! Wrong key!"

The idea of a girdle of chastity was a metaphor used by religious leaders as early as the 6th Century, long before the First Crusade. It was intended to refer to moral and spiritual protection against sin, including illicit sex, overeating, drinking and cheating at Knucklebones.

People were urged to surround themselves with a spiritual "girdle of chastity" much as today someone would implore you to wrap yourself in an "aura of respectability."

No one expects you to run down to the little shop of auras and get fitted for one.

There were seven major Crusades from 1095 to 1291.

The chastity belts purported to be relics of those times didn't appear in Europe until the 1800's; more than five centuries later, and they have proved to be more a product of the artificer's imagination than to have any basis in reality.

These fabrications were fabricated because there was a market for them.

Almost all the items that were exhibited in museums until late in the 20th Century have been proven to be phony and were removed from exhibition, or were re-captioned to reflect their bogus nature.

Back to pants . . .

The transition from robes to trousers continued. By 1629 men were dressing in baggy pants tucked into the tops of boots like the Three Musketeers, and it was not uncommon for workmen and tradesmen to wear loose long pants, but the upper classes still wore knee britches and silk hose, especially to formal affairs.

The transition from breeches to long pants was completed in the early part of the 1800s.

Beau Brummel popularized them in Europe, and the fourth president of the United States, James Madison, broke tradition then by wearing long trousers all the time, even on formal occasions.

So, two and a quarter millennia after the Scythians rode into town, long pants finally became the obligatory covering for a man's legs and I'm standing in Kmart trying to stuff my 40-inch gut into a size 38-inch waistband.

Damn those Scythians anyway.

• • •

While men had been wearing trousers for hundreds of years, long pants, as we know them, weren't worn much by women until well after WWII.

Women were stuck in corsets, which had been introduced to the French Court by Catherine de Medici in the 1500s. These were thought to be "indispensable to the beauty of the female body."

These undergarments shaped high fashion and the form of female nobility for over 500 years, until the beginning of the 20th Century.

In the middle of the 1800s, narrow waists were much admired and, even though women were smaller then, it is remarkable that some ladies got their girths to less than fifteen inches.

Carrying the fashion to such excess must have been extremely harmful. It certainly had to have been terribly uncomfortable.

If the relief I experience when I remove my shoes in the evening is any indication, the joy that women felt when the laces were loosened must have been close to ecstasy.

Nevertheless fashionable types squeezed their bodies inside whalebone corsets until shortly after 1900 when two developments occurred that changed the way women clothed themselves and what they wore under their clothes.

One event arose from the genius of a French couturier named Paul Poiret, the other from the genius of a French lingerie designer named Herminie Cadolle.

M. Poiret introduced a new, straight, upright silhouette for dresses that hung loosely and draped the body. He was influenced by classical, Middle Eastern and oriental fashion such as kimonos and harem pants.

Women loved Poiret's designs, in part because they eliminated the need for corsets and they promoted the use of what was to become the brassiere.

Which brings us to the second event that changed the course of women's wear; it was exhibited in Paris at the great Exposition of 1900.

Herminie Cadolle introduced her new take on the corset.

Mme. Cadolle had divided the corset into two pieces; a top and a bottom which, for starters, gave women much more freedom.

The bottom part was a corset for the waist.

Her genius was in the way she constructed the top.

Until then, whalebone corsets pushed the breasts together and up from a foundation at the waist creating a "monobosom."

Cadolle's new design was sturdy and practical. Each breast had its own cup, and the whole was supported in place by shoulder straps. It didn't look very much like a present-day bra, but it was revolutionary in the world of undergarments then.

Although it was a formidable apparatus, in no time at all she was selling the top part separately as a *soutien-gorge*, French for "support for the throat" – "*soutien*" being an old French appellation for "breast."

Her clientele included royalty, high society, actresses, even Mata Hari who, sadly for her, opted not to order the bulletproof model.

You have to understand that the reason these two advances – Poiret's designs and Cadolle's corsetry – were so influential is that they were introduced in Paris, the hub of world fashion. What was the *dernier cri* in Paris soon became the *cri* uttered by all women of style.

After six generations, Cadolle's atelier is still a successful business, creating custom-made lingerie in Paris at 225 Rue Saint Honoré.

M. Poiret's fortunes took an altogether different turn.

After WWI his couture fell out of fashion.

His fortunes declined and in 1929 when his house closed he was broke.

Eventually he was reduced to taking on odd jobs and peddling drawings in Paris cafés.

Once the head of a fashion empire, he scraped by until he died, forgotten and nearly friendless in 1944.

Elsa Schiaparelli paid for his funeral.

Herminie Cadolle has been given credit for inventing the proto brassiere, but she did not invent the word "brassiere." That was coined in 1904 by the DeBevoise Company, a French manufacturer, to describe their breast supporter.

The word derives from the French "upper arm"; it wasn't until the 1930s that brassiere was gradually shortened to bra.

My mother, who was born in the late 1890s, called the garment a "brassiere" all her life.

Fashions are slow to change and the corset didn't die in the early 1900s.

The *coup de grace* was delivered in WW1, when the US government asked women to stop buying corsets so that the metal used for stays could be diverted to war production. Apparently women heeded the admonition since it is estimated that some 28,000 tons of metal was saved; enough to build two battleships.

The modern brassiere was invented in New York in 1910 by a nineteen-year-old socialite named Mary Phelps Jacob.

She was dressing for a party and had chosen a gown with a sheer top and plunging neckline that showed off her ample frontage, but her whalebone-ribbed corset poked out from under her gown ruining the effect.

Until then, Ms. Jacob had let her corset push her up, but she certainly wasn't going to allow it push her around.

She decided, then and there, to invent what became the modern brassiere.

She and her maid took two handkerchiefs, sewed them together along with some ribbons and, as I once heard a lady proudly announce as she set a magnificent roast of beef on the table, "Viola!"

At the party that night the other young women wanted to know how she moved about so freely, and when they learned the reason, they all wanted one of those thingamajigs she had sewn up.

Her design was lightweight and comfortable and in 1914, she received a patent for her "Backless Brassiere."

She started a business, but it didn't do very well, and after marrying another socialite with a healthy trust fund, she sold the business to the Warner Brothers (not those Warner brothers) Corset Company for $21,000. Over the next thirty years, the Warner Brother Company made over thirty million on the patent.

However, in the teens, '20s and '30s, trousers for ladies were considered so outré that they were not worn in public except by celebrities who wanted their picture in the rotogravure.

In 1931 Sophie Tucker was one of the first women to wear long pants in public. They looked like long culottes, and the "Red Hot Mama" looked as though she was having a hellova good time wearing them.

Even though Hollywood glamour gals like Hepburn and Dietrich were photographed in elegant slacks, these garments were fashion statements to be worn at exclusive clubs, not the kit to be togged out in when cruising the local grocery.

This continued until after World War II.

Even though women had exchanged their dresses for slacks when they worked in factories, they still wore dresses and skirts at home and out to the movies.

In most of America, the "little woman" still wore a dress, stayed at home and took care of the house, the kids and the cooking. If she was ever asked what she did, her response would invariably be a self-deprecating, "I'm just a housewife."

But the social revolutions of the '60s and '70s brought tectonic changes in the way men and women thought about themselves and related to each other.

Hippies, beatniks, flower children – an explosion of personal freedom.

People wore whatever they wanted – pants or not.

Previously it was royalty or the elite couture houses that dictated the styles, but not then.

This was one of the only times, perhaps *the* only time, that a large-scale fashion change started from the bottom up.

But the change didn't complete itself overnight.

A lady friend of ours, who was a manager in a publishing company, told me that even into the '70s she demanded that her staff wear skirts to work (the women on her staff, that is); and a bon vivant friend said that during those years, in many fine New York restaurants, a woman who wore pants would not be seated at a table.

But, as Bob and Ray were wont to remind us, "Your stool is always reserved at Nedicks."

Nowadays, no one turns a hair when they see people wearing cut-offs and tee shirts to operas and theaters, where one used to see more respectful attire.

You can't blame the Scythians for that.

● ● ●

Mimi and I used to like to cook together.

I'd do the peeling and the chopping and she would put it together into a delicious meal.

She had the wonderful ability to be able to read a recipe and know if it was a good one or not.

She loved to entertain and make menus. She had a book in which she could show the seating arrangements and the names of the guests. She kept the menus and the wines.

She collected first growths from France, and although I wasn't terribly enthusiastic, it was important to her. I was happy with wines from the local liquor store and I complained about the price of wines that weren't going to be drinkable for years, but she bought them anyhow.

Once we were having a fancy dinner serving Vitello Tonato, a dish that is made from a thinly sliced veal roast slathered with a complicated tuna flavored mayonnaise.

We ordered the veal from our butcher in New York and when it was delivered we discovered to our horror that instead of leaving the roast whole the butcher had cut it into small chunks for Veal Stroganoff.

Definitely not suitable for Vitello Tonato.

What to do? I was at a loss. Not so Mimi.

She had a rather clever solution.

She braised the small pieces of veal and served them covered with the tuna sauce.

When one of the guests inquired, Mimi announced that she had decided not to make Vitello Tonato, but, instead, had made Vitello Romano.

It was a great success.

What an improviser! What a fabricator!

CHAPTER 7

• • •

Don't be Still My Heart . . . Please!

IN 1997 I was sixty-six and I was still working as a soap opera director. I'd been in the television business for forty years.

One day in the studio, during a break, someone mentioned that a colleague of mine had recently suffered a heart attack while directing his soap.

A little (maybe not so little) bell rang in my head. I realized that all three of my brothers had coronary disease in one form or another.

My oldest brother had had three bypass surgeries; my second oldest had undergone surgery replacing his aortic valve, and my younger brother had suffered a major heart attack.

It occurred to me then that it might be prudent for me to mention it to Ken Dodge. Duh!

That's how I ended up in the cardiologist's office taking a stress test, even though I was feeling great.

Compared to the tests I take now, it was rudimentary, but the results made my cardiologist uncomfortable.

If the findings made him feel uncomfortable, you can guess how they made me feel.

I could sense the winding sheet about me as I asked him what I should do.

Doctors and nurses always say "we" when thy mean "you."

"It's time for us to take our medicine." "We have to have our blood drawn now." "Have we had a good movement today?"

He said, "I think you should have an angiogram; find out what's going on in there."

I was so happy that he hadn't suggested that "we" should have an angiogram that I nearly stopped crying.

I was sixty-six and still working, I felt fine. I did not want a total stranger poking around in my heart. "No! No! No!" I said to myself. "Never! Never! Never!"

When I arrived at Saint Jude Hospital a week later, the nurse who was taking my blood pressure asked me if I was nervous. "Not exactly, I'm terrified."

After I filled out all the papers they make you fill out, showed all the insurance cards they make you show and signed all the releases they make you sign, I met the surgeon.

My cardiologist told me that this particular doctor had been doing several catheterizing procedures a day, a couple of days a week, for several years.

That's somewhat comforting, because you don't want the guy who's about the stick a catheter into your heart to come in carrying a volume labeled *The ABC's of Surgical Procedures*, and begin hunting for "Angio . . ."

Dr. Slater told me that he was going to perform an angiogram to get a picture of the condition of the heart, the valves and the arterial system around it.

There might be nothing amiss, but if he found a condition that was relatively simple to repair he would like permission to do the fix during the angiogram.

Permission granted – hopefully.

He asked me a lot more questions and explained that in about one percent of the procedures the contestant ends up dead. Occasionally someone has to be rushed to where the coronary bypass folks were standing by.

I had a vision of the surgeon pulling a lever that tilted the table, sending me rocketing down a chute like the one they have at Splish Splash, finally skidding to rest on the operating table below where the surgical team waited, masked and in scrubs, skilsaws and jackhammers at the ready.

He said, however, that these events occurred mostly in older people who had a lot of other medical complications.

Buoyed by the actuarial odds in my favor, I glided sensuously to the locker room where I disrobed and slipped into one of those naughty little hospital garments in which you don't want to be seen walking away.

● ● ●

An angio*gram* is different from an angio*plasty*. A coronary angio-gram is a picture of the heart. A catheter is threaded, usually through the femoral artery in the right side of your groin, until it reaches the coronary arteries and an opaque dye is released.

X-rays are taken to show the progress of the dye through the blood vessels, and they are fed to TV monitors so the surgeon can observe the process in real time. That way he is able to see if there are any blockages and how bad they may be. He can tell if they can be repaired by angioplasty, or if they require coronary surgery.

Angioplasty = Angio (Greek, meaning "vessel"– blood vessel in this case); plasty (Greek, meaning "to mold or repair"). The medical meaning of angioplasty is "blood vessel repair."

Angioplasty can be performed not only on the heart, but on almost any vein or artery in the human or animal body; in the bladder, the kidney, stomach, you name it.

A catheter is a thin tube that is inserted into the body. They can squirt liquid into the body through it, they day draw liquid out through it, they can use it to keep passages open. Catheters were used in ancient India to treat bladder conditions; Ancient Syrians made catheters of reeds. Hollow tubes were used by the early Greeks to treat bladder problems. So the basic function of a catheter was understood.

A catheter was introduced into the United States by none other than Benjamin Franklin in 1752.

Ben, whose inventiveness seems to have known no bounds, came up with a flexible catheter to ease the pain of his brother's kidney stones. It was made of metal tubes. The segments were strung together with on a wire to provide rigidity during insertion.

If that's how they eased pain in the 18th Century, I don't want to go back.

But it wasn't until 1929 that the first coronary catheterization was performed on a human by a twenty-five-year-old German named Werner Forssmann.

It's rather flabbergasting to note that he performed it on himself.

Forssmann figured that if you could place a catheter into the heart, you could use it to deliver medications directly, and you could also inject opaque dyes so that X-rays could show the heart's activity.

When he mentioned the idea at dinner, his boss spewed sauerkraut all over the tablecloth. He forbade him to attempt such a thing, thinking it was suicidal.

But Forssmann was determined, and he convinced a nurse to supply him with the material he needed. She did this after making him promise to do the procedure on her. (Don't ask me why.)

He strapped her to the operating table and pretended to stick her with anesthetic. He actually anesthetized his own right arm, cut it open, and inserted the catheter into one of his veins.

He released the nurse and, if you can believe it, they both walked downstairs to the radiology department. Using a fluoroscope, he guided the catheter another two feet up his arm into his right atrium and had a chest X-ray taken to prove he did it.

He was fired.

His feat was greeted with hostility and indifference by his colleagues in Germany who considered his accomplishment not much more than a circus trick.

Thirty years later he was awarded a Nobel Prize.

It took time, but eventually the use of cardiac angioplasty became the preferred treatment for many cardiovascular problems.

• • •

Meanwhile . . .

I returned to a room where I was placed on a gurney.

Thence, an orderly wheeled me through a set of swinging doors above which was a plaque emblazoned with the cheery inscription "Cardiac Catheterization Laboratory."

At least it didn't say, "Abandon hope all ye who enter here."

Once through the doors, I expected to see shelves of electrified hearts jigging around in glass jars, but it wasn't like that.

In fact, the room looked a lot like the operating room set-up we used on the soap opera.

They slid me off the gurney onto a cold, shiny black table on which the procedure was to take place.

The setup was rather interesting. From where I was laying I could see a line of TV monitors showing what the X-ray machine was seeing.

I lay there with an IV in one arm and a blood pressure cuff on the other, EKG tabs on my chest and terror in my heart.

The right side of my groin was shaved; I was happy to see that the nurse was using a safety razor, (not that there could have been a lot to damage if she was using a straight edge), then the area was numbed with an injection near my femoral artery.

They use the femoral artery because it's an easy avenue through which to thread the catheter up into the heart, although the vein in the arm is still used in some cases.

Next, they inserted a hollow sheath into my artery. The sheath is about one eighth of an inch in diameter. That might not seem like much, but, I can tell you, numbed groin or not, when they jam it in, you notice.

The catheter they use is a hollow tube about six feet long that they thread through the sheath in your groin, up your artery into your heart.

The doctor is able to direct the tip of the catheter with a control he holds in his hand.

● ● ●

After that it's tickety-boo as they say in Blighty.

The doctor stood just behind my left shoulder. Since he was in a position to see the monitors I could see them too. As the catheter was threaded into my artery I felt no sensation. In fact, I didn't feel any pain during the whole procedure.

It was a strange emotional sensation, though, as I saw my heart throbbing in the TV monitor, lub-dubbing away.

Very strange.

Then, I saw the thin black silhouette of the catheter enter the picture; stranger still.

I was completely awake and the conversation was casual. The surgeon wanted to know if I was feeling any discomfort, and how similar this was to what would happen on my soap opera.

I told him that the setup would look pretty much like this, except that the scene would end with me flat lining, and the crash cart crew rushing in.

He said he hoped that this session wouldn't end like that.

It didn't.

He told me that he was going to squirt some more juice into my heart and that I'd feel a strange sensation in my chest and lower body.

He did and I did.

I saw the contrast dye being shot into my heart.

The sensation spread from my heart to my waist so quickly that I was astonished.

I understood then how it was that the heart could circulate blood through your entire body in a minute.

It was very interesting and I was having a fascinating time; for a moment I forgot that this was actually happening to me.

He finished and I was wheeled back to the recovery room where a nurse extracted the sheath. I think she applied a collagen plug to stop the bleeding from my artery because Dr. Slater wanted me to return the next day for further work.

He told me that I did have a blockage and I would require a stent or two, but he wanted to study the video recording in order to decide exactly where and how he wanted to place them.

• • •

A coronary stent is a small wire mesh tube about one-tenth of an inch in diameter that is placed on the end of a balloon catheter and threaded up a guide wire into the heart where the *stenosis* (narrowing) is.

The balloon is inflated, expanding the stent until it presses into the wall of the artery. Then the balloon is deflated and withdrawn, leaving the stent in place.

It is a permanent addition to your coronary furniture and it is supposed to prevent the vessel from narrowing again (restenosis.)

• • •

Stents had been around for years, in fact, the word "stent" is most likely named after Dr. Charles Stent, an English dentist who, in 1856 invented the material to help him create dental impressions.

You wouldn't think that a puttylike substance called "stent" that was used for dental impressions could be the ancestor of the medical stent, but as it dried hard, it was used as a matrix around which to form tissue, and it could be molded for use in surgery to hold open body cavities.

Stents can be used to hold open almost any vessel and are used commonly in the kidney, the bladder and uterus.

Although the first human coronary stent implantation was performed in France in 1986, it wasn't until 1994 that cardiac stents were introduced in the US; three years before I got mine.

• • •

It must have been the next day that I reported to the hospital again.

Things proceeded much as they had previously except, as I learned later, the doctor had placed two stents in my left anterior descending coronary artery (LAD).

The "Widowmaker," as it is called in the rather morbid patois of medical professionals.

It's called that because the LAD provides most of the blood to the left ventricle, and the left ventricle does most of the work involved in pushing the re-oxygenated blood around the body.

If the LAD is clogged, no oxygen gets to the cells in the ventricle. If no oxygen gets to the cells in the ventricle, the ventricle stops pumping. If the left ventricle stops pumping, no oxygen gets to your body or your brain, so there's not a lot of hope even if there's a cardiologist sitting at the next table.

The fact that I'm writing about this some sixteen years after the procedure should tell you that in my case, the stenting process worked.

The doctor told me that I had had a ninety percent blockage in my LAD and if it had gone on much longer I would have been one of those guys who starts his backswing and is dead before he has a chance to shank his Mulligan 40 feet into the deep rough.

The doctor was so proud of how artfully he had placed the stents that he called a colleague in to look at the X-ray.

"Way cool!"

At that point I realized, to my amazement, lying on the table in the Cardiac Catheterization Laboratory (CCL), undergoing a Percutaneous Transluminal Coronary Angioplasty (PTCA) that I was more relaxed than when I was sitting in the control room directing Another World (AW), for the National Broadcasting Company (NBC).

Once again, that little bell in my head went "ding-a-ling".

I was sixty-six years old; I wanted badly to become sixty-seven years old.

I gave notice to my boss the next week.

Three months later I returned for another angiogram to make sure that the LAD hadn't begun to narrow again.

It hadn't.

Side note . . .

It seems that near the LAD are a bunch of small dormant vessels that normally don't get into the action. But sometimes, when the LAD has limited blood flow, these vessels begin to enlarge and become active, allowing more blood to get to the heart muscle.

During the last angiogram I had in 2007, the doctor commented that these small vessels had indeed been activated and it was a good sign.

The not-so-good news was that during my angioplasties I didn't feel any pain when the doctor inflated the balloon in my LAD, cutting off the blood supply.

This implied that I don't suffer *angina* when my heart is deprived of oxygen.

My cardiologist explained to me that the pain of angina is a signal. It's nature's way of telling you to telephone your cardiologist. Otherwise, you might not realize there is anything wrong until it's late in the game.

I have a sonogram of my heart every year, and a nuclear stress test every two years or so and everything seems to be copacetic . . . so far.

But tests are just tests, they're not guarantees. Let me tell you of an encounter I had with my cardiologist a few years ago.

He is the one who diagnosed me and sent me to the doctor who did such a great job on my LAD. As far as I'm concerned, he saved my life. Besides, he is the one who never uses "we" when he means "you."

I was sitting in his office after one of the stress tests and blood-letting binges that occur every so often to heart patients. He looked at all the reports and pronounced everything satisfactory. He told me to make an appointment for six months down the line.

As I stood up I said, "Well, Al, I guess I'm good for another 10,000 miles."

"Bob, I can't even guarantee you'll make it back to your car."

• • •

Mimi and I loved to travel and we traveled a lot; and as we all know, a trip isn't a real trip if you don't come home without a few stories to tell.

In 1987, along with another couple, we visited India.

We landed in Mumbai on New Year's Eve and in order to properly celebrate both the New Year and our forthcoming journey, we had the foresight to carry with us three bottles of Moet which we iced and drank in our room overlooking the festivities at the Gateway of India.

For three weeks we traveled from north to south beginning with the Taj Mahal and ending down past Madras in the southern part of Tamil Nadu.

On the way, I kept forgetting my charge card when I left a store. Going back to our last stop was getting to be a pain in the neck for everyone, so when we came to a hotel that had a leather shop in the lobby, I decided to solve the problem by buying a special wallet for my charge card.

After we checked in I went down and purchased a neat little leather envelope that was specially made to contain one charge card.

As I returned to our room, Mimi was just hanging up the phone.

"It was the guy at the leather shop. You left your charge card on the counter."

In Jodhpur, Mimi was attracted by a "lucky' charm being peddled by a woman on the street. The woman named a price and I started to bargain with her. She said, "Sir that is less than half a dollar in your money."

I gave her a dollar. I still have the little disk in my pocket.

We loved France and always had a good time there. We were always treated well even though my French was pretty rudimentary.

At a gallery in Paris we bought a small painting of two ducks that Mimi had admired.

Later, I showed it to a French woman we had met and asked her if she thought we had paid too much for it.

She quoted an Arabic proverb, "The beauty of the object remains long after the price is forgotten."

It's on our wall, and I forget what I paid for it.

One time we had to stay in a tiny hotel on the Left Bank. It was a three-flight climb up to our tiny room.

They said it had a double bed. In America it would have been classed as a large cot. The mattress sagged so much that when we climbed in, we both rolled into the center and lay nose-to-nose.

It was impossible get much sleep squeezed together like that, so we improvised and spent a surprisingly pleasant night.

Mimi and I traveled in the Loire Valley and attended a son-et lumiere performance at Clemenceau, a beautiful 16th Century chateau built across the River Cher.

The show didn't start until after dark, so we enjoyed a good dinner with a bottle of wine.

About halfway through Mimi said, "Bob, I've got to pee."

As the audio track was describing some historic event and the lights were blinking on and off in the rooms where the event was supposed to have taken place, Mimi and I made our way out *of the stands toward the parking lot at the end of the long, dark, tree-lined, entrance drive to the Chateau.*

"I've got to pee now!"

"Mimi, it's dark here, there's no one around. Go over near one of those trees and pee."

She moved to the side of the drive, finished her preparations and got into position just as the sound effect of galloping horses broke through and the voice announced loud and clear "The king's chariot approached along the drive."

The lights flashed on, bathing everything — and I mean "everything" — in its merciless glare.

CHAPTER 8

• • •

About Me . . .

I THOUGHT THAT this would be a good place to take a break, and let you know a little bit about how my mind works, when and where I was born, my early life – things like that.

Even though I have a full-time job taking care of Mimi and seeing to the household chores, I manage to find a few moments to relax.

I like to read detective stories.

I especially like detective stories that begin with a gunshot and a body in a locked room, where the maid screams and faints, the butler is aghast and all the guests come running to see what happened.

They all have alibis – or do they?

The inspector from the Yard will find out.

Detective stories that I do not like are about detectives who are anguished poets and have a backstory that goes on and on, and whose longtime paramour is a famous brain surgeon who has been offered a post in Tasmania that she simply can't turn down.

The detective's private angst is interrupted only by tedious descriptions of drawing rooms.

By the time someone gets shot you're 200 pages in – if you get that far.

C'mon – Bang, Bang. Whodunit?

I don't like Scandinavian detectives either. They all seem to be alcoholics or recovering alcoholics who will surely get blotto before the story goes very far. In most cases their daughters are drug addicts and their wives have long since run off with another Scandinavian (most likely a picture framer); but she's sure to show up somewhere down the line begging the detective to help find her Scandinavian picture framer who has been missing since he took up with the wife of another Scandinavian detective.

Irish detectives are trouble too.

They all seem to have the same drinking problem that the Scandinavians have except it's compounded by what happened to them when they were altar boys.

It's a sure bet that they'll run into the remorseful pedophile in a bar before the story is over.

I'm put off by a detective story that ends with the sleuth seated with friends around a table at the club, smoking cigars and sipping brandy, where he is explaining something like, ". . . As soon as I saw him duck the finesse and renege on the next trick, I knew he had to be the one. Because only someone with the foresight to void himself in trump and then double his own partner when they were vulnerable would have been able to anticipate . . ."

Puleeez!

I don't like detective stories about bizarre serial killers who dress up in rubber masks and tutus, and go about mutilating their victims on every third Wednesday after the new moon.

Of course each of the victims is horribly disfigured and painstakingly described by the author.

Yuck!

These killers invariably write taunting notes to the police and give obscure clues containing quotes from nursery rhymes or baseball players' batting averages, hinting at where they'll strike again.

And since the book has to be long enough, you know that you'll have to go through several even more disgusting descriptions before the maniac hangs himself just before the cops get there.

"My God, it's a woman!"

Isn't there enough gruesome stuff on the news?

"Some of the images in this story may be graphic."

Tell me what sort of image isn't graphic.

What they mean is that if you keep watching you'll be seeing lots of dead bodies.

What's on the Cooking Channel?

As long as I'm on the subject, I have to tell you that if I read a review of a play that begins something like, "This is a compelling story of incest and rape in the Arizona desert—"

Don't look for me in the audience.

I like to read mysteries from the Golden Age of British detective fiction: Agatha Christie, Ngaio Marsh, Dorothy Sayers, Josephine Tey.

I like Rex Stout and S.S. Van Dine.

Oldies, but goldies. You know what you're getting into.

● ● ●

I like to do crossword puzzles too.

They say it helps to stop the plasterers from troweling cement all over the inside of your brain.

I don't know if that's true but I like to do them anyway.

The first crossword puzzle was composed in 1913 by Arthur Wynne. He worked for a newspaper called *The New York World*.

You can look it up on Google.

Crosswords have come a long way since then.

Now there are crosswords not only in English, but all European languages, Japanese, Chinese, Urdu, Hindi and Swahili, Malagasy, Telugu and Lojban to name just a few.

The New York Times refrained from publishing crosswords until 1942 because it thought they were "a primitive form of mental exercise."

Can someone please tell me why so many things I'm fascinated by are referred to as "primitive" or the "lowest form" by the so-called intelligentsia?

But, after Pearl Harbor was bombed, Arthur Hays Sulzberger, *The Times* publisher, had the puzzle added to the paper so that people would have something to do during blackouts.

It took a war.

The Times puzzle starts easy on Monday and gets more difficult by degrees 'til Saturday. If you can do the Saturday puzzle regularly you probably would have been recruited for Bletchley Park.

The puzzle is carried by more than 300 papers and that doesn't include the folks who subscribe to it on the Net.

My guess is that over a million people do the puzzle daily. Maybe a couple of million; maybe more

The New York Times Crossword Puzzle presents challenges; especially to a bleary-eyed, dyslexic, bad speller with nearly illegible handwriting, who has a slight case of dry macular degeneration in his left eye so when he scans a horizontal line, the letters seem to tilt, bulge and squish.

I'm talking about me.

My old eyes are often bleary and have to be dabbed with a tissue. In certain type fonts the word "turn" reads "tum." The clue "One good tum deserves -------" will leave me perplexed.

If I fill in a box, the letter I write will often cover the number of the clue going in the other direction and it will require erasure to read the number. Otherwise, I will have to go back to a box where I can read the number and count the perpendicular-numbered boxes until I get to the particular box that I am trying to full. By then I've forgotten the clue and after I've gone back and reread it I've lost the space that the clue refers to. Annoying.

Being dyslexic is no help because I have such a terrible time spelling that I don't realize that the word I'm hearing in my head isn't a real word at all. I will read a clue as "It can be found in a hamburg." The first three letters and the last letter will already be filled in, so I have 'com---t.' Aha! I have it. A hamburg is comfort food, so I fill the remaining letters to form the word "comfort." It is only later when the crossing clues cannot possibly work with the word "comfort" that I return to the clue, and, looking more closely, see that it reads "It can be found in a "handbag," not "hamburg." Of course the word they're looking for is "compact". Later, I discovered that "hamburg" isn't even a real word. Humiliating.

Spelling is something you're either born with or without.

Wright? er, write? uh, rite? Right!

I remember a test in college when I spent a good deal of the precious time trying to decide if the word was spelled "bouth," "bowth" or "bothe." None of them looked correct, and I don't remember what I finally decided.

But "both" definitely did not look right; it still doesn't. If you want to know, "both" still looks to me as if it ought to be pronounced to rhyme with "sloth" or "broth". Go figure.

A bunch of famous individuals were bad spellers.

William Faulkner misspelled words, but you've got to cut him some slack. He had to tangle with Yoknapatawpha County. C'mon.

Alfred Butts, the man who invented Scrabble, no less, was supposed to be a lousy speller.

Hemingway's editors complained that they had to correct a lot of his spelling. He remarked that that's what they were paid to do.

Jane Austin was a poor speller; Agatha Christie too.

John Keats: Owed on a Grecian Earn?

Da Vinci, Einstein, Churchill, Jack Kennedy; all of them suffered from *cacography*.

It sounds to me like Greek for "crappy writing", and that's exactly what it is; *kakos* = "bad." It doesn't take much imagination to guess what other word is derived from "kakos."

I'm put off by people who read something I've written and shake their heads, snickering at my gaffs.

"I" before "E" except after "C" is a crock. Think about neighbor, beige, codeine, conscience, deity, deign, eight, either, foreign, freight, heifer, height, heinous, heir, heist, neither, peignoir, science, seize, sheik, society, sovereign, veil, vein, weight, weird.

There are more.

I googled "spelling rules" and there are so many exceptions to every rule, that one's eyes glaze over before you've read the first few.

The main thing I learned is that spelling rules always apply except when they don't.

When I answered the clue "Newborn farm animal as "FOLE," the "F" fitted perfectly, but I guess you can figure that there was going to be troubel ahead. Excuse me, that should be "trouble" ahead. Too bad spell-check doesn't work on the puzzle.

By the way, I looked up "fole." It's a main belt asteroid with an orbital period of 1164.4126764 days.

So, if they ever put in a clue, "Main belt asteroid with an orbital period of 1164.4126764 days" you can thank me as you fill in the answer.

When I start working the puzzle, I lay down letters that are as crisp and clear as the ones on those cards that were tacked over the blackboards in grade school.

But soon the crisp letters begin to wilt like lettuce you leave out overnight. My Ys begin to look like Ts; my Ls start to resemble Cs; Ds relax their spines and slump into Os. This causes confusion, naturally.

To compound the problem, even though I'm left-handed, I try to fill in some of the boxes with my right hand.

After all, one never knows when something terrible may happen and I'll have to depend on my right hand. So, I'm trying to improve its dexterity.

As of now, the letters I produce with my right hand bear a passing resemblance to Linear B. It's a slow process, but, I'm going to keep at it.

Digression . . .

Above I described myself as dyslexic.

As I was writing this, I happened to read an op-ed in *The New York Times* by Blake Charlton, a physician who is dyslexic.

I had been aware that I often misread words and occasionally the result would be an amusing confusion.

Dyslexic, big deal; I thought it was about as debilitating as a bad case of dandruff.

As you read this I am probably 84 or more (that is if I'm still around at all) and, until that moment, I had no idea of the profound effect that dyslexia had had, and was having, on my life.

I never underwent the ragging that Dr. Charlton and others had to endure.

I suspect that's only because in the 1940s not a lot of people had even heard of dyslexia.

I didn't think about it much except to tell jokes: "Did you hear about the suicidal dyslexic who kept throwing himself behind a bus?"

So, it was with only casual interest that I began to read Dr. Charlton's article (Very slowly. I'm a terribly slow reader.)

As I read into it, however, the noise I heard was my jaw dropping to the floor.

I thought that my misreading of words was sort of cute.

It never occurred to me that my slow reading was part of the dyslexic pattern.

It never occurred to me that my atrocious spelling was part of the dyslexic pattern.

It never occurred to me that my terrible stuttering as a child could have been part of the dyslexic pattern.

Dyslexia had been with me all my life.

I began to feel that if I hadn't been dyslexic, I could have made something more of myself; "I could'a been a contender."

As I read on, however, I learned that maybe everything wasn't in the negative column, that there were positive attributes that worked in the dyslexic mind.

A dyslexic mind has a different way of processing information.

For one, dyslexics often possess the ability to make connections that others don't see, or hear; puns, for instance, which have been a joy in my life.

But, perhaps the most extraordinary quality of dyslexic circuitry – which I have been blessed with – is the ability to visualize spatially.

I remember those tests in grammar school with pictures that showed a weight attached to a complicated series of pulleys and levers. The problem was to figure out if the weight would go up or down if you pulled the handle at the far left.

No prob, Bob.

Many dyslexics have become architects or designers.

That carried over to camera movement and staging when I became a television director.

If you visit my website – bobschwarzart.com – and look at the art I create, you will be able to see the architectural quality.

I've been asked numerous times at exhibits if I had studied architecture.

The answer is "no," but now I see how the dyslexic tendency to feel comfortable with spatial relationships has emerged in the constructivist sculptures that I make.

Back . . .

We seem to have strayed from the crossword puzzles that I was talking about a while ago, but we're not on any schedule.

The editor of the *NYT* Crossword puzzles since 1993 is a gent named Will Shortz. He doesn't construct the puzzles, though I'm sure he could if he wanted to.

Will Shortz graduated in 1974 from the University of Indiana having earned a degree in enigmatology; the scientific study of puzzles. He invented the discipline himself so that he could get a degree in it.

He also graduated from law school. That means that I've got to be careful what I say about him.

I suppose I have to preface any critical remarks with "alleged." like the news people do to protect themselves from lawsuits every time they refer to someone who was caught on surveillance cameras, guns blazing, shell casings flying and seen by dozens of witnesses performing some despicable crime, as the "alleged perpetrator."

Then the 24/7 news cycle is on it. They'll go to almost any lengths to get an exclusive interview with someone who knew the alleged perpetrator.

Those channels will send reporters trudging across burning deserts of North Africa or scampering up the mountains in South America to interview a shepherd who is alleged to be the cousin of the alleged perpetrator's alleged third grade school teacher and is alleged to have known him.

"Here I am in the tiny principality of Aymusin where an alleged sheepherder alleges that he baaaaaaaarely knew the alleged perpetrator and any allegations to the contrary would be subject to severe penalties – er – allegedly. Chet Glibley reporting from high in the Aymusin Andes. Back to you, Wolf."

Mr. Shortz alleges that he sends the puzzles out to some allegedly knowledgeable puzzle solvers who allegedly fill them in and check to see if any of the clues are incorrect.

I am not alleging that the puzzle makers make many mistakes. Most of the complaints that Mr. Shortz gets are made by people who don't fully realize the potential meaning of the clue.

Just last week there was a clue, "Big game." Four letters beginning with "B". I filled in with the word "bear."

Nothing would work with the other letters. I finally gave up. The next day I looked at the answer and, lo and behold, it was "Bowl."

Again and again I asked myself, "How could bowling be a big game?"

Then boing! Rose Bowl; a big game indeed.

You've got to believe that they put that clue in beginning with "B" just to lead me down the garden path.

I'm sure glad I didn't post an angry email alleging that the Shortz Gang had goofed.

However, I hereby allege that I know of one time when a friend of mine caught them with their Shortz down.

A few years ago the puzzle had a clue that read something like: "He wrote farces."

The answer supplied next day was "Wilde," as in Oscar Wilde.

My friend called and said, "Y'know, they got it wrong in *The Times* yesterday. Wilde wasn't a farceur; he wrote comedies of manners."

My friend was right. (I had missed it.)

So, ladies and gentlemen of the jury, the facts have proven, beyond doubt that my client was in Brisbane on the night of the – er – (wrong summation) – I allege that even the greatest minds in puzzledom can occasionally get their Shortz in a twist.

Quod erat demonstrandum.

There are times when I get frustrated doing the puzzle.

Whenever you see a question mark after a clue you know the answer is going to be tricky. The answer to "Country Kitchen?" might be "French Cuisine." See what I mean?

I'm not saying that every clue should be like "Mata ----."

And I freely admit that, being an Old Fart, I have very little interest in events or personalities that teenagers are apt to be familiar with.

But I allege that bringing Death Metal music into *The New York Times* Sunday Puzzle is not quite fair to Old Farts like me.

I don't know the names of any current teenage heartthrobs, male or female.

I can't tell you who the lead guitarist is in any musical group currently performing.

I haven't the faintest idea of the name of the bestselling Rap album of 2005, or any other year for that matter, or the "artist" who made it.

I am not familiar with any singer whose first name is BeeBee, CeeCee, DeeDee, GeeGee or any other repetitive two-letter combination.

I am ignorant of the names of almost all the players on sports teams, except, of course, the 1946 Boston Red Sox team that played against the Cardinals in the World Series that year; Williams, Doerr, Pesky, Dom DiMaggio, York, Metkivitch, Boo Ferriss, Wally Moses, et al.

It was Game 7. The Series was tied at three games each. It was the 8th inning of a 3-3 game. Enos Slaughter led off the St. Louis half with a single. The next two batters failed to advance him.

Two outs.

Next up was Harry Walker; he knocked the ball over shortstop Johnny Pesky's head into left center.

Slaughter took off. With two outs, it was naturally assumed by anyone who knew anything about baseball that Slaughter would hold up at third like any rational, prudent, God-fearing base runner should.

Pesky took the throw from the outfield. He checked Walker at first, and then turned to check Slaughter at third. But to Pesky's amazement, chagrin and alarm, third base was empty. Slaughter hadn't held up at all. He hadn't even slowed down. Rather, he was legging it down the third base line, hell-bent for leather, and straight for home. Pesky's throw was wide.

Slaughter scored.

The Red Sox lost the game 4 to 3.

The Red Sox lost the World Series.

I was fifteen.

Some think that "Slaughter's scamper" is one of the greatest plays in the history of the game.

It stinks when your home team comes out on the wrong side of one of the greatest plays in the history of the game.

I don't like to think about it.

I'm happy with clues like: "When Yuba Plays the Rumba on his Tuba Down in..." Or give me: "McCarthy who wooden take no for an answer," and I'm right at home.

You can google the answers but, somehow, I think if you do that, you break the unwritten contract you make when you begin the puzzle.

Nevertheless, I stumble through the puzzle and, usually, in spite all my handicaps, most of the time I finish the thing.

Oddly enough, I immediately begin to suffer from post-puzzle depression. Seven whole days till the next Sunday.

Depending on how hard I find the puzzle, sometimes it's only four days till Sunday.

● ● ●

In 1971 Mimi and I bought a small summer house in East Hampton.

We viewed several possibilities. Mimi was particularly taken by one that had a huge fireplace in the front room. That was the one Mimi settled on.

Of course, I was asked for my opinion, but if that was a place where she felt comfortable, then it was the one we both wanted.

The funny thing was that we hadn't intended to buy a house at all, but that afternoon we returned to NYC with a receipt for the deposit in our hands.

Mimi said that the only thing that could improve it would be a swimming pool in the back.

Sooner rather than later, a pool was in place where we spent many happy hours paddling about both alone and with friends, often skinny-dipping in the moonlight with candles burning along the edges and brandy snifters at each end.

Mimi loved having me make fires in the evening when we were having cocktails (even in July and August).

I'd tell friends that Mimi liked a fire in the fireplace, the air conditioning on and the door open to catch the evening breeze.

She decorated the place impeccably and many times she'd look about her and say how beautiful it was and how happy she was to live here.

Flowers were everywhere. Tuberous begonias were hung along the stairs and outside in the patio beside the pool. Fuchsias were on the deck and oxeye daisies in pots all around; the pool was surrounded by New Guinea impatiens.

It took me almost an hour to do all the watering.

If you have ever bought a place to live, I guess you know that your wife had better be content with it.

Mimi was more than content, she was in love with the place. She had had to flee from her home when she was sixteen and once she had settled in her nest there was no chance of prying her out of it.

Once when I was traveling I visited Asheville in North Carolina. I was quite taken by the scenery and I suggested to Mimi that we might think of moving.

She asked me two questions.

"How do you think you're going to get me there, and if you do, how do you think you're going to keep me there?"

I never mentioned it again.

CHAPTER 9

• • •

Words, word, words . . .

EVERY ONCE IN a while *The New York Times* Sunday puzzle section includes, a puzzle of puns and anagrams.

I like puns. Anagrams, eh.

According to Wikipedia: "The pun, also called *paronomasia*, is a form which suggests two or more meanings, by exploiting multiple meanings of words, or of similar-sounding words, for an intended humorous or rhetorical effect."

I don't know who wrote the Wikipedia entry about puns, but he or she wrote that puns were used by Plautus, Shakespeare, Pope, Wilde, Lewis Carroll, Joyce and George Carlin among others.

George Carlin???

The example used wasn't bad, something about atheism being a non-prophet religion, but George Carlin grouped along with those folks? I don'no.

Puns get confused with other kinds of wordplay.

A *malapropism* is not a pun. It comes from the French – "poorly placed." Mrs. Malaprop appears in Sheridan's play *The Rivals*, where she, of course, proceeds to utter a lot of malapropisms like using *allegory* for *alligator*.

One I like is attributed to Yogi Berra. He was supposed to have said, "Texas has a lot of *electrical* votes." (In typical Yogi fashion, Berra has protested that he never said half the things he said.)

Malapropisms are the product of a person unaware of the fact that the word he or she utters merely sounds similar to the intended word. They can be droll, e.g.: "In 1969 he *defecated* from Russia to the West."

Another example I like is the one of the woman who went to the pharmacy and asked to be directed to the area where they sell disposable diapers for those suffering from adult *incompetence*. Possibly the clerk should have sent her to our nation's capital.

A *spoonerism* is not a pun. This aberration is named after William Archibald Spooner, an English educator at the turn of the 20th Century who was prone to come out with them.

A spoonerism occurs when the first letter, or letters, of two words become interchanged – *belly jean* for *jelly bean*; *sea poop fog* for *pea soup fog*. I don't think much of spoonerisms.

An *eggcorn* is not a pun. The word comes from Professor of Linguistics, Max Lieberman, who in 2003 described how a woman heard the word "acorn" as *eggcorn*. When it was discovered that there was no word to describe this sort of mix-up, a colleague, Geoffrey Pullum, suggested using eggcorn itself. And, children, it was so.

I had a personal eggcorn. For years I heard the name of the Hollywood star as Donna Meechey. I thought he was a woman.

A *mondegreen* isn't a pun either, but it's an amusing phenomenon that's worth learning about.

As a child, the author Sylvia Wright was often read to by her mother. One of her favorites was a poem from an 18th Century collection, Percy's *Reliques*. It begins with the quatrain:

Ye Highlands and ye Lowlands,
Oh, where hae ye been?
They hae slain the Earl O' Moray,
And laid him on the green.

Young Sylvia heard the last line as *And Lady Mondegreen*. She thought that two people had been slain, both the Earl O' Moray and Lady Mondegreen.

When she was writing about her mis-hearing in a magazine article, she discovered that that particular phenomenon had not yet been named.

She chose "mondegreen," thereby inventing a new word in our language and at the same time honoring a phantom peeress of the realm.

Looking back on my mistaken hearing of Donna Meechey, I think that it is more likely a mondegreen.

Here's one you can tell to your grandchildren. "The mother bear made her cub clean his feet when he came home from the beach because she didn't believe in *sandy claws*."

Now, I can't decide whether that's a pun, an eggcorn or a mondegreen. It could be a combination of all three.

Then it would be a *pundegreen*. A new word certainly, but I don't expect to find it in the OED anytime soon.

As a matter of fact, I think "eggcorn" and "mondegreen" are so much alike that they are really the same thing.

But "eggcorn" sounds ugly and brutish; grating on the ear, whereas "mondegreen" fills the air with a melodic tone; it sounds elegant; I venture to say grand.

Therefore, I rise in an uncontrollable outburst of fervor and issue a clarion call urging that we transport the eggcorns of this world to barren desert ruins where they would eventually waste away, crumble and end scattering in the sirocco where lone and level sands stretch far away.

Mondegreen, on the other hand, has a sweeping arch; a grand scope to it. It should be enshrined in topless towers, locked in atmospherically-controlled glass cases for all eternity, where they can be marveled at by generations to come.

Thank you. The fever has passed. I shall now resume my seat.

A lovely mondegreen was reported to me by Jim McAllen, a soap opera director on *As the World Turns* in the '50s and '60s.

There had just been a script meeting at which one of the writers wanted make the current villain much more sympathetic.

Irna Phillips, the creator and head writer of ATWT, would not hear of it. "After all," she said, "a *leper* cannot change his spots."

Sadly, he can't.

Euphemisms are fun too. Think of "break wind" for fart. "Restroom" or "comfort station" for toilet.

I always think of a comfort station as a place you go where someone sits you down and pats your hand saying, "There, there, it isn't that bad."

An *oxymoron* is not a pun. It is usually a two-word combo uniting two contradictory terms; jumbo shrimp; rap artist; deafening silence; military intelligence; Republican compromise – that sort of thing.

A *simile* is not a pun. A simile compares two items by using the word "like" or a similar word as Robby Burns did in 1794:

My love is *like* a red red rose
That's newly sprung in June:
My love is *like* a melody
That's sweetly played in tune.

"The spider was *as big as* a Buick." – Woody Allen

One that tickled me particularly is, "It was *as cold as* a frozen fart in a dead Eskimo."

A *metaphor* is not a pun; it is a phrase that unites two different things that have something in common.

"*I Am a Camera*" is a metaphor. It is the title of a 1951 John Van Druten play taken from a Christopher Isherwood book, *Berlin Diary.*

The character is obviously not a camera, but he is saying that he is similar to a camera in that he reports things without bias.

"I Am a Camera" was famously reviewed by Walter Kerr in three words: "Me no Leica." (A very neat pun.)

Maybe it's just my cynical nature, but I think that once a reviewer comes up with something clever like that, he or she simply must use it no matter how the good the play is.

Hyperbole is not a pun, it is an exaggeration used for effect. "He had a face that could stop the Super Chief."

My mother used to say, "You look like the wreck of the Hesperus."

I wonder if anybody would catch the reference now.

Antanaclasis. I never heard of it either but the word itself is so visually arresting, that when I saw it on a website concerned with figures of speech, I had to find out what it meant. It is sort of like a pun. It is repeating the same word, but with a different meaning.

An example is what Benjamin Franklin is supposed to have said at the signing of the Declaration of Independence: "We must, indeed, all *hang* together, or assuredly we shall all *hang* separately."

I read the next one and it took me several seconds to get the joke, but when I did, I had a good laugh.

"Time *flies like* an arrow; fruit *flies like* a banana." It's a cute one, because both *flies* and *like* are used in different senses.

Epizeuxis is not a pun, but, again, the word looks so interesting that I had to find out what it means. It comes from the Greek, "fastening together." It is a term for the repetition of a word with vehemence or emphasis.

There are many famous ones in literature.

King Lear cries out: "Never, never, never, never, never."

There are plenty of others, but my fave is spoken by Claude Rains as Captain Renault in *Casablanca* (1942): "I'm shocked, *shocked* to find that gambling is going on in here!"

Acronyms are interesting.

Once I had to go to Stony Brook Hospital for an examination and I passed by a door that had the letters CACU printed on it.

I was perplexed and I was told that CACU stands for "**C**ardiac **A**cute **C**are **U**nit."

It is an acronym.

Per Wikipedia, "An *acronym* is an abbreviation formed from the initial components in a phrase or a word."

It can be simply the first letters of the words in a phrase you want to acronymize (my word).

One of the earliest acronyms was SPQR (**S**enātus **P**opulus**Q**ue **R**ōmānus): "The Senate and People of Rome." You've seen it many times embroidered on a banner carried at the forefront of Roman Legions right behind Charlton Heston.

But SPQR was an anomaly because acronyms were few and far between before the 20th Century, but believe me they've made up for that scarcity in the meantime.

I was surprised to learn that the word "acronym" didn't exist before 1943 when it was made up from the Greek *acro* "tip, end" plus another Greek word that comes into English as *onym* "name."

I'm not sure how that describes an acronym, but there you are.

There's MADD (**M**others **A**gainst **D**runk **D**riving). This is a neat one because it has the added fillip of being a homonym with the word "mad", suggesting mothers are angry about drunk driving.

But an acronym doesn't have to sound like a real word; WYSIWYG stands for "**W**hat **Y**ou **S**ee **I**s **W**hat **Y**ou **G**et." Now "wysiwyg" is in the dictionary.

An acronym can also be a conflation of two or more words: AMTRAK (American Track). AMTRAK is the acronym invented by the National Railroad Passenger Corporation. They could have used NARAPACO. I think they were wise to go with AMTRAK.

Many acronyms are specific to certain professions and you would have no way of knowing what they stand for unless you just happen to know that they stand for. They can be confusing.

Medicine has a million of 'em: AAA = **A**bdominal **A**ortic **A**neurysm for one.

You're probably ahead of me in realizing that AAA can also stand for American Automobile Association and Anti-Aircraft Artillery.

But, if you're a doctor and you are told that a patient has an AAA, you understand something quite different from someone who needs driving directions to a friend's house for Thanksgiving, and a whole other thing if you are a general ordering ordnance for your troops.

A while ago Mimi had to have an ERCP and nobody on the floor of the hospital knew exactly what the letters stand for even though they all knew what the procedure is.

They generally got through "Endoscopic," but after that they petered out.

Here's what the letters ERCP stand for, it's **E**ndoscopic **R**etrograde **C**holangio**P**ancreatography.

Frankly, I couldn't give somebody very bad marks for not coming up with Endoscopic Retrograde Cholangiopancreatography.

If a doctor had to perform several of them in the same day, he would probably take more time writing down what he was going to do than he would spend actually doing it.

In case you don't happen to know what an ERCP entails I'll tell you.

The procedure makes use of an endoscope; a pliable tube with a light and a camera leading the way.

An endoscope is similar to a colonoscope except they stick it in the other "endo."

Endoscopic Retrograde Cholangiopancreatography is a procedure during which the surgeon guides an endoscope down the throat, into the stomach, through the stomach, out of the stomach into the area of the pancreas and gallbladder where he takes a look around.

Another three-letter acronym for a twenty-five-letter procedure is EGD.

EGD is the acronym for **E**sophago**G**astro**D**uodenoscopy.

So as not to keep you in suspense, it is a test to examine the lining of the esophagus, stomach, and first part of the small intestine. It is done with a small camera on a flexible endoscope that is inserted down the throat, much like an ERCP.

It's obvious that an acronym is needed to refer to such procedures because there aren't three people in the hospital who would be capable of pronouncing Esophagogastroduodenoscopy.

Just think if a physician had to write up his report in longhand at home after dinner.

I can hear him calling out to this wife, "Phyllis, darling, are there six or seven Os in Esophagogastroduodenoscopy?"

I haven't tried to count them, but I'll bet there are hundreds of medical acronyms; you know many of them from TV or from personal experience: OR, ER, ICU and the like.

There are many too many to list here and many of them refer to diseases and functions that I'd rather not investigate.

One I thought was interesting, though, was BM, which can refer either to **B**owel **M**ovement or **B**reast **M**ilk.

You better be sure which department you're in before you order some.

Another one I found was HPE which was listed as an acronym for HPE. I didn't pursue it any further.

I like the ones that turn out to be real words.

Many acronyms have entered our vocabulary as words we use regularly, without knowing that they are in fact acronyms; LASER (**L**ight **A**mplification by **S**timulated **E**mission of **R**adiation); RADAR (**R**adio **D**etection **A**nd **R**anging); OPEC (**O**rganization of the **P**etroleum **E**xporting Countries) and sadly, AIDS (**A**cquired **I**mmune **D**eficiency **S**yndrome).

There are a gazillion of them on the Internet; they proliferate and evaporate so rapidly that there's no sense in trying to list them.

I especially like contrived acronyms that evoke the job that the acronym stands for.

Some of these were coined in WWII, like WASP (**W**omen **A**irforce **S**ervice **P**ilots).

The US Navy had WAVES (**W**omen **A**ccepted for **V**olunteer **E**mergency **S**ervice). You have to figure that a bunch of PR (PR is an acronym) types started out with the word "waves" because it sounded like water and the Navy, then they shoe-horned together words that fit; sort of.

SNAFU (**S**ituation **N**ormal **A**ll **F**ucked **U**p) is a WWII US Army acronym that is self-explanatory. It has entered our everyday language and nowadays simply means a screw-up.

FUBAR takes it one step further (**F**ucked **U**p **B**eyond **A**ll **R**ecognition).

I wanted to toss in one from the Brits and remembered WRENS (**W**omen's **R**oyal **N**aval **S**ervice).

The Germans had GESTAPO (**GE**heime **STA**ats**PO**lizei, "Secret State Police").

Nazi came from **NA**tionalso**ZI**alism; Hitler's political persuasion.

ANZAK (**A**ustralian and **N**ew **Z**ealand **A**rmy **C**orps) comes from the First World War.

AEF (**A**merican **E**xpeditionary **F**orce) was current then, too.

The acronym G.I. was originally used in the army before WWI as an abbreviation for **G**alvanized **I**ron.

It wasn't until later in the war that the letters G.I. became associated with Government Issue.

From there it took only a little imagination to refer to common soldiers as G.I.s.

There are a ton of NYM words beside acronym. There's pseudonym, synonym, homonym and a lot more.

Just go to Google and type NYM words.

And always remember, "A rose, by any other nym . . ."

• • •

As we learned above, "acro" is the Greek prefix meaning "tip end", as in acro-polis = "top of the city"; this led me to "acrophobia"— fear of heights."

Of course, my love of words forced me to investigate phobias.

I always thought that phobias were weaknesses, but many of the ones I've collected seem to me to define quite sensible attitudes.

In fact, I happen to be afflicted by most of them.

Chronophobia – Fear of time.
Gerascophobia – Fear of growing old. (Fear of becoming an Old Fart.)
Eisoptrophobia – Fear of mirrors or of seeing oneself in a mirror (how this whole thing started).
Coprastasophobia – Fear of constipation.
Diarrheaphobia – Get me to the pot on time.

Defecaloesiophobia – Fear of painful bowel movements.
Dentophobia – Fear of dentists.
Odontophobia – Fear of teeth or dental surgery.
Iatrophobia – Fear of going to the doctor.
Neopharmaphobia – Fear of new drugs.
Opiophobia – Fear of pain medications.
Nosocomephobia – Fear of hospitals.

Somehow I thought that the next two were especially closely related.

Proctophobia – Fear of rectums.
Politicophobia – Fear or abnormal dislike of politicians.
Hexakosioihexekontahexaphobia – Fear of the number 666.
Paraskavedekatriaphobia – Fear of Friday the 13th.
Hippopotomonstrosesquipedaliophobia – Fear of long words.
Ithyphallophobia – Fear of seeing, thinking about or having an erect penis.
Pentheraphobia – Fear of mother-in-law.
Zemmiphobia – Fear of the great mole rat.
Consecotaleophobia – Fear of chopsticks.
Omphalophobia – Fear of belly buttons.
Panophobia or Pantophobia – Fear of everything.

The only thing we have to be phobic about is phobia itself.

• • •

Great minds . . .

Samuel Johnson was a great literary figure of the 18th Century, and possibly the greatest man of letters in English history. He singlehandedly compiled a dictionary of the English language with over 43,000 entries that was considered the standard until, 150 years later, the OED was published.

He liked oysters and he also liked cats; two exemplary traits in any human being.

Because the square in front of his lodging was not large enough to contain a statue of Johnson, it contains instead a bronze statue of his favorite cat, Hodge, and a couple of oyster shells perched on top of his dictionary.

Wikipedia tells us that Johnson also excelled as "a poet, essayist, moralist, literary critic, biographer, editor and lexicographer." There really wasn't much left over for him to excel at.

He is also remembered for his verbal wit, which consisted of *bons mots* or aphorisms. One of his most insightful remarks was "Patriotism is the last refuge of a scoundrel." All you have to do is look at the verbiage our current politicos are spouting and you can easily see that his remark is as true today as it was then.

People who play at reconstructing IQs of smart people who died hundreds of years ago have pegged his at 165; Einstein's is thought to have been around 160.

You might think it presumptuous of me to pick a bone with a character who carries such intellectual credentials, but here I go: Samuel Johnson called puns "The lowest form of humor."

That hurts.

The punster has a special mind.

Punning requires a truly nimble, one might say ambidextrous, mind that reverberates to the echoes of sounds and multiple meanings of words.

Like: "When the human cannonball quit, Barnum and Bailey had a hard time finding another man of his caliber."

OK?

If you have a punning mind you "hear" the sound/meaning of the ePUNymous word, in the punning word.

Let's get "eponym" out of the way right now.

An eponym is the person, place or thing which is the name source for what is to be named. It comes from the Greek *eponumous* – "giving a significant name."

For example, our current president (2015) is named Barak Obama. His name is the name source for the word "Obamacare." President Obama is the eponymous individual who gave his name to Obamacare. Barak Obama is the eponym.

I don't want to hear any more about it!

• • •

I drove to the beach last summer; Mimi and I live about three miles from the Atlantic Ocean and most afternoons we drive down to watch the waves roll in and split a Häagen-Dazs chocolate covered coffee ice cream bar with crushed almonds.

As I pulled up to the barricade separating the parking area from the strand, a woman pointed out that I had run over a pair of sandals which had been lying there. "Oh, dear," I cried, "I've committed shoe-icide."

I thought it was pretty good, off the cuff like that. The woman applauded.

I was at a party a while ago. As is usual with folks my age, the conversation started out with ordinary small talk, and as usual with folks my age, the conversation soon turned into an organ recital.

One of the ladies was describing a dream she had while coming out of anesthesia. She dreamt that the Queen of England came into her room and asked to use the toilet.

"Talk about the royal wee." I couldn't help it.

I can't get away from it even when I'm asleep.

Years ago I dreamt I was sitting on a porch. There was a goose nearby and I asked what it was doing there.

"I'm a porch-a-goose."

That's really a very clever double pun.

I wonder who thought it up.

Sometimes when I'm smoking a pipe, puns come to me. I smoke one pipe a day. I don't inhale. My cardiologist told me I shouldn't smoke at all. Ken Dodge, my internist for over forty years said: "A cardiologist has to say that, Bob; you're over eighty-four – smoke your pipe."

Continuing this digression – On TV a year or two ago, there was a story about a lady in an assisted living facility who was going to be 100. She was being interviewed, and the reporter asked her what she wanted for her 100th birthday. Without hesitation she snapped, "A martini and a cigarette."

I'd like to know why, at 100, the old dame shouldn't have a martini and a cigarette every day. It surely isn't going to stunt her growth.

Back to my pipe and my puns. While puffing away, a pun arose spontaneously about a neurotic chef who suffered from fear of frying. While turning that over in my mind, it occurred to me that it would be great if I could somehow combine it with the *Ritual Fire Dance*. Y'know, cooking and fire. But no matter how I tried (and I tried for a long time) I was never able to get out of the frying pun and into de Falla.

• • •

At Christmastime, Mimi's family had always decorated a Christmas tree, and she carried that tradition with her when she came to America.

Besides it was a great excuse for a party.

Mimi and I would drive to a tree farm and hunt for a balsam fir; the kind that looks like the one Charlie Brown had.

There had to be space between the layers of branches because we always put real candles on our tree.

If we were lucky enough to find two of them at the same tree farm, there was always a long discussion as to the merits of each tree, the symmetry, the spread of the branches, the height; all the subtle differences discernable only to us.

When we finally made our choice, the lucky winner was brought home and set in the living room.

Then began three days of decoration.

The first thing that had to be done was to place the clip-on candles.

I had to be very careful to make sure that there was no branch directly above any candle. It took a good amount of clipping and snipping, but eventually I was able to put about twenty candles where they would be able to burn in the clear.

We had collected many, many ornaments over the years and Mimi treated them like old friends.

The first one she placed every year was a little Satan that she always hung at the bottom of the tree.

Mimi felt that if you don't invite the devil in, He'll find a way to crash the party. Besides he had a broken wing and she felt sorry for him.

Then she would hang all the angels and the birds and the glass balls and on and on until the tree was thick with ornaments.

At last came the moment when Mimi would sit back and adjust the ornamentation; that is she would direct me to move various angels and other baubles until she felt that every one was displayed to its best advantage.

When she was finally satisfied, I had the duty and the honor of mounting the ladder and placing the angel on the very top – ta-da!

It was something to see.

On the afternoon of Christmas Eve, thirty or more guests would arrive for the lighting of the tree.

Mimi especially liked to have youngsters see the tree because none of them had ever seen real candles on a Christmas tree and were not likely to again.

She would have laid out a variety of German Christmas cookies and candies as well as Dresdner stollen.

And there was always gluhwein, the German hot mulled wine punch, and apple juice for the kids.

When the time came, two of us took long tapers and, as the stereo played carols, we lit the candles on the tree.

The moment was silent and spiritual.

After most of the guests had left, actually after I announced that it was time for them to leave, about eight of us would sit down for Mimi's Eastern European Christmas dinner.

The table was set with special Christmas plates and glasses.

The centerpiece was Santa's sled filled with a lovely bouquet.

Mimi spent her childhood in Silesia, so her Christmas meals were influenced by Eastern European cooking.

The original recipe called for a carp to be served.

Mimi told me that some families bought the fish at the beginning of the month and put into the bathtub where it would swim contentedly until the fateful day when Papa would remove it and prepare it for the holiday meal. It would be cleaned, cut into serving pieces and be poached in a liquid spiced with vinegar, thyme, peppercorns, allspice and cloves.

The poaching liquid would be strained and mixed into a sauce made of cooked prunes, beer, pumpernickel, gingersnaps, raisins and almonds.

We didn't use carp; instead we slathered the sauce over red and white bratwurst.

Let me tell you, it was yummy!

Along with the bratwurst the meal consisted of boiled white potatoes and Mimi's extraordinary sauerkraut.

The first time she made her special kraut we had somehow forgotten to buy juniper berries, so Mimi, with her usual resourcefulness, compensated for our oversight by administering copious dollops of gin throughout. This produced such an eminently satisfactory result that henceforth, whenever she made sauerkraut, she followed the same procedure.

There was never any left over.

Most of the diners had wine with their meal; I drank beer from a Bohemian cut-glass beer stein.

For dessert, we served an Austrian cake I made that is something like a stollen but with a lot of chocolate bits in it.

Champagne was served.

CHAPTER 10

• • •

When I was a lad . . .

YOU EMBARK ON becoming an Old Fart on the day you were born (maybe before), and although I haven't made any groundbreaking discoveries and don't have a star with my name on it embedded in the middle of a sidewalk anywhere, I think it's important to let you know a bit about what my life has been like and how I got to be an octogenarian.

I was born in the Lying-in Hospital in Boston, Massachusetts on August 4th, 1931, at a little past midnight.

My Sun is in Leo, my Moon is in Aries and I have Scorpio rising. I have very little idea of what this means anymore.

Shortly thereafter, I had my first experience with a scalpel; a schmeklectomy was performed.

I am slightly disbelieving of those who say they remember the very earliest moments of their life. I don't remember those very earliest moments. Lately I have trouble remembering what I had for lunch, unless I burp.

But I do remember snowy winters in Massachusetts. I remember Saturday mornings speeding down the hill on my Flexible Flyer; trudging back up and doing it again and again until my feet were nearly frozen and my woolen mittens were covered with little ice balls.

My mother would ring a cowbell when it was time for lunch.

The kitchen was full of the smell of my mother's corn chowder. She would set a bowlful next to chunks of buttered Jewish rye. Dessert could be a dish of apple pie covered with sugar sitting in heavy cream: "mishy-mashy."

I was a skinny kid; would you believe it?

I remember the 1939 New York World's Fair. My father was a newspaperman and he often had business in New York. One time he took me and my two older brothers out to Flushing Meadows to visit the Fair.

The architectural symbols of the Fair were the Trylon and the Perisphere. The Trylon was a narrow pointed needle that towered over 600 feet next to the Perisphere which was a sphere nearly 200 feet in diameter. They must have been pretty impressive, but I don't remember them at all.

I was nine years old.

While Leon, my seventeen-year-old brother, was engaged in an exhibit on something called "Television" or some other improbable futuristic gimmick, my nineteen-year-old brother, Edward, led me along with no apparent goal until we got to the entertainment area. There, seemingly by chance, we came upon a marquee bearing the legend "The Streets of Paris."

One of the entertainers appearing on the bill, surely a complete surprise to my brother, was a performer by the name of Gypsy Rose Lee.

Now, you may ask how it is possible that I would have no memory of a 600-foot needle-shaped column next to a 200-foot sphere, and yet I have a particularly vivid memory of a five foot eight, half-Jewish dancer who was born with the name of Rose Louise Hovick.

You had to have been there.

My mother's name was Frances; she was short and stout. Everybody said she looked like the actress Sophie Tucker: she did.

I never found out how far she got in her formal education, but she read voraciously. At school she had memorized a vast repertoire of poems she could spout at any moment, and a seemingly never-ending stock of popular songs from the '20s and '30s.

She had a great sense of humor.

Once I caught her talking to herself. When I asked her why she did it, she responded, "Sometimes I like to have a conversation with someone as intelligent as I am."

While working on a stew she might suddenly stop and, pointing the wooden spoon at me, declaim "'Who is the father of my child? She cried in accents wild, as she shook her wooden leg and staggered down the stairs.'" (I never learned where it came from.)

If I have a sense of humor, and I think I do, it came from her.

She worked hard. She raised four boys (My younger brother Marc was born in 1937). She cooked and took care of a 10-room house.

We seldom had help. That included me; I wasn't very helpful.

My mother's toughest job was putting up with my father.

Percy was about six feet tall and extremely imposing. When he walked into a room you knew it.

He was in charge of special advertising for *The Boston Herald,* and he worked hard, too.

When he was in company he was engaging; he was the life of the party; the center of attention.

At home it was a different matter.

In the evening when the front door swung open you never knew who would be stepping across the threshold, Doctor Jekyll or Mister Schwarz.

If he had had a bad day . . . look out!

Frankly, at times like that I tried to fade into the scenery.

It wasn't easy.

"Have you seen my pipe?"

"No."

"I left it right here on the table by the couch."

"I haven't seen it."

"Well, somebody took it. I left it right here."

It would start like that and I would be sent to scour the house.

My mother would usually find the object in the overcoat he wore the day before or some other place where he had forgotten he put it.

But he would be sure that someone had hidden it there, probably Mom.

Then voices would be raised and the battle would start accompanied by slamming doors and much, much shouting.

Dinner would be sort of a staring contest, or rather a non-staring contest, eyes on your plate.

"What are you looking at!"

"Nothing."

It wasn't fun.

I remember where I was on Sunday morning, December 7th, 1941.

We lived at the bottom of a hill on a dead-end street; I was riding my bicycle in the turnaround. Edward, my oldest brother, came running out of the house yelling, "The Japs have just bombed Pearl Harbor!"

I was ten, and I didn't have the foggiest idea what a pearl harbor was or where it was, but I knew that it was big news.

Shortly thereafter, both of my older brothers joined the army, and if you ask me, they were prompted by a desire to get out of the house as much as they were by patriotic fervor. They had taken the brunt of my father's black moods one way or another, and were probably more comfortable preparing for combat than they were at home.

My oldest brother had run away several times and had been returned in a police car. He did not get along with my father.

They were always at each other and there was tension when they were in close proximity.

Of course that contributed to serious sibling rivalry between my two older brothers which, sadly, was never resolved, even to the end of their lives some seventy years later.

One of them would say something and Edward and Leon would start. I mean fights that ended with doors being broken down, tables turned over, and bloody noses. It was like the movies.

It was scary.

That, and the shouting matches between my father and mother in the background.

People on the street knew when we were home.

Now, with my two brothers in the army, my younger brother and I were on the front line of the home front.

My younger brother Marc was only five; you couldn't blame him for much. Besides he was as cute as a button and very precocious. (You don't hear that word much anymore.)

I was eleven; just the right age to be given the responsibility for mowing the lawn, weeding the garden, cleaning out the cellar and generally fulfilling the function of handyman/gardener cum janitor.

The problem was that I wasn't the sort of character who enjoyed doing any of those things.

To add to the problem, it turned out that I was the possessor of two characteristics which mitigated against competent workmanship.

I was impatient and sloppy; not a good combo when the one who checked the quality of the work was my eagle-eyed father.

We had a beautiful perennial garden in the back of our house. My father loved the garden, he just didn't see himself working in it very much.

He saw me working in it.

When I did, I'd leave a "holiday" in the middle of the lawn when I was mowing, or I'd miss some obvious weeds when I was weeding, or I'd skip a long stretch when I was edging a particular flower bed.

"Do it again tomorrow, and do it right, you lazy bastard." He swore a lot; mainly "son-of-a-bitch" and "bastard." I never heard him use any really foul language.

He was actually right in calling me lazy. I was lazy.

I'm continually surprised by the fact that when Mimi and I bought a summer house East Hampton in 1971, I created a garden which I kept in meticulous order for thirty years; it contained over 500 varieties of daylilies.

Later, Mimi and I hybridized daylilies.

At times we had nine or ten thousand seedlings growing in the lot next door; all planted by me and all taken care of by me.

I often thought of my father when I was on my hands and knees, dripping sweat, hands caked with dirt, happily weeding.

I didn't like being around my father because you never knew what would set him off.

Along with a lot of other people, he had had a nervous breakdown in the late 1920s.

Maybe that's why he smoked so many Pall Malls and was so hard to get along with.

He had hobbies as therapy.

He collected stamps. He had hundreds of proof sheets, stamps that commemorated a national park or a hero or an historic event or some other topic that the US Postal Service thought would pry some money out of philatelists.

He hooked wool rugs too. The fabric with the pattern would be tacked to a frame on a stand. He'd sit there, hour after hour, late into the night, smoking and plugging yarn through the fabric.

Over the years, I've latch-hooked several rugs, done needlepoint and stitched several large Bargello pieces that have ended up as pillows. I couldn't help thinking of Percy now and then.

Dad collected antiques.

Barrels from the Morgan Memorial filled with the residue of foreclosed homes would arrive, to be gone through by my father and gleaned for "good" pieces of glass or other objects that were saved.

One of the most seat-squirming events usually took place on a Saturday afternoon when Dad was feeling expansive; he took me "antiquing" with him.

I was a selfish little brat, I had very little interest in antiques, and I didn't want my Saturday afternoon stolen from me.

I had probably planned to do something terribly important, like play football or do some bike-riding with my friends.

I think it was his way of spending what we now call "quality time" with me. The effort was lost.

I felt cheated because instead of having a good time screwing around with kids my age, I was going to be treated to a tense afternoon being carted around to inspect dusty musty storefronts.

He knew all the shops around Boston; we'd drive out towards Framingham, for instance, but there would be no conversation in the car.

We'd stop at every shop along the way.

I was always embarrassed when we entered a shop. Dad transmogrified from the silent automobile driver to his salesman's persona.

He knew all the owners and he approached each of them with a glad-handing and exuberant bluster that I had, from long experience, come to recognize as bullshit.

I'm sure the owners recognized it too, but that was the way my father approached people.

It was the same when we entered a restaurant, or a grocery store or any other establishment; hail-fellow-well-met, loud voice, always attracting attention.

I was embarrassed.

If he saw something he wanted, he and the owner argued about the price, and after a good deal of haggling he usually got what he was after, although I don't think the dealer ever lost money on the sale.

These were $5 and $10 items; he wasn't into Renaissance masterworks.

Percy was very tight with money. Looking back I think that, even though he was making a good salary, he was spending a lot.

He ran two homes, two cars and had four children to support and clothe. He traded in his Buick Roadmaster every year.

He bought all our clothes, on sale, from Filene's Basement, and all our bed linens and furnishings were "seconds". You'd have to look hard to tell, but they were seconds.

I think he was trying to scrimp and save wherever he could.

Maybe it was skating so close to the danger sign that kept him up late some nights, playing solitaire in the living room, smoking Pall Malls.

But I have to say that he had a nearly unbelievable appreciation for American antiques.

He had a fabulous collection of American pressed glass including Moon and Star, the Lion Pattern and the Cable pattern – compotes, goblets, challises, creamers, celery dishes, cups, saucers, platters, tureens, ladles, salts, sugar flower baskets and more.

He had antique toy fire engines made of cast iron, some with three sets of horses that bobbed up and down as you pulled them along. He had toy banks, glass shoes, barber bottles and seventy or eighty music boxes.

A couple of the music boxes were as big as coffins. Some had drums and bells that accompanied the music. I remember one that had half a dozen interchangeable rolls the size of fireplace logs; another played perforated disks over two feet in diameter that rotated across the surface of the box, picking out tunes on the teeth of the music box's comb; proto LPs.

It was a bewildering collection that filled the whole space of what was supposed to have been a two-car garage when the house was built.

It was appropriately called the "Glass Room."

It was always locked.

It was locked because it was his private room and he didn't want anybody messing around in there.

It was where he kept things away from you.

Because he was in the newspaper business, he was able to get all sorts of magazines gratis.

These included comic books. You can imagine how I yearned for those. But they were kept locked in the glass room.

They would be kept, and released only as a reward for good conduct.

But I didn't want to wait for a good conduct reward.

So, when he wasn't around I adopted the artful shortcut of unscrewing the "T" hinges from the outside of the door and lifting the whole thing off.

I was a brat, but I was a resourceful brat.

I don't think my dad was happy.

He complained of not being well a good deal of the time. He had high blood pressure; he was on a salt-free diet.

He suffered from headaches; he suffered from constipation and he suffered from bursitis.

I don't know what he took for his headaches, but I know that he often underwent high colonic enemas for his general well-being and to ease his constipation.

At times he would have me rub his shoulder with capsicum ointment. It seemed to help his bursitis.

My father didn't like me to listen to the radio late at night.

His bedroom was in the front of the house; mine was at the back of the house. It was as far away as you could get and still be in the same house.

I used to turn my radio on so low that I could just make out what was being said.

"Turn that goddamned thing off!"

He knew I was listening to it.

"Don't make me come in there!"

That was the threat he always used when he wanted you to stop doing something.

But he never ever laid a hand on me.

He would shout and swear and threaten and withhold and he was an emotional bully. That was plenty.

More than once he told me that I would cry when he died and that I would miss him.

I didn't.

Several years later, at his funeral, I discovered from his colleagues that I was one of his favorite topics of conversation – what a great son I was; how proud he was that I was at Harvard; on and on.

It was all news to me, and I did feel sad.

I felt sad because I understood that if, in fact, his influence did get me into Harvard, it was simply so he could have a kid at Harvard to brag about.

I don't think I'm being unfair or ungrateful. I don't resent having gone to Harvard.

It was the realization of the manipulation that made me feel sad.

In the '60s when I was in analysis I tried to explain what a tyrant my father was, and how difficult he was to live with.

My analyst asked me if I thought he was like that when my mother married him fifty years before.

He suggested that I write a letter to my long dead father and ask him what had happened.

My parents met in Atlantic City during the First World War but they hadn't talked about it much.

There was a photograph of them, though, taken at the time.

My mother wore a light-colored coat with a fur collar and a cloche.

She was smiling a beautiful smile. She looked happy.

He was wearing a navy seaman's dress uniform, silk tie around the open collar, white sailor hat perched on his head.

He was smiling too. He looked young and quite handsome.

I wrote the letter.

A few days later, in a dream, I received a response.

This is the dream.

I was at the end of a pier in Atlantic City. I looked down at the water. There, undulating on the surface, was the photograph of my father in his sailor's uniform, young and handsome, smiling up at me, ready to take on the world.

I wept then, I'm weeping now.

• • •

When we got back to America, it didn't take long for Mimi and me to hook up with a bunch of people our age who rented a group house on Fire Island every summer.

Fire Island is a barrier sandbar separated from the southern coast of Long Island by the Great South Bay.

No automobiles are allowed so folks travel by bicycle or foot-back.

The year-round population is about 400, but from June through September it's packed.

It's only a few hundred yards wide in most places so the beach is never far.

That's a good thing, because it happens to be one of the most beautiful beaches in the world with fine golden sand – thirty miles of it, stretching to the horizon in both directions.

On a calm sunbaked day, the Atlantic Ocean provides a never-ending supply of gentle curlers easing in leisurely along the shore.

It's hard to imagine a more ideal spot to plant an umbrella and plop down next to someone you love, an icy six-pack and The Times *puzzle*.

Mimi and I spent our summer weekends there for ten years.

Most of the time we shared a rickety old house with other "groupies."

It was communal living and we all chipped in for food and drink.

During the day there was always plenty of beer and cold cuts for sandwiches, and in the evening while dinner was being pre-pared, there were cocktails.

Sometimes cocktails started a little early.

If Mimi and I had arrived before the others, we would meet our fellow renters, frazzled from a hot week of work in New York, as they stepped off the ferry.

We greeted them standing beside a little red wagon contain-ing a pitcher of cold martinis and a sign which quoted the Alka-Seltzer slogan at the time: "Relief is Just a Swallow Away."

As you may imagine, dinner was often a haphazard event.

Different members of the group would volunteer to cook their specialties – with varying degrees of success.

"Doesn't anybody like my baked salmon balls?"

A rejection like that often resulted in the chef making a tearful exit to the front porch firmly clutching another martini.

Mimi took her turn in the kitchen. I don't know what possessed her but, one time, she decided to roast a turkey.

It had been in the oven for a while and when she went to baste it, the pan slipped out of her hands on the floor – upside down.

Several of us responded to Mimi's cries for help and, with a team effort, we cajoled the bird back into the roaster.

When we had the floor cleaned up, and Mimi calmed down, we realized that we had been at it for a while. There then ensued a spirited discussion about how much time, if any, should be added to the roasting process.

Various opinions were expressed and when, at last, we had finished arguing, no one was sure exactly how much time had elapsed since the eagle had landed.

We opted for fifteen minutes, or something like it, and in the end the turkey came out OK.

This event gave rise to "Mimi's Famous Turkey Recipe" which included the following unorthodox steps:

1. When taking turkey out to baste, drop it in on floor.
2. Holler for others to rush in and clean up the mess.
3. Argue about how much additional cooking time.
4. Return bird to oven and hope for the best.
5. Have a martini.

• • •

Whenever the moon was full. Mimi and I would go down to the beach, bathe in the gentle glow, and splash along the shore, kicking up cascades.

If the tide and temperature were right, the water would be filled with tiny luminescences that glowed like comet trails when our feet moved through them.

Marching together in the moonlight, singing and holding hands – it doesn't get much better than that.

CHAPTER 11

• • •

Memory . . .

I'M 84.

Like so many people our age, Mimi and I forget things.

I forget to bring my wallet when I get into the car. So I wrote a note and glued it to the dashboard. It said "WALLET".

It didn't do much good, because after the first few times, the piece of paper became part of the dashboard and I began forgetting my wallet again.

Taking a cue from what I had done, Mimi stuck a note on the bathroom mirror. On it was written "ZIP". Same result.

I began to get worried; but all our friends complain about forgetting things, misplacing things; and when they do everybody in the room starts nodding in agreement.

Some memory loss and forgetfulness is a natural consequence of evolving into Old Fartdom.

Martha Weinmann Lear wrote a book titled, *Where Did I Leave My Glasses?* There's a cute picture on the cover of a woman with her glasses shoved up on her head.

Ms. Lear interviews several professionals who study memory loss in adults, and it leaves you with a better understanding of why our normal memory works the way it does when we grow older.

Ms. Weinmann pointed out that there's a big difference between someone asking "Where are my glasses?" and "What are my glasses?"

That made me feel pretty good because I know what my glasses are and, since I need them, they're seldom far from me. But that doesn't mean that when I take a shower they are going to be where I put them before I entered the stall.

I don't usually lose things; I do misplace things, though.

For example, I'll be looking for my drink, I know I had it, because I made it when I made Mimi's. I look all over and finally, after a frustrating search, and a short conversation with the Management (as Mimi calls Him or Her), I make myself another drink.

The next morning I go into the laundry room to take the towels out of the dryer. There, on the shelf stands a glass; the watery remnants of last night's drink. I must have taken it into the laundry when I took the socks and pajamas out of the dryer and put them on the table and then took the towels out of the washer and put them into the dryer and then took the socks and pajamas into the bedroom and put them away.

"I'm innocent, Your Honor. I plead *Distractus Maximus*. All that counting of socks and folding of towels; loading and unloading; traipsing back and forth would put anyone off his game and, I just remembered, I was interrupted by a phone call from a fundraiser soliciting donations for the International Alliance of Lady Mud Wrestlers. That's how that wee drop of Laphroaig got forgotten on the shelf. I plead not guilty."

Distractions are a root cause of misplacing things; you have to avoid them at any cost.

Keep your eye and mind on the prize. Move toward it unswervingly. Do it now!

When, on Monday, you agree to let your nephew use your beach buggy for the weekend, put the key under the pot of chrysanthemums near the garage that very minute. Otherwise you're sure to discover it in your pocket Friday afternoon, when you're 600 miles away checking into a motel on Cape Cod.

I was making croutons the other day. I had made some split pea and ham soup and I wanted to sprinkle a few croutons when I served the soup to Mimi and me. I dribbled a little EVO on the bread cubes in a cookie pan and slid them into a 350-degree oven for the prescribed fifteen minutes. Uh-oh, I remembered I had left the hose running out back. I went out and turned it off. There were some goldfinches at the feeder and I love watching goldfinches. They look like streaks of liquid gold in the air.

"Bob, something is burning." That was Mimi calling from inside. Oh, m'gosh! I'd been gone for nearly a half hour. I ran in through a miasma of black smoke.

When you are cooking do not answer the phone, do not try to finish the crossword puzzle, and do not pick up an English detective novel at the point where the inspector from the Yard is explaining that the Bishop could not possibly have ridden his bicycle from the vestry to the train station in the blizzard, sidesaddle.

If you do any of the above things I guarantee you will pay the price, and dinner will be lousy pizza from that place down the block.

I'm going to cook a shrimp dish. I go the market with the recipe. I make sure that I buy the olive oil, the garlic, the rice, the onions, the tomato sauce, the oregano, the basil, the chicken broth and the chipotles in adobo sauce. Yum.

I get home and, sure enough, I forgot the shrimp. Man!

It should be easy to follow a recipe but, my memory is so short, that while the food is cooking I constantly have to refer back to the recipe to remind myself if it was two tsp or two tbsp. of olive oil; 1/3 cup or ½ cup of balsamic vinegar, and what the next eight ingredients are that have to be added simultaneously.

By the time I get back to the sauté pan, the garlic is turning black.

Then comes the point when the recipe instructs me to add the rest of the sour cream.

What do you mean "the rest"? I added all of it when I mixed the beef stock in.

• • •

As Kurt Vonnegut wrote so poignantly in *Slaughterhouse Five*, "So it goes."

Mimi and I were having dinner at a local restaurant a few years ago when I looked up and saw that Mr. Vonnegut and his party had just taken a table not far away. In East Hampton we see a lot of celebrities. I normally try to ignore them; give them their space, and I hate it when some other guest intrudes on their privacy.

But I have been an admirer of Vonnegut's since *Cat's Cradle* in 1963, (Ice-nine, remember?), and I began to feel an unfamiliar and uncontrollable urge taking hold of me. I fought it through the meal, but as we started to leave, I knew I would give in.

I finally decided that a simple "Thank you" would be appropriate and not too intrusive. I had had a Rob Roy and some wine, and I was nervous. As we approached Mr. V's table – it was only eight or ten feet away – I vacillated. Should I simply walk on by? But when would I get another chance to express my thanks to a man who had provided me with so much pleasure over the years. Should I, shouldn't I; should I, shouldn't I? What the Hell! I'll do it.

I paused by the table, leaned in and said in my most sincere voice, "Thank you, Mister Blonigup."

• • •

When I cook, *Mise en place* doesn't help. I will have gone through the process of composing the meal and be ready to march to the table with a bright "Ta-da," when I look at the counter and realize that I never added the chopped olives or the parsley. The roux sits patiently waiting. No wonder the gravy is so thin.

What is it with parsley, anyway? I have to spend $2.99 for a bunch of parsley in order to chop a tablespoon of it to sprinkle over the carrot puree.

Then the parsley goes into a plastic bag in the vegetable bin where I find it a month later reincarnated as semi-liquid greenish ooze.

A couple of weeks ago I was watching Jacques Pepin on the cooking channel; he was making *oeufs en cocotte*.

It looked so good and so easy that I decided to make it.

I followed his directions and after I sautéed the shallots and the mushrooms I put in a splash of cognac and some heavy cream, which I cooked down, and poured the mixture into a ramekin.

Easy peasey.

I cracked an egg on the top and as I was lowering the ramekin into the boiling water bath I actually felt as if I should have a cordon bleu draped over my shoulder.

Unfortunately, I hadn't measured the depth of the water accurately and the ramekin sank beneath the surface.

Au revoir ma petite cocotte.

Soups are almost always easy. I make a lot of soups. A basic flavoring ingredient in many soups is *mirepoix* (meer-pwah). It's generally made up of onions, carrots and celery.

Mirepoix is named after Charles-Pierre-Gaston François de Lévis, duc de Lévis-Mirepoix. He was a 17th Century French field marshal and diplomat distinguished primarily by his incompetence. He held his fortune only because Louis XV was boffing his wife, and it is extremely unlikely he ever made mirepoix himself, or saw the inside of a kitchen, for that matter. But, if he did, I feel confident he would have forgotten the roux too.

It does nothing for my ego to know that I am related to French nobility only by incompetence.

• • •

Even though I like to cook, food doesn't taste the way it used to. I remember a lot of things as having been more flavorful years ago.

Because of that, Mimi and I have both developed an inordinate craving for an herb we had previously distained.

In my mind's eye I envision its discovery.

Somewhere in East Africa, long, long ago, man descended from the trees and began a tentative exploration of the surrounding land.

One of our distant ancestors, naked beneath the blazing sun, lumbered aimlessly across the grassy plain, his posture stooped, his face devoid of expression, his hairy arms dangling by his side.

Suddenly he is drawn up short. His dull glance is replaced by a questioning one. He turns his head in the breeze, his nostrils flaring.

He begins to shuffle in the direction toward which his acute olfactory preceptors are prompting him.

He breaks into a shambling run as he finally approaches the green shoot from which the intoxicating aroma emanates.

He sinks to his knees as he reverently withdraws the plump bulb from the earth.

He holds it to his nose, takes in the glorious aroma and, without further ado, chomp, chomp, chomp.

With tears of happiness he lifts his brutish head to the heavens and in a paroxysm of joy, loudly grunts, "Ugsh, grummtle, fougle, bung!"

Which I freely translate as, "I say, this is a truly laudable comestible. We simply must include it in our culinary repertoire. And to commemorate this historic gastronomic moment, I hereby use the power vested in me to name this treasure 'Garlic.'"

Thereupon a low rumple of approving thunder sounded across the plain.

And that, children, is undoubtedly how it happened.

• • •

I used to think that the problem with our taste was the chemicals they're putting in, or maybe I'm missing the chemicals they've stopped putting in, or perhaps the vegetables and spices are less potent than they used to be; I know I am.

I came to the conclusion, though, that it's me: that my taste buds are dying out, and that's why I'm not tasting the flavor as I used to.

But it probably isn't my taste buds that are the major problem, more likely it's my nose.

Taste and flavor are two different things.

Taste really refers to four sensitivities we derive from our taste buds; sweet, sour, salty, bitter, are the four well known ones.

A fifth sensitivity – *umami* – was isolated in Japan in the early part of the last century. It is described as imparting a brothy meaty taste like that found in mushrooms and parmesan cheese.

If you like pasta with Bolognese ragout, your sensitivity to umami is responsible.

It is also contained in mother's milk, so it is possible that you got your first exposure to umami from you-mammie.

However, awareness of flavor is tied to aroma.

Flavor is a combination of several different senses: the taste buds make their contribution, but the most important contribution comes from your olfactory system. In fact, some estimates suggest that as much as seventy-five percent of what we perceive of as flavor is aroma, that's why food doesn't taste like much when you have a stuffed nose.

The loss of acuity (either partial or total) in the sense of smell – *anosmia* (from the Greek) – occurs because the cells in olfactory sensors are not replaced as often when you are old.

Some people are not aware that they lack a sense of smell in certain areas.

It can be a big problem if you are anosmic and unaware of the telltale odor of leaking gas as you're lighting the candles on the dinner table.

Years ago a lab advertised for people whose urine did not change odor when they ate asparagus. They had several responses and when they fed the volunteers asparagus it was discovered that the odor of their urine *did in fact change*, but the volunteers couldn't smell the difference.

Many people have powerful memories of particular flavors from childhood; re-experiencing them in adulthood can instantly bring back moments from years past.

Sniff, sniff – "Ah, just like mother used to make."

The most famous reference to food memory in literature is in *Swann's Way*.

Of course, it is Marcel's memory, evoked by the taste and smell, of a morsel of a madeleine soaked in tea, which he used to share with his aunt when he was a child.

That recollection allowed Proust to tap a reservoir of memories out of which poured, what I found to be, an incredibly boring work of more than one and a quarter million words.

I don't want to intimate that I have read all of *In Search of Lost Time*. In fact, after several decades of attempts I finally finished the first chapter of *Swann's Way*, at the end of which the madeleine and tea recollection occurs.

• • •

Often I'll be in the supermarket trying to decide if the bananas are ripe enough for the smoothies or too ripe and will spoil before I get to them.

Someone will approach and greet me like an old friend. He'll tell me how good it is to see me again and ask how I'm doing and after several moments of cheerful chatter he'll move away leaving me with no idea of who he was, or how I used to know him.

It's easiest to nod and shake hands and act as if you actually remember the chap.

If I feel the urge, I'll ask him, "Where do I know you from?"

"Oh, I used to come into your garden and look at your beautiful daylilies."

"Ah, yes," I respond. "I didn't recognize you with your clothes on."

That's a thing I say to lighten what might otherwise have been an awkward moment; besides it's so stupid that the other fellow always laughs and quickly moves away.

• • •

Cooking is a dangerous sport for an Old Fart. The kitchen is a regular minefield, and you have to keep your wits about you as you navigate through it.

There are a lot of sharp pointy things that have the habit reminding you that they are sharp and pointy if you make the mistake of trying to slice the tomatoes while you are watching the Super Bowl.

I discovered that the only good thing about slicing your thumb on Super Bowl Sunday is that the emergency room is nearly empty.

There are really dangerous contraptions with motors and blades that spin around and are apt to do severe digital damage if you don't unplug them before you clean them.

Please, if one of those machines gets stuck, take the plug out before you try to unstick it.

Just the thought . . .

If something spills, wipe it up NOW!

There are lots of hot pots and pans handy. You do not want to pick anything up that's just come out of the oven without an oven mitt, or you will be a little bit wiser when you let go of it.

A couple of months ago I was making pasta; simple enough. I usually use two oven mitts to carry the pot to the sink.

I had seen a chef on television use a towel to carry the pot. He held an end of the towel in each hand and picked up the pot that way. It looked pretty professional to me.

I don't know exactly how it happened but the towel slipped and scalding water poured over my hand.

Friends, I could cover two or three pages with "Ow, ow, ow, ow, ow, ow . . ." and it wouldn't do justice to the pain. It hurt so much I couldn't even swear; I think I hopped around nearly as much as Mimi did when the cat chased a chipmunk up her pants leg.

It was a good thing that I keep cold packs in the freezer compartment of the fridge, because as soon as I stopped hopping around and got my brain together, I slapped one on my hand and kept it there for three or four minutes even though it hurt like hell.

The next day my doctor gave me some pills and some salve and bandaged the hand.

I kept changing the bandage and peeling skin, and a month later there was no sign of the burn.

I was lucky and the experience taught me two things: 1) scalds are excruciatingly painful; 2) I shouldn't be screwing around pretending I am a celebrity chef.

Of course I'll forget that as soon as I start trying to flip omelets in the pan.

I now make sure that the sauté pans are placed so that the handles don't stick out over the front of the stove. Also, I've moved all the equipment and serving utensils near to where I work. It's a big help.

I have a big garbage can in the corner with a fifty-gallon liner in it. It doesn't look pretty, but it sure saves steps.

The kitchen isn't the only place where danger lurks.

Try the bathroom.

Each year over a quarter million people go to the emergency room because of injuries sustained in the bathroom; more than ten percent are hospitalized.

It's a fact that more than sixty percent of the injuries happen to women.

Of course, the tub and the shower are the locations where a lot of accidents happen for all age groups.

People have rubber mats they put on the bottom of the tub, but most injuries occur when getting out of the tub or the shower. That makes sense because by then the tiles on the bathroom floor are wet and slippery.

Why they put tile on the bathroom floor in the first place is a mystery to me. Wet tile is not a safe surface.

There are some non-slip floorings that are suitable for the bathroom, but they are expensive and not generally in use.

Carpeting would be a big help, but it would stain and get moldy.

I have taken several launderable rubber backed bathroom rugs I bought at Kmart (about four feet by two feet) and pretty much covered the bathroom floor with them. They seem to do the trick; inexpensive too.

Most of the falls that happen to people over eighty-five happen around the toilet.

A lot of times the falls happen when folks are transferring from a wheelchair to the pot.

Grab bars could help.

For nighttime visits I have an automatic LED night light in our bathroom; when the room grows dim in the afternoon, it lights up.

People who live alone and are prone (pun intended) to falling should think about one of those devices that you carry about with you to summon help if you've fallen and can't help yourself.

I just got one. It fits on my wrist; people think it's one of those fancy new things from Apple.

Look, if you're old like I am, you should scout around your dwelling and try, within reason, to remove booby traps and other obvious stumbling blocks.

You most likely won't be able to cover all the bases, but at least you can make sure you've closed all the open trap doors in the floor.

• • •

I keep forgetting why I went into a room.

"I know I came in here for something."

When I go to the grocery, I know that there are three things I need, but I can remember only two of them when I step through the door.

It takes me some time to remember what we had for lunch and what it was that we wanted to do in the afternoon.

I know there was something I wanted to put into this part of what I'm writing, but it's slipped my mind right now. "Slipped my mind" is a wonderfully graphic way to describe it.

Sometimes, for no apparent reason, things "slip" back. Last week "Penny Singleton" suddenly came to mind. Where did she slip back from? She played Blondie on the radio show of that name from 1939 to the mid-1940s.

I looked her up to see if I could find any reason why her name suddenly appeared.

The only interesting thing I could find was that Penny Singleton's birth name was Marianna Dorothy Agnes Letitia McNulty.

Sometimes I get the feeling that there's somebody else up there in my head sitting at the same desk writing a different book.

When I first got the idea to write this – whatever it is – I realized that I would have to carry a small note pad and a pencil to write down the ideas that would pop up, because I knew that I could never remember them. I bought a spiral notebook like the kind that police inspectors in the movies use to take down a statement from a witness. Of course I misplaced it that afternoon.

Since then I've been writing brief notes on paper table coverings in restaurants, on paper towels if I happen to be in the small room, on the backs of receipts, recipes, envelopes, margins of magazines or anything else handy when the idea strikes me.

It's not pretty when I unload my pockets.

My desktop is littered with scraps and bits of various sizes and shapes with one or two words written on them. But my handwriting is so illegible that I generally can't make out what the great idea was.

A technique I read about to help you avoid standing in the study in front of your desk, without the faintest idea why you are in the study standing in front of your desk, is to have announced your mission out loud before you left the living room: "I am going into the study to get the stereo remote that I put there before I went looking for the batteries which I finally found."

This procedure may help you remember why you are in the study, but chances are it will be of no help when you try to discover where you put the batteries you just found.

"They were right here a minute ago."

How many times have you gone through the alphabet trying to attach a forgotten name to the proper signature letter, "I know it began with an 'L'... Larry? ... Lonny? ... Lindsay? ... Aha! Peter, that's it."

The above doesn't mean that I haven't developed my own aide-mémoire system.

The way I do it takes me around Robin Hood's barn, but it works for me.

Here's an example:

At 3:00 a.m. one morning many years ago I was trying to remember the name of that comedienne (I use the feminine) who starred Sunday night on CBS television. You know, the one who had the little caricature of a charwoman with a wash bucket that she used as her logo at the end of the show.

Yeah, that one. What was her name anyway?

Don't ask me why I was trying to come up with that particular name at that particular time. Who knows what little gremlins, like hobos hopping a slow freight, clamber into your head as you shuffle back to bed after a trip to the small room in the middle of the night.

Anyway, there I was, unable to sleep trying to remember her name.

After what must have been an hour or more of tossing, the sticky file in my brain suddenly flew open.

Carol Burnett!

What a relief.

I carefully printed the name in the book I keep by my bed.

Blissful sleep ensued.

In the morning I tried to invent a system so that I would not forget the name again.

It's a riff on a widely used system, but it's tailored to my particular memory quirks.

I had already remembered that she used the character of a charwoman and that hadn't helped.

I needed something more specific to my memory.

Carol Burnett's initials are C.B. She appeared on CBS. If I could remember CBS and remember that CB stood for Carol Burnett, I was home free.

"Who was that woman? She was on CBS. Aha! I've got it."

I test it occasionally, and I have always been able to retrieve CB's name.

My system doesn't start with the name, but it shows me the way to get to the name. It's a mystery to me, but it allows me to remember.

I love the word "remember" (I've used it often enough); to me it means putting things together, the opposite of dismember.

I visualize "re-membering" as gathering all the disparate segments of an event and, like assembling a jug-saw puzzle, piecing the parts together until they form the picture.

I get to Julie Andrews via June Christy – Julie Christie – Julie Andrews; a three- bank shot.

I don't know why I can easily call up Jack Benny, or Fred Allen, or Joe Penner for that matter ("Wanna buy a duck?"). It doesn't make any sense.

But there is soooooooo much in life that doesn't make sense to me, that I just keep putting one foot in front of the other ignoring things like that.

• • •

It wasn't always a little bit of heaven.

Over the years Mimi and I had our bad times; especially when I was depressed about my job.

When I'd show up after a particularly hard day at the studio, I would be on edge; I might say confrontational.

I would be easily upset and when I arrived home I would expect a warm hug, a cold drink and a hot dinner.

But things didn't always turn out that way.

If something had gotten under Mimi's skin during the day, it was a moderately sure bet that there would be a blow-up.

It didn't need much, and most of the time I couldn't even remember what started things off.

Mimi was stubborn, I was irrational. It made for a noisy evening.

And when everything had been said, and occasionally, when the broken crockery had been cleaned up – yes there were times when plates flew – or when furniture had to be put back on its feet – Mimi would seem to have gotten whatever it was out of her system and she was ready to move on.

I, on the other hand, was usually remorseful and sullen, and although I got back into the swing of things relatively quickly, I found it hard to forgive myself for losing my temper.

These events didn't happen often, but they did happen.

Each of us had our dark side, and if you don't cast a shadow, you're not human.

CHAPTER 12

— • • • —

Say what? . . .

I WEAR HEARING aids.

I never knew I needed them until a few years ago when Mimi complained that she often had to repeat what she was saying.

Hearing deteriorates in many of us as we grow older.

One of the reasons is that organs in the ears called *hair cells*, which transmit neural impulses to the brain, become damaged, either from disease or having been exposed to too much noise during the person's lifetime.

I had been working for over forty years in video editing rooms which had loud air compressors operating all the time.

I thank that is probably the cause of my problem.

A third of people over sixty, and half of those older than eighty-five have hearing loss.

Hearing loss generally occurs in the higher frequencies. You miss a lot if you don't hear what's going on up there.

You don't hear high sounds, like birds tweeting merrily, or the tinkling tone of the tiny triangle in the symphony orchestra, and you probably also have trouble distinguishing plosive sounds.

P, B, K, G, T and D are the (ex)plosive letters, and it is easy to mis-hear one for the other; especially P and T.

This accounts for the odd look you receive from a hard-of-hearing neighbor at the dinner table when you remark casually that you have a small pit caught between your teeth.

A real life example occurred when I was trying to discover the name of a particularly nasty weed that was growing in our garden. I described it to a fellow gardener over the phone. She recognized it and told me the name. After I hung up I called out to Mimi in the other room.

"Linda Sue told me the name of that weed."

"Yes?"

"Yeah, it's 'liverwort'."

A short pause. "Liverwurst?"

They say that the inability to distinguish between plosives only worsens as you age.

Also, as your brain becomes unaccustomed to a once familiar sound, it doesn't recognize the sound for what it is anymore.

After I got my hearing aids I took a pee. It sounded to me like someone had thrown a brick through a plate glass window.

That only shows that you didn't realize what you were missing.

But like many improvements in life, this improvement carries with it a double-edged sword.

Yes, I can now hear the goldfinches tweeting merrily at the feeder. Yes, I am now able to tell the tinkling tone of the tiny triangle in the symphony orchestra.

The downside is that when Mimi and I are sitting down to lunch, I am now able to be traumatized by the piercing scream coming from the five-year-old at the table behind me, when he is denied another helping of something covered with marshmallows and M&Ms.

The amazing part of it is that while Mimi is covering her ears I have tears running down my cheeks, the parents aren't bothered by it at all.

They shake their heads at each other with parental pride, and the mother lightly admonishes the child with something like, "No, no, Davenport, two Pingos are enough. You don't want to go home and throw up all over Mommy's new sofa the way you did last week."

My fork clanks to the plate, and for a moment I think of anonymously sending a double Pingo to little Davenport.

I don't know what it is with parents nowadays.

Nowadays kids play with their noisy battery-powered toys in restaurants. They use remote controls to run their G.I. Joe Super-Atomic Tanks (klack! klack! klack! klack!) under adjoining tables and, without a thought, scramble between the legs of patrons to retrieve it.

Kids play tag among the tables hiding behind bemused diners.

How do their parents allow it? Where is the management?

Occasionally I wonder if would not be a good thing to return to the days when children were whisked away to wet nurses and nannies and not returned until they needed a shave.

Mimi and I eat lunch out several times a week. We try to make our doctors' appointments around lunchtime – and we have plenty of doctors' appointments.

Sometimes it seems as if the only time the phone rings is when a receptionist calls reminding us of an appointment with a physician – unless it's that mud wrestlers group.

When Mimi and I are in a restaurant I still think it's strange when the server (there are no waiters and waitresses anymore) asks, "Are you 'guys' ready to order?"

I saw *Guys and Dolls* in 1951 and I still have a definite image of what gender a Guy or a Doll should be.

Doll is not PC, though, and I can hardly imagine the server greeting a mixed group, or especially a group of women, with, "Are you dolls ready to order?"

After several minutes, I finally attract the attention of our server who has been busy punching her thumbs into her cell phone.

She approaches, "Are you done?"

I explain patronizingly, "'Done' is what a chicken breast is when it has been in a 350-degree oven for thirty-five minutes. In answer to your question, we have finished."

I can really be a pain in the ass.

While I'm at it, whatever happened to "You're welcome"?

You remember, it used to come back at you after you said "Thank you."

Nowadays when you thank someone, the response, more often than not, is "No prahm."

No prahm? It took me a while to figure out what it meant, and I still don't understand how it relates to "Thank you."

On our way out of the restaurant I say to the waitress – er – server, "I guess I sounded like a frustrated English teacher."

She looks up from her phone, "No prahm."

In restaurants today it's not unusual to see a group of people seated at a table ignoring each other pecking away at their cells.

Occasionally one will pause and turn the phone to a neighbor in order to share an especially noteworthy event, such as a picture of a kitten scattering a roll of toilet paper.

No conversation.

I keep a cell phone in the car for emergencies; I've had it for years.

It's so old, I tell people that when I turn it on the operator asks, "Number please?"

I don't mean to be sexist, but sometimes you can say something that is sexist and true at the same time.

Women generally have higher-pitched voices than men.

Whenever I catch sight of a table that seats half a dozen women who are obviously enjoying a good time, I head for the opposite side of the room. Even there, the voices and the laughter are nearly enough to shatter the mirrors on the wall.

I know I'm sounding like a grumpy Old Fart, but as Popeye often observed, "I yam what I yam."

I was told that when I was in a crowd my hearing aids would filter out extraneous noise.

In my case, not true!

It should come as no surprise that the microphones in my behind-the-ear aids are behind my ears. They face backwards. Therefore, the mikes pick up all the conversations and extraneous noise that happen behind me.

The conversation at my table becomes muffled and barely audible, but the gossip from the table behind me comes in loud and clear.

My only recourse is to stick my hearing aids in my breast pocket and ask my dining partners to speak up.

It was more than nine years ago that I discovered (for which read "When Mimi informed me") that I had a hearing problem. I searched the Web to find some suggestions about what to do. Here's a quote from one site: "Your doctor may refer you to an otolaryngologist (oh-toe-lair-in-GAH-luh-jist)." What condescension.

My mind immediately conjured up that movie shot we've all seen. It's taken from the point of view of the baby in the crib. The uncle leans in, his face huge in the lens. He's going to have some fun with you. He pokes you in your tummy and asks "Can you say 'oh-toe-lair-in-GAH-luh-jist?'"

At any rate, an otolaryngologist is an ENT (Ear, Nose and Throat) doctor. He'll send you to an audiologist.

This was in 2007, so some of what I am saying may be outdated, but not so outdated as all that.

I made an appointment with an audiologist.

I should have taken warning from the fact that the walls of his office were decorated with photos of him astride a show horse, leaping hurdles.

"That you?"

"Yep. Me and my Betsy."

"Neat."

After the preliminaries, he sat me in a soundproof booth with a pair of headphones and gave me a test with an audiometer. The audiometer produces tones at specific frequencies. It sends out a beep at various volume levels and tests each ear independently.

I had to press a button every time I heard a beep.

The beeps kept getting softer until I couldn't hear them anymore and I stopped pressing the button. That way he could tell the limit of my hearing ability in each ear at that particular frequency.

You will be relieved to know that normal hearing at any frequency is a sound pressure of 20 dBSPL or quieter.

He told me that I hear low sounds well, but my ability to hear higher sounds is severely curtailed.

Hearing aids that fit behind the ears (BTEs) would help with that problem.

I tell you now that a HA is basically a device with just two parts: a microphone and a loudspeaker (amplifier).

The earliest amplifier for use with the hard-of-hearing was the SHOUT! The SHOUT! required no mechanical apparatus, just a healthy set of lungs.

It was used with varying degrees of success for hundreds of thousands of years (maybe millions of years), and I have no doubt that it is still the method of choice in quarters where the cost of HAs is prohibitive.

Ear trumpets and similar devices provided some relief, and in the 20th Century, when telephone technology was developed, cumbersome devices using vacuum tubes were the cutting edge; but it wasn't until the introduction of the transistor and ultimately the computer chip that HAs evolved into those tiny ear adornments that are in use today.

BTEs have banana-shaped devices that fit behind the ears to hold the microphones that transmit the amplified sounds through a thin plastic tube into your ear.

What I didn't know when I visited the audiologist (dispenser or salesperson in this case) is that most dispensers work on commission, and unless you have the audio acuity of a snowy owl, you'd have a hard time getting out of the office without having ordered some expensive amplifying equipment to stick in your ears.

If this is the first time you are buying hearing aids, you have no way of knowing exactly what you need and have no idea what price range to expect.

It's sort of embarrassing to say, "Look, I want the absolutely cheapest thing you have that will allow me to hear well enough so that my wife will stop telling me I need hearing aids."

And you don't really want to say that, because it's *your* hearing after all, and you want what's best for it. So you speak the fatal words, "What do you suggest?"

He began, "Mister Schwarz, I'm happy to tell you we have three wonderful plans."

Then he described the $2,000 type – that's $2,000 per ear. I thought he had started out at the top.

He hadn't. He had started out at the bottom.

He wasn't disparaging about that low-priced model, but he wasn't exactly enthusiastic either.

The mid-priced model was $2,500 per ear, and while it was good, it didn't have all the features of the $3,000 per ear model. That is, crowd noise suppression, clarity on the telephone and a couple of other things that I didn't understand very well, but which made it special.

Well, I figured if these HAs were meant for someone else, the lowest-priced ones would surely be adequate.

But these things were for me! My insurance would chip in for about some of the cost.

After I was apprised of all the geegaws and doodads of the premium model, that's what I opted for.

$3,000 – per ear.

The price included the test by a professional (which I just had), the fitting fees, as many adjustments as I required, all the batteries I needed for five years, office visits for cleanings, and another audiology test halfway through the five year period.

These particular aids had the crowd-noise suppression system; feedback cancellation system and the "make phone calls clearer" system. It also included an insurance policy in case I lost them in the first two years.

The cost of the HA has to cover the salesperson's commission, office space, the receptionist, the equipment, the administration, the advertising and the jelly beans in the waiting room, not to mention a profit.

That's a lot of expenses and services, but $6,000 is a lot of money, considering that each top-of-the-line aid probably costs less than $500 to manufacture. Yeah, less than $500.

There are online sites that sell HAs for bargain prices; some under $100 per ear with adjustments that you fiddle around with until they work for you.

You can get "sound amplifiers" for less than $40 per ear. Not recommended.

You can even take a hearing test online, but they warn you that they might not be as accurate as a test administered by an audiologist.

Many people are happy with their pricy model, and those who dispense them will tell you that you get what you pay for, and all the testing and maintenance are worth the price.

Still it's a good chunk of dough.

I got used to my HAs quickly, though, and now I'm seldom without them; except at restaurants and parties. I hear fine and I thought that I had been treated well.

But, as in fairy tales, when the time agreed upon has elapsed and the poor farmer must give his only daughter to the fellow in the black cape with the red silk lining, the five years of my service agreement had expired.

Five years, so quickly, so quickly. Ah, me.

Now, once again, I had to face the audiologist/dispenser.

I hope I'm not being too hard on him. He was just trying to keep Betsy in hay.

He started off with what seemed like a sensible proposal.

Keep my old HAs, pay $100, and get four cleanings and a year's worth of batteries; that was the basic plan.

But, he quickly added, there have been so many nearly miraculous advances in HA technology, that I should consider replacing the old models with the spiffy new types that were now available.

They had all the features of the old ones but now there was so much more. Everything is digital and controlled by microprocessors.

They could connect wirelessly to the TV (with an added attachment to the TV). You can change the audio level remotely; sixteen channels. Bluetooth to your cell phone was available, as well as a host of other electronic features to enhance your HA experience.

I said, "Talk to me."

He began, "Mister Schwarz, I'm happy to tell you that we have three wonderful plans—"

Uh-oh.

"—The first one is the Silver Plan . . ."

I held up my hand. There was no use in him going on.

I knew that if he was starting with the Silver Plan there was sure to be a Gold Plan, which would include everything the Silver Plan contained, but would make the HA experience even more exciting and more rewarding.

I knew as well that, as sure as the walrus liked oysters, there was going to be a Platinum Plan produced forthwith, which comes complete with air conditioning, swimming pool and a three-car garage. This HA would be such a prodigious leap forward that you would be able to hear the Gettysburg Address – live.

I passed on all of them and decided to take the $100 maintenance plan.

I was content; that is until last summer, when we had a guest who wore HAs. He had had to buy new ones a short time previously, and I was surprised to learn he had purchased them at Costco.

He had paid over $5,000 for his original set. At Costco, for the top of the line, he had paid a little over $2,000.

He was very happy with them.

Really?

I thought that if, as I had been told, the current models were so much better than the five year old ones, I would give Costco a try.

I am probably one of the few living Americans who had not previously visited a big box store; but I can tell you this.

They don't call 'em BIG box stores fer nuthin'.

I was bowled over.

I have since learned that you can buy an automobile or a piano at Costco. I never did see Buicks or Steinways stacked one upon the other, but I saw only a fraction of the place.

After a long walk, I finally arrived at the audiologist/dispenser's desk.

The desk was out in the open next to a soundproof booth. Not a large space; nothing fancy.

The audiologist and her assistant were at the desk waiting for me.

I noticed with satisfaction that taped to the computer on the desk was a picture of a cute young girl with pigtails; no leaping Betsys or supercharged hydroplanes.

I told them that I was just looking; that I wanted to discover if the new hearing aids had improved enough to warrant me upgrading.

The audiologist said that was fine with her. She does not work on commission; her wages are not dependent on my buying HAs.

She said she would be glad to test me and let me try a set of their hearing aids.

She led me to the booth and began the test.

Tuning forks held against my skull, recordings with words that could be easily confused, plus the usual beeps.

When we had finished she popped a set of HAs into a machine, and presto, the computer which had kept track of all the testing info, automatically adjusted them to the optimum settings for my hearing capabilities.

The whole thing took about an hour, and it was more thorough than the one I had been given at the high-priced place.

If I bought them it would be about $2,000 for the pair.

She presented me with the HAs and said that I could go to lunch give them a try.

I drove to the local McDonald's and dined on Mc-fishy things with tartar sauce, fries and diet soda. I like McDonald's every once in a while. They still make some of the best fries around, although not quite as tasty as when they were using real beef fat.

All the while I was cocking my head like a randy rooster, trying to detect any of the amazing advances I had been told had occurred in the past five years.

I couldn't.

What I heard, and the way I heard it, seemed exactly the same as in my old aids.

I guess that the advances had been made in the peripheral aspects; Bluetooth, remote control, connections to the TV, etc.

I returned to the audiologist/dispenser and thanked her for her work, but I said that I might as well stick with my old aids.

She was very gracious, and before things got maudlin we parted company.

I have to say that another reason why I didn't go with the new HAs was that this particular Costco is almost a two-hour drive from my home and if I needed any adjustments it would take a day out of my life.

There would have to be a marked difference for that to be worthwhile.

Costco has since built an outlet much closer to where I live, so you never know.

But my experience was positive and if I find I need new hearing aids I certainly will consider them as an option.

● ● ●

We loved sailing.

We never owned a sailboat, but twice in our marriage we have been deep sea sailing together.

The first time was in Greece.

Mimi had done some work teaching German on a television show, and with the money she earned she invited me to Greece where we would hire a sailing boat and cruise around.

175

I couldn't refuse.

Athens is a beautiful city and Constitution Square at its center is filled with cafés which have a fine view of the Acropolis on a nearby hill.

There was going to be a full moon the night we arrived so we decided to go up and view the moonrise from the ruins.

As we climbed the hill, it was a little scary. It wasn't very well lit, and when we finally approached the two pillars at the end of the path they seemed like a doorway to eternity.

For a moment the thought crossed my mind that when we passed between them, we'd come out in ancient Greece on the other side.

I'm glad to say we did not get transported into the past, and when the moon rose over the hill in the East it flooded the place with an incredibly romantic light – eerie, but romantic.

The next day we went to Piraeus, the harbor near Athens, and boarded a 35-foot sloop – Toxotis "The Archer" – it was a beautiful thing. I had imagined a tub, but this was sleek and elegant. I suspected she was yar.

She came with a skipper, Markos – and a deck hand, Zoi.

They took care of everything, and for the next five days we island-hopped; leaving port in the morning, stopping to picnic and swim at an intermediate islet and reaching the next harbor in time for dinner at a dockside restaurant.

Marcos insisted that we dress when we entered a new harbor, no swimsuits allowed.

He had standards.

Near the end of our charter, we pulled into the harbor of Monemvasia on the East coast of southern Greece.

What makes this place so memorable is a mile-long island off shore. Its salient feature is a huge volcanic plug rising nearly 300 feet.

Very impressive.

Seeing that there was only a day or so left, and the scenery was so dramatic, Mimi decided to have her party.

She unpacked a dozen paper lanterns which Marko had and strung them along the boom.

Zoi went into town and brought back a feast of cold cuts, bread and that light Greek white wine that goes down so easily.

So with the remnants of an ancient volcano looming over us, we shared our meal, toasting to the trip, accompanied sporadically by Zoi doing his best to improvise "Give My Regards to Broadway" on his harmonica.

The candles had burned down, and the sky was (as Oliver Sacks quoted Milton) "powdered with stars" when we finally called it quits.

CHAPTER 13

• • •

We return to those thrilling days of yesteryear . . .

MY FIRST REAL experience with serious medical procedures that prolonged my life and set me on the path to becoming an Old Fart happened in 1942, when I was eleven years old.

I came down with appendicitis.

The funny part of it is that nobody really knows why we have an appendix. It's a little dingily tube about three inches long that hangs off the bottom off the large intestine.

It doesn't seem to do much of anything except get infected occasionally and have to be removed.

Darwin thought it bolstered his theory of evolution, since it must have had a use at one time, but now the body has evolved so that the appendix is no longer needed.

Some anatomists are not happy with the concept that there is an anatomical anomaly inside you that doesn't seem to have any use. They are sure that it must have a purpose, they just can't agree on what the purpose is.

Nobody thought much about my stomach problem because it started out like a bad bellyache and I'd had bellyaches before.

The pain got worse, though, and during a break in a bridge game, one of my father's cronies, a doctor, put his cigar down long enough to examine me.

"Bellyache."

Two days later I was screaming. My father finally called a specialist who came and examined me. Doctors came to the house in those days.

He said that I was suffering from acute appendicitis. I was rushed to the hospital where I underwent an emergency appendectomy.

My appendix had ruptured and I was suffering from peritonitis; my peritoneum was badly infected and they thought I might die.

I didn't.

Without WWII, I probably would have died.

Luckily for me, sulfa drugs had been introduced and were working miracles on the battlefield curing bacterial infections.

It took a war.

After the appendectomy, I discovered that there was a drain sticking out of my stomach. It looked like a large size rigatoni. Sorry, but that's what it looked like.

Every so often a nurse would come into my hospital room and empty a packet of powder into the drain; sulfanilamide?

Whatever it was, it had the desired effect because several days later an intern caught my attention by yanking the drain out without warning.

Here I am, over seventy years later.

It took a long time for me to recover, but ultimately, I regained my health and had successfully passed a rather daunting hurdle on the road to becoming an Old Fart.

I sometimes think that if all that surgery hadn't interrupted my education, I might have done better later on. But in retrospect, I believe that my cloak of academic mediocrity had already been measured and was being stitched, and even if the disruption had not occurred nothing much would have improved.

I was attending the John Ward Elementary School in Newton Massachusetts, which was experimenting with a new concept called "Progressive Education."

The idea of Progressive Education was put forth in the US in the late 19th Century by John Dewey, a philosopher and educator. He was no relation to Melvil Dewey who invented the eponymous library cataloging system in 1876, nor was he related to New York Governor Thomas E. Dewey, who invented a way to lose a slam-dunk presidential election to Harry S. Truman in 1948.

Anyway, I never knew what progressive education was. I knew that the John Ward School was involved in it, but to be perfectly honest I didn't know much about it until I looked it up on Google a couple of days ago.

As it turns out, Progressive Education was a lot about how things worked in the real world.

Dewey felt that young students should learn by doing. They should participate in their own education; not just sit there and try to absorb the facts being thrown at them. We went on field trips to museums, the police station and the firehouse.

One of the things I remember best was sewing oilcloth into mats and filling them with cotton batting. We used them to lie on when we took our naps.

Thanks Mr. Dewey.

I don't remember much of the curriculum at Ward School.

But I do remember that we recited the Lord's Prayer every morning before we started class; heads bowed, hands clasped.

I don't think reciting it did much good or any harm, it was simply another one of those things you did in school.

And even though the Lord's Prayer is a central prayer in Christianity, and even though the John Ward School's student body was overwhelmingly Jewish, nobody, as far as I know, ever found occasion to complain about it.

It wasn't until the mid-'50s, long after I left school, that the legal wrangling about the First Amendment and the "establishment clause" started in earnest.

We also repeated the Pledge of Allegiance.

The Pledge was written in 1892 by a Baptist minister named Francis Bellamy.

The original pledge went this way; "I pledge allegiance to my Flag and the Republic for which it stands, one nation indivisible, with liberty and justice for all."

In 1923-4 the words "of the United States of America" were added.

"Under God" was grafted on in 1954, during the Anti-Communist frenzy at the time of the Eisenhower administration.

Eisenhower stated that the inclusion of these two words "recognized the dedication of our nation and our people to the Almighty." It seems that he thought the words "under God" had a religious connotation.

Since that time a host of lawsuits have been instituted with the aim of having the two words stricken from the pledge when it is recited in public schools.

I don't like the insertion of those words mainly because they break up the rhythm of the pledge. Say the pledge to yourself (or out loud if you choose) and you'll see.

Also, it irks me a bit to be forced to succumb to the fervor of religious zealots who derive satisfaction by forcing you to acknowledge a deity whenever they can.

All of which brings me to our national anthem; a work of which I am an admirer even though it is really hard to sing well. You need a broad *tessitura*. The melody ranges from the C below the staff to the G above the staff; one-and-a-half octaves. I can tell you that near the end when the lyric gets to "the land of the free," you had better have your dance belt on tight if you expect to hit that high G.

Francis Scott Key wrote this poem commemorating a tense night during the War of 1812 when the British Navy was bombarding Fort McHenry near Baltimore.

His verse was written to the cadence of a particular tune he had in mind. It was one that had been used previously used for patriotic songs he and others had written.

In fact, the same melody was, for a time, used for the national anthem of Luxemburg, so there can be no denying that it had a certain patriotic resonance.

The tune was originally written in the late 18th Century by John Stafford Smith. It was the official song of the Anacreontic Society, a group of amateur gentlemen musicians.

Anacreon was a poet in ancient Greece known particularly for his poems dedicated to love and wine. Therefore, the tune has often been characterized as a drinking song, but with a vocal range like that, I can't imagine what you'd have to be drinking to hit all the notes.

All you have to do, to judge just how difficult it is to sing, is sit through some of the excruciating renditions sung by celebrities at sporting events.

"The Star-Spangled Banner" contains some wonderfully patriotic language, and when it is played with enthusiasm, it's certainly one of the most stirring pieces of music I have ever heard.

By the end of the 19th Century the song was performed whenever a national anthem was appropriate, but when, in 1928, Robert Ripley (of Believe It or Not . . .) pointed out that, in fact, the United States Congress had never officially voted on a national anthem, both houses rushed to remedy that deficiency.

After some wrangling over whether the words were too bellicose and the melody too hard to sing, the scales were tipped by the unimpeachable authority of none other than John Philip Sousa, who expressed his admiration by describing "The

Star-Spangled Banner" thusly, "Besides its soul-stirring words – it is the spirit of the music that inspires."

In 1931, Herbert Hoover, in one of the signal events of his administration – possibly *the* signal event – signed a law making "The Star-Spangled Banner" the official national anthem of the United States of America.

I know this is going to upset most of you, and I hate to be the one to break the news, but there is serious doubt that Betsy Ross designed the first American flag in 1777.

Wait a minute! Resume your seats . . . please! Order! Order! Calm down!

Whew!

What I'm trying to tell you is that there is no evidence that she had a hand in the flag's creation at all, except a much-disputed claim made by her grandson nearly one hundred years later.

Besides, up until 1777 the flag that represented the thirteen colonies – the Grand Union Flag – looked exactly like the flag we have today except the canton (the box in the upper left) contained a miniature British flag.

The only change was that the British flag in the canton was replaced with a blue field on which were affixed thirteen five-pointed white stars.

So, there wasn't much of a change after all.

Caught in the middle . . .

When I went to John Ward Elementary, I didn't know I had been immersed in a special type of educational process; to me it was just school.

That would not have been a problem except that John Ward was the only school in the system involved with progressive education.

When I got to the 7th grade at Bigelow Middle School, I was unprepared for what they taught there.

For example, I had learned nothing about sentence structure or grammar. I couldn't tell the difference between a dangling participle and a flying Wallenda.

Breaking a sentence down to its component parts was something I had never done. Adverbs and infinitives . . . Huh?

Nevertheless, I've always been able to write fairly well, and from time to time I've wondered why an American with a good ear ever really needed to be bothered with all those tiresome grammatical definitions and rules.

I'll admit that when I hear a newscaster report that "The politician told my cameraman and I to leave," it bothers me.

I wonder how that newscaster ever got the job of casting news in the first place. And even more, I wonder how his or her boss doesn't catch him or her up on this basic grammatical error.

Funny, I'm listening to a classical music station at this very moment and the presenter, in order to create an intimate atmosphere, I presume, has just said, "There's no one here except you and I."

Ugh.

I think that the error must come from a mistaken impression that somehow "I" sounds more refined than "me." and in my time as a director of TV Soap Operas I've had to explain to many young (and not so young) performers the proper use of "I" and "me" in those situations.

In order to find out what I might be missing by not being more fluent in grammar, I went to the website of Robin Simmons, a grammarian who dispenses examples of grammatical rules.

Here's a sentence I found describing the infinitive. In case you are as ignorant as I am, I have set the infinitive in italics: "The best way *to survive* Dr. Peterson's boring history lectures is a sharp pencil *to stab* in your thigh if you catch yourself drifting off."

So?

I'd like to know why I should spend any time at all, or how it would improve my syntax, learning that *to survive* and *to stab* are infinitives. What's the point?

But I am grateful to Ms. Simmons because her sentence can be used as an example of a different sort of writing, i.e. humor.

She is not only explaining a grammatical rule, she is trying to leaven the lesson by making a joke, and I think she has stepped on her own punch line.

My definition of humor is, "The unexpected."

A joke must have at least two parts: A) a *setup*, which explains the context of the joke, and B) a *payoff*, which contains the unexpected "hook" or "reversal" which makes the joke funny.

The punch line is the payoff to the joke. The punch line is always unexpected and it is always at the end.

The unexpected punch line of Ms. Simmons' joke is "a sharp pencil to stab in your thigh." Nobody expected that.

Her sentence might just as well end there, since it's implicit that the boring history lectures of Dr. Peterson would put anybody to sleep.

But if you feel it is helpful to add the phrase "if you catch yourself drifting off" it should not step on your punch line.

Place it elsewhere, as in "If you catch yourself drifting off during Dr. Peterson's boring history lectures, the best way to survive is to stab a sharp pencil in your thigh."

The infinitives are still there, but you should always save the punch line for the end. That might not be a grammatical rule, but for a humorist it's axiomatic.

Meantime . . .

I got through the three years of middle school.

The Second World War ended and I moved on to Newton High School for three more years of what turned out to be mediocre attainment.

The remarks appended to my report card said that I could do better if I would only "apply myself."

Each September, I would promise myself that this year I would "apply myself." I started out with high hopes.

But sooner rather than later it always turned out that my application wasn't sticky enough and I would be reissued my old cloak of mediocrity.

I always dreaded bringing my report card home to be signed.

I don't remember much else of what happened at Newton High.

I do remember algebra, however.

At first, I thought that math was a subject that I could get along with. A mathematical discipline that challenges you with problems like X+6=10 was right up my alley.

But it was not long before I was disabused of that comforting notion.

From out of the blue, there appeared the infamous gang of three: A, B and C.

A, B and C showed up in various permutations; always going someplace, building something, or engaged in the improbable activity of pumping liquid into and out of cisterns for reasons that were never explained.

Whenever I sighted the three of them, I was filled with despair. I knew there was a formula and, if you could plug in the correct numbers, it would enable you come up with just how much faster A could dig his trench than B or C, or how many miles out of the station A's express would go whizzing past C's, but I could never master it.

My ability to cope with geometry was the only way I made it through math. I have learned lately that my dyslexic ability to imagine shapes in space may have helped me.

I did graduate from high school, class of '49, and I was accepted at Emerson College in Boston.

Emerson was, and still is, a place where students study communication and the dramatic arts.

It was founded in 1800 by Charles Wesley Emerson as a "school of oratory." Drama and acting were the major concerns.

In my imagination I saw my future as an actor, skipping happily toward fame and fortune, down the road toward Old-Fartdom – "Hi-diddle-dee-dee . . ."

At Emerson I was at home; satisfied.

My father, who was footing the bill, wasn't satisfied.

You know why? He wanted a son who went to Harvard.

I had two older brothers, one of whom graduated from M.I.T. with honors, but that wasn't enough.

Our next-door neighbor had a son who was going to Harvard and my father wanted one too.

The only difference was that the next-door neighbor's son was a genius.

I, on the other hand, was swathed in a cloak of mediocrity.

But this was 1949, and where there was a will and some influence there was sure to be a way.

My father sent me to a prestigious prep school that concentrated on test preparation for Harvard.

I took the tests and, not long after, I received a letter announcing that I had been accepted at Harvard for the class of 1954.

I have to tell you that I was thrilled, even though my acting career would be put on hold.

I believed that I must have scored really well on the tests, and I began to feel a little proud of myself.

My brothers quickly slapped me back to earth and let me know, in no uncertain terms, that the publisher of the newspaper my father worked for had used his influence to get me admitted.

It wasn't anything I had done.

In the intervening years, I have come to the conclusion that I couldn't have done that badly on the test, because I don't think Harvard would have accepted a complete idiot.

But you never know.

During the year I was at Emerson, my father arranged an interview with an actor who was appearing in Boston.

As I was admitted to his dressing room, I knew this was a set up and the actor had been prompted to deliver a mendacious sermon recommending the straight and narrow; "Life upon the Wicked Stage" and all that.

After I graduated, if I still wanted to get on the stage, but the stage left without me, I would always have a solid college education to fall back on.

The actor proceeded exactly as I expected, while I sat peeking at the fascinating jars of cold cream and tubes of make-up in front of the mirror at his table.

When he had concluded his cautionary tale, he offered me a pearl of great wisdom fetched up from the vast depths of his experience.

Leaning close, he confided that if I ever appeared on stage in a scene where I had to make love to a beautiful and seductive actress, I should always wear a jockstrap.

He had obviously learned the hard way.

Fair Harvard . . .

I did graduate from Harvard, Class of '54.

Barely.

I know I graduated because I have a diploma, and my picture is in the yearbook; but it took a summer school class to accumulate the required credits.

I had majored in English Literature, but since I have told you that I am the world's slowest reader, I didn't finish a lot of books.

Nowadays whenever someone recommends a book to me, I go into a bookstore to take a look. Sadly, the book is usually about four inches thick. I say to the clerk, "It better have big print and a lot of pictures."

• • •

As I was saying, I graduated from Harvard, class of '54.

If I majored in anything, I majored in drinking.

I know, I know, it was a waste of a good education, but I wasn't thinking of that, I was thinking of having a good time.

I was interested in the theater and I was interested in writing.

The first thing I ever wrote was my acceptance speech for the Nobel Prize. I'm still touching it up.

The first thing I ever sold was a set of lyrics for a Ladies Garden Club show.

I was paid $75 and I spent it on a magnum of pre-war Hennessy. Remember this was in 1953.

My roommate and I sat in my room one weekend and drank it.

I don't regret it.

I wanted to be an actor in those days and I took part in several Harvard Dramatic Club productions: *Murder in the Cathedral* and *Marco's Millions.*

I wrote some of the lyrics and took the lead in *Ad Man Out*; the Hasty Pudding Theatrical of 1954.

The show was a hit and one of the Boston reviewers said that I was Broadway material.

Apparently no one else thought so, but it was great fun.

During the Christmas hiatus we trooped the show and even got to perform at Barbara Warner's coming-out party at the Rainbow Room.

As the party was breaking up and we were leaving, we were approached by Mr. Warner who wanted to thank us.

The opportunity was too much for one of our group, a wag named Freddy Faucet.

As Mr. Warner was shaking our hands, Freddy asked him, "Are you really one of the Warner brothers?"

"Yes, I am."

"Which one are you, Harpo, Groucho or Chico?"

Stage name . . .

Before I went to Harvard, I had my stage debut at the Coonammesset Summer Theater in Falmouth on Cape Cod. It must have been in the late 1940s.

I was an extra in a production of Shaw's *The Devil's Disciple* starring Maurice Evans.

My role was this: After Mr. Evans had leapt onto a table and made a rousing anti-British speech to the American colonists I, costumed as a Red Coat, was the one designated to pull him off the table to be marched off stage.

During the dress rehearsal, I reached up and yanked, then three of us marched him off.

Rubbing his arm, Mr. Evans motioned me over.

He then imparted a one-sentence acting lesson so precise and clear that Stanislavski or Clurman could not have framed it better.

"Young man, if you *pretend* to pull me off the table, I will *pretend* that you are pulling me off the table."

Oh.

In that brief summer of treading the boards, I realized that I ought to come up with a stage name.

Nowadays most performers use their own names but in that era, I wasn't the only one in the world who took a stage name. Take Cyd Charisse, for example. She was born Tula Ellice Finklea; hardly a moniker you'd want to see beside Fred Astaire's on a marquee. Apparently Fred Astaire (Frederick Austerlitz) didn't think his given name was appropriate for a marquee either.

Robert Schwarz simply would not do; too Jewish, and I didn't intend to go into the Yiddish Art Theater.

Remember this was in the 1940s. There weren't a lot of performers with Jewish names, even though there were a lot of Jewish performers.

Frieda Lipschitz ended up as "Her Nibs, Miss Georgia Gibbs." One of her hit records was "If I Knew You Were Comin' I'd've Baked a Cake." It wouldn't have been the same is she sang, "If I Knew You Were Comin' I'd've Baked a Kugel."

Edward Israel Iskowitz, became Eddie Cantor. Asa Yoelson, born in Poland, grew up to be Al Jolson. The three stooges were all Horowitzs before they were Howards.

David Daniel Kaminsky turned out to be Danny Kay. Irwin Alan Kniberg would become Alan King; Pincus Leff – Pinky Lee; Joseph Levitch – Jerry Lewis. Rosetta Jacobs was morphed into Piper Laurie, Benjamin Kubelsky became Jack Benny; the list goes on. By a happy coincidence, the Marx Brothers started out with that name.

Sophie Tucker, "the Last of the Red Hot Mamas," started out in Russia as Sonya Kalish.

She introduced such memorable songs as "Some of these Days" and "My Yiddishe Momme."

In her act she wasn't above using some numbers that weren't so memorable: "Nobody Loves a Fat Girl, But Oh How a Fat Girl Can Love" and "Who Paid the Rent for Mrs. Rip van Winkle When Rip Van Winkle Went Away?"

Pseudonyms and *noms de plume, noms de theatre, noms de guerre, et noms d'autre choses* are always interesting to peruse.

You might not have known that the name on Picasso's birth certificate is "Pablo Diego José Francisco de Paula Juan Nepomuceno María de los Remedios Cipriano de la Santísima Trinidad Ruiz y Picasso." His mother must have had to take a deep breath before she called him to dinner.

Back to my problem . . .
Schwarz means "black" in German, so for a while I considered Robert Black.

Not suave enough, no, no, no. I wanted something more man-about-townish. What about Robert Blake? Close, but still too ordinary.

Aha! Blake Roberts! That was just the ticket. It had a certain mystery about it. Yes! Blake Roberts it was.

So, if you happen to have preserved a program from the Coonammesset Summer Theater for a late '40s summer that includes the cast listing for *The Devil's Disciple* and you look under "extras" you will find Sam Schultz, Ronnie Wiener, Dan Baumgarten and Blake Roberts.

My father wanted to know why my name wasn't on the cast list.

I squirm whenever I remember it.

• • •

Two side trips . . .

When I was at Harvard, a friend came home on leave from the Air Force. We decided to take in the show at the Old Howard.

The Old Howard was simply and unabashedly a burlesque house. It was located in the then seamy Scollay Square area of downtown Boston.

Wikipedia describes burlesque as "a literary, dramatic or musical work intended to cause laughter by caricaturing the manner or spirit of serious works, or by ludicrous treatment of their subjects."

Fugedaboudit!

The Old Howard featured strippers, and it was to see the strippers that folks bought their tickets.

My friend and I were folks.

The strippers' routines were interspersed with baggy-pants comics, an Irish tenor, an occasional dance number slogged through by a rather mature lady's chorus and a pause during which the hawkers would peddle merchandise such as Fanny Farmer Candy: "Everybody's got to have a piece of fanny once in a while."

Harvard students would embarrass their dates by paying ushers to cruise the aisle during intermission and holler out, "Phone call for Miss Sarah Johnson and the like."

A bit tawdry and a whole lot of fun.

It was not always thus . . .

Boston's Howard Athenaeum, at 34 Howard Street, a structure capable of seating 1,360 patrons, was completed in 1846.

In its first years it presented high quality entertainment; ballet and serious drama; Edwin Booth played Hamlet there. His younger brother, John Wilkes, acted in the same role before he became famous for acting badly on a different stage; Sarah

Bernhardt also appeared there; vaudeville, minstrels; opera too: Verdi's *Ernani* had its American debut there, as did Donizetti's *Linda di Chamounix.*

After a couple of decades, though, the theater lost much of its high class glamour and high class customers. It presented mostly vaudeville, and eventually switched over to what we now call burlesque.

Harvard students (as well as some of their professors) frequented the place. Jack Kennedy was supposed to be a regular.

But the shows became more and more risqué, until 1953 when the Howard Athenaeum was shuttered for being too lewd.

As you might have guessed, the night with my Air Force friend was not the first time I had crossed the threshold of the Old Howard. I was not a frequent attendee, but I had been there once or twice before.

On one of my visits I was fortunate enough to observe the efforts of Willis Marie Van Schaack, better known to the burlesque cognoscenti as Lili St. Cyr.

Ms. St. Cyr came at the stripping game from a unique angle. She didn't strip, she un-stripped.

When the curtain parted she was discovered in a bubble bath, from which, after some entertaining moments, she arose, appropriately shielded from the curious eye by a large square of fabric artfully managed by her maid.

For the next several minutes she proceeded to enrobe herself in a leisurely manner which to my youthful eyes seemed appropriate and eminently satisfactory.

When she had completed her levee, dressed in an elegant black outfit complete with a parasol and a lap dog on a leash, she not so much exited the stage as withdrew from our sight with great style and dignity.

In 1960 the Old Howard was razed in order to make way for urban renewal.

But the place was open for business the night the two of us walked up to the ticket window and plunked our money down.

My friend was wearing his Air Force uniform and, though he was in his early 20s, he had lost most of his hair, so when we entered the hallowed precincts, much to our embarrassment, we were ushered to the front row where, for some reason, they sat all the baldies.

One of the strippers had a particularly active routine, shaking and quaking all over the place, tossing her garments hither and thither until she got down to where there wasn't much of anything left to toss. Then she seemed to discover my friend in the military uniform, and she chose him as the object of her gyrations. Scantily clad, she danced over and leaned out above him. She shook and shook; she winked and smiled, she wiggled and jiggled.

I was not in a position to ignore her; after all I was sitting right next to the guy.

Looking up I noticed, along with her jiggling, a gold chain around her neck on which hung a Star of David.

My first thought was, "How can a nice Jewish girl be here doing this?"

● ● ●

One time a classmate of mine invited me to spend a weekend with him and his family on Martha's Vineyard.

They owned a large piece of property in Edgartown.

It so happened that their next-door neighbor was James Cagney.

My friend's mother was a fine cook and every Sunday, Mr. Cagney would come over to sample her monumental breakfast.

He joined us at the table and I remember being amazed that he looked and acted exactly like James Cagney.

When we were introduced and he heard my name was "Schwarz," he began speaking to me in Yiddish.

He had learned it growing up on the Lower East Side in New York earning pocket money by being a Shabbos Goy. He performed small tasks that were forbidden to Orthodox Jews on the Sabbath, like starting the stove and turning on the lights.

What he couldn't realize was that, even though my mother spoke Yiddish, much to my regret, she thought it was low class, and didn't speak it around the children.

Mr. Cagney was disappointed and, although he was cordial throughout, I think he would have had a lot of fun practicing his Yiddish.

If I had been able, I would have had a lot of fun too.

• • •

Mimi and I used to live in an apartment near Central Park.

When there were concerts in the Sheep Meadow, we often packed a picnic and moseyed over.

It was always pleasant; out in the open like that, with the city lights silhouetting the skyline.

Some people brought folding chairs, but most spread blankets, and a goodly number brought sandwiches and wine.

On one particular occasion (I don't remember what was so celebratory about it) Mimi decided to do something special.

That was the reason I ended up lugging a heavy picnic basket and a large shopping bag into the park.

Mimi carried the blanket.

When everything was unpacked, all I could do was shake my head in wonderment.

She had laid out silverware, and cloth napkins; had unpacked plates which she decorated with country pate, roasted chicken, French bread, grapes, Camembert and a nice bottle of cabernet with real wine glasses.

The Roxy finish was the lighting of a hurricane candle that burned cheerily as it sat in a protective glass sleeve.

Passersby applauded.

Word must have gotten around because, not long after, a reporter showed up to interview Mimi.

When he asked her why she had done up such a fancy feast, she replied, with a straight face, "To give the butler a night off."

The reporter snapped a photo and, believe it or not, the picture showed up the next day in the fashion section of The New York Times.

Typical Mimi.

CHAPTER 14

• • •

Moving on . . .

IF THIS WERE a 1930s film drama, right about now you'd be seeing pages flying off the calendar as my years at Harvard flew by.

My father had died in 1950 of a cerebral hemorrhage, and my dear mother footed the bill for the rest of my education.

I was an average student and, considering the lack of preparation for tests and the general goofing off I indulged in, it was a pretty remarkable accomplishment.

After I graduated in the spring of 1954, I fooled around until the fall and then volunteered for the draft.

The Korean War had ended the previous year and at that time there were no wars going on.

I had no desire to be in a war and I thought it would be a good time to get my military service out of the way while the getting was peaceful.

I took my basic training that January at Fort Dix in New Jersey. It was cold, cold, cold.

Most of my fellow inductees had just graduated from law school; they thought they would be assigned to the Adjutant General's Department, but there were so many of them that they got sent to Korea to help with the armistice.

I missed out on that plum assignment because I came down with a pneumonia-like infection that sent me to the infirmary.

When I got out, I was shipped to Germany . . . Joy! Joy! Joy!

I ended up in Mainz, as a heavy weapons infantryman; a member of the 7th Army's 42nd Armored Infantry Battalion, "Hell on Wheels," which we troops referred to privately as "Wie gehts on roller skates."

This was early in 1955 and Germany was still pretty much a wreck. The war's devastation was all too visible.

I arrived in the last few days of the occupation and, if I choose, I am authorized to wear the Army of Occupation Medal beside my Good Conduct Medal.

I don't do it often.

I was designated a squad leader; after all, I was a Harvard graduate.

We trained setting up heavy mortars, taking target practice, marching back and forth, enduring inspections and waiting for Saturday nights when we could get passes to go into town, where we ate schnitzels and drank beer.

There were some bikers from Brooklyn in my squad. They didn't take orders very well, and a lot of the time they sat around on the edge of their bunks pretending they were revving their motorcycles, "Wahpoom! Wahpoom! Wahpoom!"

It was very disconcerting; I was not comfortable.

Coincidences have played a large part in my life, and a coincidence was on the way.

A couple of months later we were on a training exercise, camped in an ugly area near Baumholder where Rommel had trained his desert troops. It was rainy and muddy and unbelievably cold; icy water was dripping from my nose; I was wet and miserable.

In the next tent, the bikers were "wahpooming" away.

I was called to Company Headquarters to answer a phone call.

It was a former classmate who was with 7th Army Special Services.

He had heard that I was serving in Germany and he asked me if I would consider a temporary assignment to Special Services managing a touring 7th Army variety show.

I considered it.

A week or two later I received orders and, with a light heart I reported to Special Services in Stuttgart.

It was *the* pivotal point in my undistinguished military career.

During my three-month temporary duty assignment with Special Services, we happened to pass through Frankfurt which was the headquarters of AFN (American Forces Network).

They were holding auditions for announcers.

I auditioned.

I had had a year of speech training at Emerson, I had lost any Boston accent, and had no trace of the twangy southern accent that so many of the soldiers had.

I was moderately conversant with the names of classical music composers and their works, so I thought I did pretty well on the audition.

That turned out to be an accurate assessment because in a week or two I received a notice informing me that I was accepted as an announcer on AFN.

With the recommendation of my sympathetic Company Commander, the transfer was accomplished, and by another lucky coincidence, three announcers from the Munich studios were rotating back to the States. I was assigned there.

Then began the only two years in my eighty-odd-year life during which I was completely carefree.

The AFN studios were located in the late 19th Century villa of Friedrich August von Kaulbach, a prominent Munich artist of the time.

We announcers were billeted, two to a room, in the servants' quarters three flights up; they were luxury suites compared to the barracks in Mainz.

Because there were no mess facilities, we were put on separate-rations pay so we could buy our meals on the German economy.

We did not wear uniforms and, to protect our vocal cords, we were not allowed to work more than four hours a day on the air.

We did have to write promotional announcements, though, and submit record lists.

All in all, it was not what you would call arduous duty, but somebody had to do it.

Gasthaus Wilhelm Tell was just down the street.

The Deutsche mark was over 4.20 to the dollar (6 or 8 on the black market), and even on army pay one could live pretty well.

That's where I met Mimi.

● ● ●

Mimi – Annamaria Wojaczek – was born in Breslau, Poland in 1929. She and her mother had fled from the East in January of 1945. They somehow survived the bombing of Dresden as they made their way to southern Bavaria and ended up in Munich, where they were reunited with Mimi's father.

He was a doctor. He had been a colonel in the German Army Medical Corps and had served on the Russian front. He was OK, a little bit too "German" for my taste, but there he was. He began a new and successful practice in Munich and they lived in a very pleasant apartment near Roten Kreuz Platz.

Her mother was a housewife and a lovely lady. She liked me a lot and she was right to, because Mimi and I turned out to be a very good couple.

There was also a younger brother– Christian. Today he is a retired doctor living near Munich, with two grown children and a grandchild. It does go on, doesn't it.

The family was nominally Catholic, but I don't ever remember them going to church.

Mimi told me that she overheard her father say to her mother that all they needed was a Jew in the family.

Well, they got one, and it didn't seem to matter.

You might ask how a twenty-three-year-old Jewish man could come to Germany during those post-war years and even think of falling in love with a German woman.

I have no answer.

It happened.

Mimi and I continued our relationship.

We visited Salzburg, and drove along the Danube to Vienna. We visited the wine taverns in Grinzing and picnicked in the Vienna Woods. We drove all over Bavaria, went Fasching (the German version of Mardi Gras) together, visiting the towns large and small and we were becoming very close.

Ultimately it became time to make a decision, so I took a three-day leave and went to London to think about it.

It didn't take me long to realize that I was having more fun with Mimi than I'd ever had with any other person in my life. She was beautiful, and clever and the possibility of somehow being without her filled me with a terrible emptiness. It was something I didn't want to face.

I was smart enough to figure out what that meant.

I sent her a telegram, "Be back Tuesday. I love you." It wasn't very romantic, but they charged by the word.

She had a tough decision to make. She was two years older than I, she would have to leave her homeland for someone who had no trade and no prospects. It was not the prospect of a very solid and secure future.

But she had balls and she had faith in me, and we (she) set the date – 2/2/57.

I also think that the idea of America with its much freer society that contrasted so much with the rather stiff German model appealed to Mimi. She was much too much of an individual to feel comfortable with the rather conformist society in Germany. Even when we went back to visit her parents she was not really at ease there.

"Too many Germans," she would say.

We were married at the City Hall and moved on to Humplmeyer's, one of the best restaurants in town, to celebrate with a lavish meal arranged for the wedding party by my new father-in-law.

Mimi was a stunning bride and I'll tell you that, looking at the pictures, I was pretty handsome too.

After the meal and the speeches, the good doctor collected all the leftover hors d'oeuvres, boxed them and escorted us to our used VW beetle, where they all cheered and waved us off.

We overnighted at the Garmischer Hoff, a splendid hotel, which was still under US Army control. Then we drove on to Lech in the Austrian Alps and spent our honeymoon skiing, and doing honeymoon things.

That was in February 1957, and we were hardly settled in an apartment before orders arrived shipping me back to the States for an early discharge into civilian life.

Reality was about to set in.

• • •

Mimi and I landed at Idlewild (now JFK) early in July in 1957 on one of the hottest days in years. The temperature was something like 110 degrees.

Thence to Elizabeth, New Jersey, where my mother lived with her two sisters in an apartment with an extra room large enough for Mimi and me.

Reality had set in with a vengeance.

Here I was – a couple of hundred dollars in my pocket, married and living with my brand new wife in the spare room of my mother's apartment in Elizabeth, New Jersey.

It was crowded and my aunts looked at Mimi as if she were a lab specimen.

On the second night we all went to the movies and Mimi and I had to select a cup and a saucer to add to the dinner service that one of my aunts was collecting.

Not the way I expected my married life to start out.

I'll break the suspense right away by telling you that the mother of my roommate at Harvard knew a vice president at CBS and got me an interview.

A couple of days later, I was hired as a Production Assistant at CBS-TV.

I was hired because I went to Harvard, and that was the only time in my entire career that Harvard was ever mentioned.

It opened the door.

It was a huge load off my shoulders.

I worked in television for the next forty years.

I think the salary was $40 a week (plus overtime); not very much even then, but it was the way to break into a new and exciting theatrical business, and those who were starting out coveted the job.

The first day on the job, when I walked into a studio and saw what was going on, I understood how it all worked. I didn't know the technical terms, but I understood cross-cutting. I was aware of how the cameras had to move, how the booms had to be placed, where the actors had to be; the whole shooting match.

I think that must have been my special visualization kicking in.

In those days, New York was a hot spot for up-and-comers.

Live TV drama was everywhere: *Studio One*, *Playhouse 90*, *Kraft Television Theatre*, *The United States Steel Hour*.

Directors like Sidney Lumet, Norman Jewison, Frank Schaffner, John Frankenheimer and Delbert Mann; authors like Reginald Rose, Horton Foote, Rod Serling and Paddy Chayefski were all working in TV in New York.

There was talent all around, and the place tingled with excitement.

We, who were just beginning, were sure that this was the start of a National Theater that would raise the American public's level of appreciation for the dramatic arts.

Sadly, the American public didn't want the level of its appreciation raised. It wanted to watch variety shows and quizzes and wrestling. By the early '60s, those live dramatic shows began to leave the air.

But, this was 1957, and here I was fresh out of the Army and eager to get going.

The Production Assistant had a lot of responsibilities.

He or she had to order all the studio facilities, give out the cast calls, keep the script up-to-date, clear the music, order lunches and always be useful, available, pleasant and courteous.

TV was live then, and timing the show was a major responsibility of the PA.

A musical variety show could be especially tricky because there were so many segments: songs, dances, comics, jugglers, commercials.

During rehearsals I timed each segment and worked with the director and producer to trim or stretch the show so that it would time out correctly.

Then I back-timed the show, adding up the times of all the segments in order. That way when the show was on the air, I could tell after each segment ended if we were on schedule.

For example, you knew that a commercial should hit at 8:23:30.

If it hit at 8:24:00, you would announce we're thirty seconds long, and the host would get a "speed-up."

There was always a little cushion at the end of the show one way or the other, so things generally worked out.

Another function of the PA during dry rehearsal, was to call the performers when the director and the producers were ready for them.

I PA'd *The Ed Sullivan Show* for a while. Ed liked to book old-timers on the show. He loved them.

Ted Lewis was on – Do you remember his signiture line: "Is everybody happy?" Do you remember him singing "Me and My Shadow"?

If you don't, you're probably not a real Old Fart.

I went to call him for rehearsal; he was sitting outside the hall reading the paper.

"Mister Lewis, you're on."

"I am? How'm I doin'?"

When Janette McDonald and Nelson Eddy appeared, there was a discussion about how to introduce an act that "needs no introduction."

Some wag suggested Ed introduce them by saying simply, "What has four legs and sings?"

I was promoted to Stage Manager a year later.

I learned how the "floor" worked. I counted down the commercials, cued performer's entrances, assigned dressing rooms, cued set changes and made sure that the actors were content with their situation in the studio.

In fact the decorum in the studio was set by the Stage Manager. He or she had to deal with the technical crew and the stagehands as well as performers. With a good SM, things produced smoothly.

I worked on game shows, news shows, religious shows, weather shows, science shows, variety shows, children's shows, dramatic shows, beauty pageants, sporting events, and space shots at Cape Canaveral.

I worked on *The United States Steel Hour*. Sir Cedrick Hardwicke appeared on one of the episodes. Dave Fox, the other Stage Manager, always referred to him as "Sir Seldom." The old man loved it.

Three years later I was bumped up to Associate Director.

I sat in the control room next to the Director and readied the camera shots according the markings in the director's script.

Once, I was AD-ing for an up-and-coming stage director. After he had discussed the motivation with the performers and staged the piece, he stepped into the control room and handed his book to me. It was completely empty of any camera markings. When I asked him where he had marked the shots, he looked a little surprised and said, "Oh, I don't do that."

I shot the show from my memory of the staging.

It only dawned on me later that it was most likely my dyslexic wiring that enabled me to do it.

I became a very good AD; assisting the director, and because I have a great – well good – sense of humor, I was able to keep the normally tense mood in the control room light and relaxed.

People liked working with me.

● ● ●

In 1963 an AD assignment took me to La Quinta Golf Club in Palm Springs for the CBS Golf Classic.

The "color" announcer was Tommy Armour.

He was a great golfer. He had won the 1927 US Open, the 1930 PGA Championship, and the 1931 Open Championship plus a total of 25 PGA tour wins; 23rd on the list of top tournament winners.

During a gas attack in World War I, he had lost the use of his left eye, so he accomplished all those victories with only one eye. What do you think of that?

However, he had his bad days too.

One week after winning the US Open, he is reputed to have scored the very first "Archaeopteryx." That is, 15 or more over par for a single hole. He is supposed to have shot a 23 on a par 5 hole for an 18 over. There are those who dispute it and say that it was only 8 over par. But still.

Anyway, one afternoon when things were quiet at La Quinta, Tommy approached me and suggested we play some golf. I had never held a golf club in my hands and told him so. I don't think Mr. Armour could have conceived of anyone in his mid-thirties who had never played golf, but being the gentleman that he was, he still urged me to play. He said golf was easy. So, with nothing to do and nothing to lose, I went with him.

I have played only one hole of golf in my life and I played it with Tommy Armour.

Tommy thanked me graciously; he said I had potential, and I should take up the game.

He really was a nice guy; a bit of a fibber, but a nice guy.

When I look back on it now, I'm pretty sure I scored an Archaeopteryx myself.

That's a distinction, after all.

• • •

My reputation as an AD grew, and one of my assignments was to be the backup AD on *The Ed Sullivan Show*.

Ed used to have audience bows. Celebrities would be invited to come and sit in the audience. During the show, sometimes to cover a set change, he would ask the person to stand up and take a bow.

Sometimes, too, if a Broadway show was not doing so well, the producers would ask Ed to give one of their cast members a bow in order to generate a little publicity.

Now, I have to tell you that I worked on that show, off and on, for what must have been half a dozen years. I never once saw Ed do anything mean. It was just that sometimes he said what he thought before he thought about what he was saying.

It's spring 1967 and the musical, *Sherry* – a version of Kaufman and Hart's *The Man Who Came to Dinner* – was playing on Broadway.

It got awful reviews and it was not doing well.

So the producers called Ed and asked him to give one of the stars a bow.

The task fell to the leading lady, Dolores Gray.

Ms. Gray was seated in the audience and when the moment to introduce her arrived, Ed called for the houselights.

"In our audience tonight we have Dolores Gray. Stand up, Dolores."

Applause.

Dolores dutifully arose.

Ed went on, "Dolores is currently *starving* on Broadway in the musical 'Sherry'. Let's give her a big hand."

Scattered applause.

Dolores, slightly abashed, seated herself.

We went to a commercial, and Ken Campbell who was Ed's onstage assistant, explained Ed's gaff to him.

In the control room we saw Ed nod when he realized what he had said. He wanted to repair the damage.

As we came out of commercial, Ed called for his camera. "Let's have the audience lights."

On they came.

"Stand up, Dolores."

A slightly apprehensive Dolores Gray rose to her feet.

(At this point it should be told that Dolores had put on a bit of weight during the run of the musical.)

Ed went on, "I've been told that I said Dolores was starving on Broadway. Well, just take one look at her. You can see she's not starving."

• • •

Another time we had an act that featured a wrestling bear.

It went this way.

The bear and his trainer would get into a stage set of a boxing ring and slap each other around.

The bear participated in this indignity because at the end of the act the trainer would present him with an ice cream on a stick.

It never got that far, though.

Just as the act was beginning, Ed told our Stage Manager, Ed Brinkman that he wanted to give the ice cream to the bear.

In the control room, we had no way of knowing what was happening off camera.

Halfway through the act, as the bear and the trainer were going through their routine, Ed walked into the picture.

He was eating the bear's ice cream.

The control room grew deathly silent.

Ed's actions did not escape the bear's attention, I can tell you.

He started toward Ed, dragging the whole boxing ring with him.

The trainer prudently leapt out of the way.

Ed saw the bear coming, and took the ice cream out of his mouth.

The bear made a swipe at it.

The silence in the control room was broken only by the audio man saying, "I hope that bear can introduce acts."

The bear had made a perfectly coordinated grab of the ice cream out of Ed's hand and by now was happily licking away at his reward.

Everyone in the control room breathed a huge sigh of relief, and the next thing we heard was Ed's inevitable accolade, "Let's hear it for the bear!"

● ● ●

In the summer of 1968, the Democrats held their National Convention in Chicago, in the International Amphitheater, a huge building next to the stockyards.

Vern Diamond was the director for the CBS Network coverage, I was the AD.

The Vietnam War was still going on and there were rumors of large protests being organized with the aim of disrupting the convention.

Richard J. Daley was the mayor of Chicago and he was not the sort to accommodate rioters in his city.

He was very proud of his town and he was not going to allow any demonstrations to disrupt the convention.

He organized a formidable police presence.

Many of the cops around the amphitheater had two pistols strapped on, and a few supplemented them with additional firearms tucked into their leather boots; tough-looking cookies.

Late one night, after the convention had concluded for the day, I got lost driving back to my motel from where my car was parked in the stockyards, and was pulled over by a heavily armed officer.

I rolled down my window; he leaned in. "Where the fuck do you think you're going?"

"Anywhere you want me to."

He directed me to the exit.

The next day Red McSpadden, a fine cameraman, took a portable camera. He and I roamed the convention area taking shots of the firearms that festooned the police, the barbed wire that festooned the fences and the billboards festooned with blowups of a smiling, benign Mayor Daley.

I edited them into a two-minute sequence with the musical background of "My Kind of Town (Chicago Is)."

CBS aired it.

We had cameras positioned all around town; in the hotels, in the parks, all over. I counted nearly fifty monitors in the control room.

In spite of the heavy police presence, the demonstrations had started.

We had several remote trucks stationed around town.

One of them – I think it was in Lincoln Park – was in the middle of things.

There was a lot of action going on there. The police were roughing up demonstrators and tossing tear gas.

There were reports of Molotov Cocktails being thrown by the demonstrators.

The police were rolling tear gas canisters under the TV trucks, trying to prevent us from showing what was going on.

Everyone inside was wearing gas masks.

Harvey Glick, the AD in the remote truck was overheard to mutter," My mother thinks I'm in television."

After the day was over, I looked under the console where I was sitting. There were five empty Lucky Strike packs.

I haven't smoked a cigarette since.

● ● ●

We had been raising daylilies in East Hampton for years on a lot we owned next to us.

My work on the soap opera required me to be in NYC only two or three days a week, so I could take a break from working on the scripts and work in the garden for a couple of hours.

It isn't very difficult to make seed on most daylilies, and hybridizing, as I practiced it, was pretty straightforward.

If I had a plant "X", which produced a blossom I liked, but didn't have a lot of buds, I'd look for a plant "Y", in the same color range that had a good bud count.

Wedding bells would begin to chime.

You simply break off a stamen from "X" and stoke the anther across "Y"'s pistil, leaving a pile of pollen there.

You hope that a pollen tube will grow down the style, into the ovary and in about forty days and forty nights, a seed pod would have formed, containing seeds which you hope – when the flowers bloom two years hence – will display the best attributes of both "X" and "Y."

But, most often the result resembled the anecdote which supposedly recounted an interchange between Isadora Duncan and George Bernard Shaw.

They say she proposed that she and Shaw produce a child together because it would have her beauty and his brains.

He declined on the grounds that the child would more likely have his beauty and her brains.

The same is true of hybridizing.

Most often the progeny produced by "Y" times "X" are disappointing.

But I made many different crosses during a season so, when all the plants bloomed, there were bound to be a few "pants-wetters."

This, of course, intrigued Mimi, so she asked me if I would mind if she made a few crosses herself.

"No, go right ahead."

You know the one about the camel getting its nose under the tent flap.

In short order Mimi was cracking open seed pods full of glistening black daylily seeds that I had to plant and take care of along with my own.

My aching back!

But it was worth it. We had a wonderful time "talking daylilies" and being in the garden together.

She had good instincts, and a good eye; her efforts produced introductions.

● ● ●

In the north, daylilies (which grow from rhizomes, not bulbs) take two years to bloom from the time the seeds are put in the ground.

The seeds I planted in April of 1995, would bloom for the first time in June/July of 1997.

214

So, in late June, when the first year seedlings began to bloom, it was a heady time.

Early in the summer morning, armed with high hopes and mugs of coffee, Mimi and I would trot out to the seedling patch to see what treasures might await.

Now and again I would hear her exclaim, "Come here, look at this one!"

It would often be a nicely budded cream lavender with a ruffled edge.

I'd check the marker that had the names of the parents and say to Mimi, "How did you get that stunner out of those two pieces of junk?"

She'd shrug, "Talent."

Then she'd pump her fists back and forth, do a silly little dance and give me a kiss.

Believe me when, out of all the hundreds of seedlings, you bloomed a winner, it was a special occasion.

We hybridized together for over twenty years. Mimi's introductions had names like, Ain't Misbehavin', Singin' in the Rain, Sittin' on a Rainbow and Laughing All the Way.

She favored song titles while I, on the other hand, came up with Aphrodite's Nighty, Alone With Maud, Lavender Lingerie and Million Dollar Legs. What did you expect?

Over the years we introduced about fifty different cultivars.

If you feel like taking a glance at the flowers we hybridized you can google them at Rainbow Daylily Garden.

Don't order any – we're out of that business.

We traveled all over the United States and Canada, going to conventions and looking at gardens. I was often invited to give talks at various gardening clubs. Meanwhile, Mimi would have a group of younger hybridizers gathered around her; she was a magnate.

CHAPTER 15

• • •

I'm not an Old Fart yet . . .

I WAS THIRTY-SEVEN at that time; thirty-seven and desperate.

I had a pretty good job. I was an Associate Director at CBS Television, but I'd been there for twelve years and there seemed to be no end in sight. I hadn't made many friends and all the men and women I'd started out with had gravitated to Hollywood or moved up the corporate ladder.

I felt I was at a dead end; I was going out of my mind.

At that point I was offered a job as a Studio Manager.

It was a lower-middle level job, the responsibilities of which were exactly what the job title implied.

You managed a studio.

You filled out forms, pushed paper around your desk, bargained with the head stagehand about how many men he needed to set up each particular show.

If the rehearsals or tape times were running over, you were the one on the phone with the Facilities Manager arranging extensions for video tape machines and studio time.

I said I would take the job.

When I got home that night, I told Mimi I was going quit being an AD and become a member of management.

"Don't do it, Bob, you're not like them. You're a poet, they'll kill you."

She saved my life.

The next day I withdrew my name from consideration.

Still, my problem hadn't been solved and I grew more and more unhappy and depressed.

I was in midlife, and I was having a crisis.

At that time, I didn't make the connection to a 14th Century Florentine literary figure who'd experienced his own midlife crisis.

"Midway thru life's journey, I found myself in a dark forest.

For I had lost my way . . ."

I too needed a guide to set me back on the path.

In the midst of my depression, by yet another lucky coincidence, I met a man who told me about a psychologist who worked with people in the arts.

I needed a shrink? I couldn't believe it! My God, how could I have fallen so low?

Two weeks later I was walking up the steps of the brownstone on 73rd St.

I was flooded with shame and anxiety.

They say that when the pupil is ready, the teacher appears.

Erlo Van Waveren was tall and slim and elegant; he was in his late sixties, had silver hair, was handsome and spoke with a slight Dutch accent.

He welcomed me and offered me the wing chair across from the small secretary in that green room. He sat in a wing chair opposite me.

He said that we should have a talk and he would decide if he thought we were right for each other.

He folded his hands in his lap, crossed his ankles on that strange wooden footstool of his and waited.

It was up to me, so I began. I wish I could remember what I blurted out; maybe it's just as well I can't.

It must have been an anguished, desperate and guilt-ridden semi-coherent mish-mash of the frustrations of the recent years of my life.

I finished, having made liberal use of the Kleenex on the table next to me.

Erlo said that that he thought we could work together. I had no idea how many times I would climb the steps to the green room and converse with that kind, generous, strong, wise man.

It is not my purpose to recreate my analysis which continued intermittently for the next fifteen years with Erlo, and for the thirty years since he died.

We were not only student and teacher, but he was a father to me, and we became fast friends. He and his wife Ann, and Mimi and I, visited each other in our homes and dined together, many times over the years.

I looked up to him as I have to no other person, and without his support during the rocky years of my adult growing process I have no idea what would have become of me.

Once he told me that if you're going through Hell, it's important to have someone who has been there to tell you what to expect.

Throughout his mature life he worked hard on his own psyche and had gone through his own Hell.

His dreams convinced him that reincarnation was a reality. He kept dream books for years until his unconscious forced him to write his dreams into a tale of his journey, along with his psychic ancestors, to the birth of Aquarius: *Pilgrimage to the Rebirth*. It is available on Kindle at Amazon.

Erlo had analyzed with Carl Jung both before and after WWII.

I had not read much psychology before then and I wasn't aware of what Jung's approach was. I knew he was a famous psychiatrist and that was about it.

I knew nothing about his ideas on individuation, his study of alchemy, myth, and fairy tales; his analysis of dreams, his respect for the unconscious, the collective, the Archetypes – none of it.

During his years as an analyst, Jung discovered that some of his patients who were cured of their neuroses were still unhappy and unfulfilled.

He came to believe that this anxiety was caused by the awakening of a need to go deeper, to try to understand who we *really* are, not just what our conscious mind thinks we are.

He believed that the heart of our psyche, which he called the *Self*, strives for integration and a balance between consciousness and the unconscious.

He called this equipoise "Individuation."

It takes time and effort to arrive at that point; if you ever do.

I remember phoning Erlo once when he and Ann were about to fly back from Switzerland where they vacationed every summer. When they arrived in the US they would stay in East Hampton with Mimi and me for a few days to decompress; I wanted to make the arrangements to pick them up at Kennedy.

He answered the phone and asked me how I was doing.

"I'm still waiting for enlightenment, Erlo."

He laughed, "So am I, my boy, so am I."

A Gnostic saying goes: "There are those who are born with 'It'; those for whom 'It' is possible to obtain, and all the rest."

"It" is the gold the alchemists were trying to distill; the Grail the Round Table quested for.

I certainly was not born with "It." but I have an intuition that "It" is out there, or inside somewhere.

The quest to obtain "It" or arrive at "It" is what my life has been about for the last forty-five years.

To tell you the truth, I don't think you ever really arrive at "It."

The journey is like a spiral. You make your way around and around, and there's always another round ahead; but each time around you realize you have changed.

You go as far as you can with the tools you have. It's an ongoing process, and you must commit yourself to working with your unconscious throughout your life.

A little bit about Jung's theory.

Jung felt that we have not only a personal unconscious which arises from personal experience, but that each of us also has an inborn "collective unconscious," a "part of the unconscious mind that is derived from ancestral memory and experience. It is common to all humankind, as distinct from the individual's unconscious."

In other words, we are not a blank slate when we come into this world, but we carry in our psyche an inherited package of latent images and instincts that Jung called "Archetypes."

Archetypes are universal; they are basic patterns or forms; prototypes.

They include physical archetypes like the Hero, the Great Mother, the Wise Man, the Wizard, the Eternal Child, the Eagle, the Horse, the Elephant, Serpents and many, many others.

They include other concepts like the Journey, Mandalas, Spirals, Squares and Circles, Temples, Rivers, Ships, The Spiritual Wedding and more.

We come upon these archetypes in our dreams (or they come upon us). When we do, they leave us with a sense that we have experienced something extraordinary.

If you should ever waken from a "big dream," one in which archetypes are at play, it would be surprising if you were not touched by its numinous quality.

This sort of experience is not to be doubted, or pooh-poohed away.

It is experiential evidence and its effect on you is "proof" *per se*; it cannot be denied; cannot be argued.

I don't have to convince you it was a real event; and it's impossible for you to convince me, as Scrooge tried to convince himself, that Marley's ghost was just the product of a piece of undigested cheese.

Jung's psychology suited me very well. I was fascinated by his work on Alchemy, and it made perfect sense that the "gold" for which the alchemists were searching was really their own inner gold; their own essence.

If you feel a desire to immerse yourself in his work, do not hesitate to dip into his collected works which comprise twenty-four dense volumes, not including his lectures, letters, post cards and restaurant receipts.

The nearest Jung ever came to writing an autobiography is *Memories, Dreams and Reflections*. It's very readable and it includes a good bit of material about his "mystical" side.

Jungian psychology and Erlo's support got me through the time I was fired from a job by people who I thought were my best friends, and the time I fell into a depression after I talked myself out of a job I was qualified for and wanted very much.

I was unemployed, going through a psychological desert, and would have to keep trudging until I came to the other side.

For eighteen months, Erlo saw me every week and accepted no money.

This was during 1971-1972; then things started to improve.

I began to work in soap operas. They were produced in New York then, and Mimi and I wanted to stay in New York.

I found I was good at the work and, as it turned out, I directed for Procter and Gamble Productions from 1972 until 1995.

For me, it was a period of inner growth.

I became calmer and more confident. I brought to the studio a sense that the day was going to be relaxed and productive.

Since then I have been trying to keep on keeping on.

Every individual's growth is just that – individual.

As Woody Guthrie wrote: "You gotta walk that lonesome valley, you gotta walk it by yourself."

Erlo once told me that the process is like the circus rider standing with one foot on the back of each of two horses galloping side by side. One horse represents the outer world and the other the inner. There must to be a balance.

You must be strong and balanced in the outer world in order to keep your balance in the inner world.

So, here I am at 84, still riding in the circus.

All these "sayings" by teachers are not in themselves revelatory, but they are like blazes on trees indicating the path. They have the cumulative effect of letting you know that others have passed this way.

● ● ●

I read a lot of Jung, and I'd be lying if I said I understood even most of it.

It is very dense, and for those who can't believe in anything you can't weigh, or put a pin through, it probably seems like mystical speculation, or fanciful hogwash.

However: 1) If your psychological makeup allows you to accept the irrational aspects of life, and 2) if your unconscious forces you to experience these aspects, and 3) if you are lucky enough to have been given a competent guide, Jung's Analytical Psychology can prove itself to be a solid life-affirming reality.

But the process isn't easy, and it isn't guaranteed.

At any rate, the psychological work was going on as I was working in television; but when I was in the studio I had to keep my mind in the moment.

I didn't realize that the journey continues even if you are unaware of it.

I think that is why my days in the studio were generally smooth and people enjoyed working with me.

Erlo said, "You teach by being."

• • •

Mimi handled all our finances; she paid the bills, and she wrote the checks.

If we were looking for an apartment and she felt comfortable with a certain layout, we rented that apartment.

She bought all our furniture and decorated our home beautifully.

She went shopping with me and passed on all my clothes.

She pretty much managed our life (which was fine with me) and instigated our outings and our trips.

But she never understood baseball.

I tried my best to explain it to her but I never came close.

She never understood why the man with the "stick" didn't hit the ball more often.

When I told her that the man who threw the ball was throwing it in a way that made it hard for the man with the stick to hit it, she thought it was unfair.

The strike zone was impossible for her; balls and strikes were a lost cause, and why the man with the stick would suddenly throw it down and jog to first base remained a mystery. Why wasn't he running?

I tried to explain that a foul ball counted as a strike except if the man already had two strikes. "Why?"

Why were there three bases; why did they call it "home", what exactly was an inning and why were there nine of them?

Football wasn't much different.

"Why do they all fall down?"

The one thing Mimi liked about football was the tight pants they wear when they bend over in the huddle.

A friend tried to teach her how to play bridge.

I told him that Mimi was going to be a hard student to deal with.

He was a Grand Master, and told me that he had taught dozens of difficult beginners successfully, so he didn't expect a problem.

He began by telling her that there is a ranking order of the suits in bridge. Spades is the most important; hearts is next, then diamonds and last is clubs.

"Why?"

He got up and walked away.

CHAPTER 16

• • •

Eye-Eye-Eye! . . .

AFTER I RETIRED, I noticed that, as I was driving, my right eye would see a slightly displaced double image of a telephone pole where only one should exist. The same was true when I looked at the yellow line down the center of the road; two yellow lines. It was disconcerting.

Because I had been working as a television director, I wanted to make sure my eyes were in shape so I always saw an ophthalmologist twice a year.

I made an appointment; Dr. O'Malley tested my eyes and she said that I had a slight cataract and within a year or so I would have to decide if I wanted a lens replacement.

A cataract is the clouding of the eye's natural crystalline lens. It's called a cataract because the light-colored cloud is supposed to resemble the foaming water in a waterfall. I think that's a little far-fetched, but that's what they call it and why they call it that.

There are a few things that can cause a cataract, including diabetes and smoking. In other words, it could be your fault.

Why do medical people always try to blame you for things that happen to you? "If you hadn't eaten so much pickled cauliflower, you wouldn't be hearing those strange voices."

I was at an arboretum once and the docent led us up to a maple tree that was more than 200 years old. She explained that the tree hadn't been doing well for the past few years; they had asked arborists from all over the country examine it. In spite of all the special advice they followed and all the special treatment it had received, the tree didn't respond.

No one knew what was wrong.

A white-haired lady leaning on her four-footed cane remarked quietly, "Didn't anyone think the tree was just old?"

In fact, most cataracts, as mine were, are related to becoming an Old Fart; they are the leading cause of vision loss in people over the age of fifty-five. If you reach eighty, the chances are better than 50/50 that you will have a cataract, or will have had a lens replaced (maybe both).

Mimi had had cataracts successfully replaced with artificial lenses two years previously; cataract surgery is quite common.

Without getting too technical, I'm going to try to explain how the eye works. It hasn't got a lot of moving parts, but it's still a complicated mechanism.

I'm a little reluctant to begin, because I'm always leery about books that claim to make complicated things simple. They have titles like *Relativity Explained So That Even YOU Can Understand It*.

This sort of book always begins with somebody in an elevator, or trains passing each other in opposite directions, and ends with a drawing of a bowling ball suspended in a rubber sheet.

Thanks a lot!

Anyhow, it is with some trepidation that I embark on my sketchy explanation of how the eye works.

Here goes.

A cross section of the eyeball would show a nearly round object; that's why they call it an eye "ball."

Have I lost you yet?

Good.

When you are born, your eyeball is almost as big as it will ever get. That's why babies have such big adorable eyes. The eye will grow only a little bit, to nearly one inch in diameter by the time you are five.

The eye's movements are cleverly controlled by six muscles in each eye. They work in tandem and allow you to rotate your eyes simultaneously in all directions; they are able to work in opposition too, so you can cross your eyes to look at that mosquito sitting on the tip of your nose.

There are two folds of skin (the eyelids) which help protect the eye. They keep the cornea from drying out by spreading tears and other moisturizers every time you blink.

Eyelids are also able to communicate a desire for closer association with a member of the opposite sex (or the same sex, for that matter) as part of a combination of a wink, a smile and a movement of the head that combines into what is referred to as a "come hither" look.

Eyelashes, which adorn the edges of the eyelids, not only keep small particles of dust out of the eye, they are also a necessary component of a process called "batting" the eyelids. Batting is rapid fluttering of the eyelid, and is considered to be flirtatious.

Non-batting can also be a sign of inner equanimity: "When they told her that her next-door neighbor was an escaped serial killer, she didn't bat an eyelash."

Here are the parts of the eye from the front to the back.

That transparent bump on the front surface of the eyeball is the *cornea*. It lets the light in; it is also a lens, but it is a fixed lens and can't adjust the parallel rays of light as they pass through.

Surrounding the cornea is the *sclera*. This is the white fibrous surface of the eyeball – the white of your eye.

It is sometimes used as a convenient measure of good aiming distance in time of battle. "Don't fire until you see the whites of their eyes" was supposed to have been shouted during the American Revolutionary War at the battle of Breed's Hill.

The sclera covers the rest of ball all the way to the optic nerve at the back of the eye and up into the brain.

Behind the cornea you will find some clear watery fluid called the *aqueous humor.*

It should come as no surprise that aqueous humor means "clear watery fluid."

The light rays which enter through the cornea pass through the aqueous humor and through the *iris.*

The iris is a sphincter muscle that is like a flat elastic dough-nut; a flat disc with a hole in the center. By changing the diameter of the hole, the iris helps control the brightness of the light entering the eye.

The iris is the colored part of the eye. It comes in so many different colors it was named after the Greek goddess of the rainbow.

The color is controlled by the genetic mix of the colors of your parents' eyes; brown, green, gray, hazel, blue, and sometimes by the application of tinted cosmetic discs called contact lenses.

The color of the iris can be striking and has been the stuff of romantic poetry and song for a long time.

"Those cool and limpid green eyes, a pool wherein my love lies . . ." Helen O'Connell, Ray Eberle, Jimmy Dorsey, 1941; the time of the two-step, touch dancing. Ah, well.

Elizabeth Taylor (actually Dame Elizabeth Taylor; Hilton, Wilding, Todd, Fisher, Burton, Burton [She was married twice to Richard Burton], Warner, Fortensky) had violet blue eyes which apparently were a large part of her considerable charm. But the light pigmentation of her irises probably made her light shy.

I, on the other hand, have chocolate brown irises. While they do not attract the same level of attention as Dame Elizabeth's, I don't often need to wear sunglasses.

I was surprised to learn that the pupil, that black circle in the center of the eye is really the hole in the center of the iris.

I thought the pupil was something, but it is nothing. I feel like Homer Simpson: "Doh!"

What you are seeing through that hole is the surface of the crystalline, or natural lens, (the one that gets the cataracts). It appears black because almost all the light that enters the eye is absorbed by the retina on the inner wall of the eyeball and very little escapes.

The word "*pupil*" comes from the Latin "pupa" = "little girl" or "puppet." because of the tiny images it reflects. I've tried to see the tiny image of myself by leaning close to a hand mirror, but I've never been able to.

The hole in the center of the iris is bordered by the *pupillary constrictor*. This is a sphincter which acts like the drawstring closure of a duffel bag.

When the light is too bright, the sphincter tightens and, it narrows the diameter of the pupil limiting the amount of light that comes through.

If there is less light, the pupillary sphincter relaxes and the *dilator muscles* go into action. Those muscles are attached around the center of the iris and radiate out like spokes in a wheel.

When the dilator muscles contract, they enlarge the diameter of the hole in the center of the iris, allowing more light in, and make the pupil look large.

"Grandma, what big eyes you have."

"Yes, Little Red, it's because this is a dim room which causes my dilator muscles to contract increasing the diameter of my irises; you are seeing more of my crystalline lens which appears dark to you. Now, dear, do me a favor; turn the oven on and open the catsup."

Continuing our inventory, we come to the *lens*. The name for the lens comes in a roundabout way from the Greek, meaning "lentil," which should give you an idea of the shape of the crystalline or natural lens.

The cornea in the front of the eye is a lens, but it is a fixed lens. Light hits the cornea in parallel rays and the rays remain parallel as they pass through the iris to the lens.

Seen head-on, the lens is clear and round; it is held in the *lens sack*. The sack is held in place and supported all the way around by the *ciliary* muscles in the same way a trampoline is supported in its frame.

I always supposed that the lens in the eye was hard like the lens in a magnifying glass; it's not. The lens in the eye is soft and pliable; it has to be in order to focus the parallel rays of light that come to it through the cornea.

Dr. Tim Root compares the lens to a very pliable transparent M&M.

Think of the candy coating of the M&M as the lens sack, the transparent elastic covering of the lens.

Think of the chocolate in the M&M as the soft lens.

Think of the peanut in the center of the M&M as the harder nucleus of the lens.

Try not to think of this description the next time you are munching a fistful of M&M's.

The thickness of the lens is regulated by the contraction of those ciliary muscles around the edge. As they pull around the rim of the lens sack, they stretch it, causing the lens to become flatter; as they relax the lens fattens out.

Changing the thickness of the lens is what focuses the incoming light rays.

When the parallel rays of light from the cornea pass through the lens, they are bent toward each other in the shape of a cone.

In artists' renderings, the rays of light passing through the lens are shown converging in a point. In the real world, however, lenses do not focus perfectly, and what is shown in the drawings as a point is really a spot or image.

If the light converges as much as possible when it falls on the sensitive cells at the back of the eye, the image is in focus.

In normal eyes the natural lens always attempts to focus what you are looking at.

To prove it, close one eye and focus on something far away while you hold up your finger about a foot away from your eye.

You'll see that the finger is fuzzy.

Fuzzy finger is no good.

Now shift your focus to the tip of your finger and you'll see it come into focus and the background will become a little soft.

The ciliary muscles surrounding the lens have just relaxed, allowing the crystalline lens to become rounder – and you never felt a thing.

The rounder lens bends the light rays passing through it, shifting the focus from the distant object to your dainty digit.

The natural lens in your eye is constantly changing its shape as you move your eyes about, allowing them to focus on objects near or far.

If you have ever used a magnifying glass to start a fire in a piece of paper, you know what a focal point is. As you move the glass closer and farther from the paper, you see that there is one distance where the sun's rays are refracted by the glass lens into a tiny image. Hold that spot for a few seconds and the paper begins to smolder.

That is why you should not look at the sun. Your eye will focus the sunlight near the back of your eyeball. If it can burn a hole in a piece of paper, or light a fire in a pile of dry shavings, imagine what it can do if it is focused on the back of your eye for any length of time.

That's the story of the front part of a healthy eye – the cornea, iris, and lens.

They comprise the mechanism that captures the light and sends the image into the rear part of the eyeball, where it will be transformed into chemical and electrical impulses that will eventually be passed on to the visual center in the brain.

• • •

The back part of the eyeball is filled with a gelatinous glass-like liquid called the *vitreous humor*, which means, not surprisingly "glass-like liquid." It makes up about eighty percent of the eye.

Together, the aqueous humor and the vitreous humor fill up the eyeball so that it doesn't get squishy. I'm sure there's a medical term for "squishy eye" but I don't want to know it.

We come to the *retina*.

The retina is a thin, light-sensitive layer that lines more than half the interior surface behind the lens.

It is actually an extension for the optic nerve, which is embedded in the back of the eyeball, near the center.

The optic nerve is the cable that transports the information gathered by the various parts of the eye to the optical center in the brain where it is processed and put into a form which enables you to enjoy seeing the New York Giants beat the New England Patriots (occasionally).

The retina contains two kinds of receptor cells that detect light; *rods* and *cones.*

There are about 120 million rods scattered around the retina and only six or seven million cones.

Rods are extremely sensitive; they can detect images in light too dim for cones to "see." Since they are scattered around the retina, they also work for peripheral vision; they allow you to detect the cat hopping up on the table out of the corner of your eye.

But they have limitations.

The images they produce are not very sharp, and an important deficiency is that rods do not see color.

Yes, there are many fewer cones, but they give you a special bang for your buck because they are the ones that see color, and they are the ones that provide high resolution vision.

They don't do well in dim light, but in bright light they shine.

That's why you see Old Farts like me taking the medicine bottle over to the window to make sure that the pill you're taking is supposed to help with your acid reflux and doesn't try give you an erection.

Almost all the cones are to be found in the center of the *macula*, a "dimple" about one-tenth of an inch in diameter at the back of the eye.

The macula is the sweet spot near the optic nerve. At its center, at the bottom of the dimple, is yet another even sweeter sweet spot called the *fovea* (Latin – "pit").

The fovea is only about 1/100th of an inch in diameter but it is absolutely packed chockablock (not a scientific term) with cones.

This chockablock-ness forms a powerful concentration of cones, and enables them to produce detailed high resolution color images.

A normal field of vision can be as wide as 200 degrees, which means that with your peripheral vision you are pretty much aware of everything in front of you.

Being aware, however, doesn't mean that you see the whole area clearly.

If the cat that you casually registered with your peripheral vision decides to nudge the dish of jellybeans off the table, your peripheral vision won't be able to reveal the extent of the disaster.

You must turn your head and focus the scene on your foveae (plural of fovea) in order to observe, in high resolution and in color, the cat crouched innocently on the edge of the table, craning her neck from side to side, following the higgledy-piggledy scattering of the red, green, yellow, black, orange, brown and purple jellybeans as they disperse under the sofa, behind the étagère, or simply wobble to rest on the floor to form a haphazard color pattern reminiscent of some expensive modern paintings.

Though it takes up only about one percent of the retina, the fovea is so important that more than fifty percent of the visual part of the brain is devoted to it.

When you look at something intently, like when you're visiting one of those "blue" websites that nobody you know ever admits visiting, your lens is concentrating the focus of the image on the fovea.

Still, the fovea "sees" only the central two percent of the field of vision at a time.

If you hold your arm out all the way, the foveae will see clearly only about twice the diameter of your thumbnail; that's all. You take in the rest with your peripheral vision.

However, when you are reading, your peripheral vision isn't sharp enough to read all the words on the page at once, so you have to move your eyes to the next group of words for them to be brought into focus on the foveae; left to right if you're reading English; right to left if you're reading Hebrew; up and down if your reading ancient Chinese.

Try it now. Pick out a word in the center of a line and stare at it. See how many words to the right and the left you are able to read.

My guess is that you'll be able to make out the two (maybe three) words to either side.

Your peripheral vision will let you know that there is a whole line of words and a whole stack of lines, but if you want to see them clearly enough to read them, you're going to have to move your eyes so the next group of words come into focus on your foveae, and you have to keep doing that again and again until many hundreds of pages later, Natasha is safely, if not so romantically, married to Pierre.

The eye moves continually to keep the light from the object of interest falling on the foveae where the bulk of the cones reside.

That's the way it goes, all day long.

While the cones see best in bright light, they do not see well at night.

The rods see best in dim light, but it takes about a half hour for the eyes to fully adapt to the night sky.

That's why at night, when you are looking at the stars, you are told to look a little bit away from the ones you are interested in; this focuses the light on the rods next to the cones in the fovea. You will notice then that the stars you are interested in are clearer when you look at them that way.

The cones are not totally helpless in that situation; you can still tell that Mars is reddish and you easily see the red and white blinking lights on aircraft as they pass over.

So the retina, the macula and the fovea translate the image presented to them by the cornea and the lens into electrical impulses which in turn are transmitted by the optic nerve to the brain.

The brain decodes these impulses and turns them into the pictures that we "see."

This pretty much concludes my sketchy description of the eye's *modus operandi*. It is not intended to be scientifically exhaustive, but I hope it gives you some idea of what's going on. OK?

• • •

A cataract is a clouding of the crystalline lens. It is painless but it affects the clarity of the lens by fogging it up, and as the fogging gets worse, vision gradually becomes impaired. If the fogging becomes too bad, you may have to replace the whole fogging thing.

As you age, dead cells shed from your lens, there they gather and form clouded spots. Since new lens cells form on the outside of the lens, all of the older cells are compacted into the center of the lens where they harden, resulting in a cataract.

This is one of the few instances of something hardening as a man grows older.

Throughout the United States and around the world, almost a million and a half people have cataract eye surgery each year, and most of them end up seeing a lot better than they had and almost as well as they ever did.

• • •

It didn't used to be that way.

Couching (with the accent on "ouch") is a primitive form of cataract "surgery" (if you could call it that). It was first performed as early as the 6th or 5th Century BCE in India, described in the papers of a Hindu surgeon; a real historical person named Sushruta.

The practice of couching was adopted by the Greeks, the Romans and the Arabs. It spread to China and to Sub-Saharan Africa where, if you can imagine, it is still done today. It is one of the oldest surgical procedures known; and probably the most painful.

In couching, the lens with the cataract is pushed into the back part of the eyeball to get it out of the way.

You may rightly inquire how this is accomplished.

It is accomplished by a "coucheur" (my word) in one of a few ways.

In the first instance the coucheur uses a sharp instrument like a solid gold needle. If you don't happen to have a golden needle on you, use a thorn. He then pierces the top of the cornea or the white sclera just above it.

This has to be an excruciatingly painful procedure to the couchee since the density of pain receptors in the cornea is 300-600 times greater than skin and 20-40 times greater than dental pulp. So this must be really awful.

Next, the coucheur pokes the clouded lens out of the ring of muscles that holds it, and tries to coax it down toward the bottom of the back of the eyeball out of the way.

Secondly, there is the old "blunt instrument" method, where the practitioner uses something like a small pool cue and strikes the cornea with a stroke similar to the one he'd use on the "break" to scatter the balls. That is supposed to jar the hardened lens out of its setting and send it back into the eyeball where, with the help of gravity, it would sink out of sight into the side pocket, as it were.

A third method (my fave) was to massage the eyeball really hard to force the lens out of its ring of muscles and hope that it has enough sense to sink down and get out of the way.

There is an early description of couching in the *Book of Tobit*, written about 600 BCE.

Tobit attributed the whiteness in his eyes to birds pooping onto them. (Old saying I just invented: "Never look up at a pigeon for too long.")

Years later his son, on the advice of some angels, put some fish gall into his father's eyes. The bile, being an irritant, caused Tobit to rub his own eyes, and he apparently rubbed hard enough to displace the cloudy lenses, affording him some level of restored sight.

All of which seems to suggest that if you ever run into an angel and it gives you some advice, you can't go wrong if you follow it.

Apparently J.S. Bach, even though he created some of the world's most glorious religious music, never happened to run into any helpful angels. In 1750 he underwent couching on both his eyes. The procedure left him completely blind; four months later he was completely dead.

In 1758, Georg Friedrich Handel underwent the procedure. He too was left completely blind and died the next year.

The best result that could have been hoped for from any of these procedures would be the restoration of limited but completely unfocused vision.

In fact, when couching is performed these days (and it still is in Sub-Saharan Africa) thick eyeglass lenses may help the focus.

I guess it is better than being blind; at least you can probably tell the difference between an elephant and an aardvark.

In light of modern advances, couching is probably not a procedure the ophthalmologist will recommend.

"Way back when," however, there weren't a lot of choices to be made between remaining blind and Sushruta's 5th Century BCE "cure."

In 1748, topical anesthetics came into use. That made it possible to do eye surgery without too much pain – for the doctor, at least.

The first cataract surgery was performed by Jacques Daviel in Paris around the middle of the 18th Century.

The cornea was cut about half off the eyeball and lifted up. Then the surgeon removed the opaque lens out of the eye and the cornea was set back into place.

The patient had to lie still with his or her head packed between sandbags until the cornea healed – if the cornea healed.

But a great problem still remained. With the lens missing, there was no easy way of focusing the light rays in order to see anything clearly.

The answer was eyeglasses with very thick lenses, those "Coke bottle" glasses, although back then they were probably called "sherry bottle" lenses.

For the next century and a half, most of the progress in cataract surgery was made by devising more efficient ways to remove the lens, and although different kinds of glasses and some contact lenses were tried with varying measures of success, no one could figure out a way to replace the discarded lens.

It took a war. World War II.

In 1949, an English surgeon, Sir Harold Ridley, observed that the hard PMMA shards from spitfire canopies had remained inert in the injured eyes of pilots since the war.

PMMA is the acronym for the acrylic plastic **PolyMethylMethAcrylate**.

You might be more familiar with polymathic methacrylate under a couple of its trade names – Lucite, or Plexiglass.

Using PMMA, Ridley designed the first implantable plastic lens, and implanted it. But thermoplastic is relatively heavy and the operation was tricky; not many other surgeons tried to emulate Ridley's accomplishment.

Although the implantable lenses became less bulky and the surgical process advanced, the idea of these lenses was met with resistance, and it took a while before surgeons felt that implants were a practical method of treatment.

Even so, the cornea still had to be cut and flipped open in order to get at the cloudy lens, and a patient could expect to spend around ten days in the hospital, head wedged between two sandbags, immobilized.

In the 1960s, Dr. Charles Kelman, an ophthalmologic surgeon, was trying to figure out a way to improve this state of affairs.

After a long series of failures, his "Aha!" moment came when he was in the dentist's chair having his teeth cleaned.

Kelman felt the silver tipped instrument vibrating against his teeth.

"What is that thing that's breaking up the plaque on my teeth?"

"An ultrasonic probe."

That was the moment.

The *phacoemulsification* procedure was introduced in 1967 ("phaco" is another Greek word related to lentil which is related to lens and *emulsification* which, in this case, means break down into tiny pieces). Surgeons no longer had to make a large incision in the eye before removing the lens. Now they could do the job with just a teeny weenie one.

This was because now they could remove remnants of the lens through a tiny hole.

After a small incision was made, they would insert a sharp instrument and scrape off the front of the lens sack.

The back of the lens sack was left intact to serve as a receptacle for the new lens and to prevent the vitreous humor from oozing into the front of the eye.

Next, in went the ultrasonic probe vibrating thousands of times a second. It broke up the lens into smithereens (not a medical term). The smithereens were vacuumed out by a tiny smithereen-sucking mini-Hoover.

Everything became a lot simpler and a lot safer.

Dr. Kelman's introduction of phacoemulsification and the evolution of smaller surgical incisions was matched by the development of new lens implants created out of newer materials (such as acrylic and silicone) that could be rolled up and inserted through the tiny wound.

Nowadays, lenses can be inserted through wounds as small as .07th of an inch.

• • •

After the lens sack is empty, the eye is ready to accept the new artificial lens, the power of which has been determined by tests beforehand.

How they stuff these lenses into your eye is a tribute to mechanical ingenuity.

The new artificial lens is about one-third the diameter of a dime and it is very pliable. It is rolled up into a tubular shape and inserted into something like a hypodermic syringe, then injected into the empty lens sack through the same miniscule hole through which the foggy lens was vacuumed.

The lens "opens like a flower." That is, it unrolls in place, with two "stabilizer arms" that stretch out against the walls of the now empty sack and hold the lens in the center.

All of this changed cataract surgery to a common outpatient procedure. Each year two million people receive artificial lenses in the US as an outpatient procedure.

Usually the artificial lens will give you a good picture of distant objects, but you may still need glasses for reading.

If you are having both eyes treated, you can opt to have a lens put into one eye that will give you good focus for distance, and a different lens in the other eye that will focus closer for reading.

The brain is supposed to compensate so that you see both distant and close objects clearly.

I have a friend who has such an arrangement and she says she's very happy with it.

There is also a progressive lens available at a considerable premium which they say, allows you to focus your eyes both near and far without the need for glasses.

I happen to like glasses. They keep all sorts of dusty, sandy, unfriendly motes out of my eyes. I also think they make me look intelligent, and they hide my baggies.

Therefore, I never inquired about contact lenses.

But I investigated them.

The first contact lenses were produced in Germany more than a hundred years ago; they were made of glass. They were heavy and covered not only the cornea, but part of the white part of the surface of the eye as well.

Fifty years later they made contact lenses out of PMMA. Yes, that same thermoplastic that Dr. Ridley used.

They were not as heavy as glass and were more comfortable. They covered only the cornea and floated on the eyes' tears.

Progress continued, and in 1971 a thin flexible lens was first imported into the US. Because it was much more comfortable, it prompted many more people to opt for contacts.

Now there are lenses that can be worn for extended periods of time instead of having to be removed overnight, cosmetic lenses to change your eye color, lenses that allow you can see both far and near, and even disposable lenses that you can wear for up to a month.

• • •

I've had both eyes done a year apart and my experience has been satisfactory each time.

I put drops in for a week or two before the procedure.

Got to the hospital at about 9:00 a.m. Lots of drops to dilate the iris. Light anesthetic in the IV drip. I was asked my name and birthdate many times, and which eye was to be worked on. Dr. O'Malley came in and she marked the eye.

Wheeled into the operating room.

Chatted with surgeon as she applied more drops. Bright bright light as I was silently reciting *Casey at the Bat* to myself.

Told that I was doing fine several times.

Wheeled back to the room.

Dr. O'Malley came in and told me that everything went perfectly. An hour later I was being driven home. Eye bleary for two or three days; more drops in for two or three weeks to prevent infection and that's all; no pain, no strain.

After my eye was feeling OK I tried on my old eyeglasses. Of course the formula for the lens of the fixed eye was no longer valid.

The sight had improved so much that I had to have the eyeglass lens removed. I could see much better without the lens.

The greatest inconvenience was that the doctor wanted to wait for a month before writing a new prescription for that eye.

It was an inconvenience, but I did have fun. When having a conversation with someone I would stick my finger out through the empty frame and wiggle it. The effect was predictable; old ladies would faint dead away; children would scream and flee.

It was great!

I'm a caution. As you can tell from the above, I can be hilariously funny at times.

After I got my new prescription for the second eye, I discovered that the new lenses did sharpen things up, and my sight had improved so much I was able to see pretty well without the glasses.

Occasionally I forget to put them on.

• • •

Lenses go back quite a way. The so-called "Nimrud" lens was used nearly 3000 years ago in Assyria. It may have been used as a magnifying glass or a lens to start fires, or it could have been both, but fire-producing lenses are mentioned early on, so it's probable that their main use was starting fires.

A thousand years ago, not many people could read, but those who could (monks) were able to use "reading stones" to aid them. These devices were hemispheres made out of rock crystal that magnified the portion of the page beneath them. One simply moved the crystal along the line, enlarging the words so that they could be more easily read.

I have seen descendants of these reading stones sold in pharmacies and used by old folks as a reading aid, much as it must have been done a millennium ago.

The first pair of eyeglasses, if you want to call them that, were made in Italy in 1286. It seems to have been nothing more than a couple of reading stones joined together; one over each eye.

The science of lenses progressed. Around 1230, an Englishman with the visually intriguing name of Robert Grosseteste writes that optics could be used to "read the smallest letters at incredible distances."

In the early 14th Century in Venice and Florence, lenses of different strengths were manufactured and eyeglasses started to come into their own.

Early glasses were either held in place with your hand or by spring-loaded pince-nez. It wasn't until the early part of the 18th Century someone thought of putting on "temples," the hooks that hold the glasses on to your ears.

Ben Franklin invented bifocals; I used to wear them.

But in museums, I got tired of stepping back to view the painting and then stepping forward to get near enough to read that, yes, it's a Ghirlandaio.

Then I switched to trifocals; a slight improvement. From there it is only a short step to "progressive" lenses, which I now wear comfortably.

Estimates suggest that over one hundred and ninety million Americans wear eyeglasses, and well over thirty million are sold each year in the US alone.

The eyeglass business is a good business.

• • •

Mimi used to give a garden party every summer when the daylilies were in bloom. It was spectacular.

There were balloons everywhere. There was punch and drinks and lots of little cakes and cucumber sandwiches.

Thousands of seedlings had opened for the first time and the place was an absolutely unbelievable mishmash of exuberant color.

I say mishmash because I never planted the lilies in our garden in any particular order; I just stuck them in in the order they arrived.

Mimi had labeled them all on metal stakes including the name of the hybridizer, the year the plant was put into commerce, and if it was bred in the southern part of the country, or up north.

She had index boxes recording the date when each of the hundreds of our plants bloomed each season, and she kept meticulous records of all the crosses we made during the hybridizing season.

She loved keeping records, and I think that came from her German background.

During those parties I led tours into the seedling patch and gave the women a thrill by demonstrating, with pollen and pistil, the way daylilies made babies.

Mimi always invited a lot of people; I don't know how many had much of an interest in daylilies, but she was pleased and happy as anything.

I was too.

As they say, "Happy wife, happy life."

We kept hybridizing together, but by 2005 Mimi had trouble standing for any length of time.

She'd walk her seedling patch and make a list of the crosses she wanted me to make.

When we went into the seedling patch then, Mimi had to use a cane, and when she got to the end of a row of seedlings, she'd call me to help her turn around.

Twenty years after she fell and developed diabetes, the neuropathy in her feet was becoming a problem.

CHAPTER 17

• • •

Where there's a Will . . .

IF YOU'RE OLD enough to be classified as an Old Fart, you'd better have a last will and testament made in cooperation with a competent lawyer.

If there is no will and you have left no instructions about what to do with your vast fortune or more modest residue, there might be a whole lot of grabbing and backstabbing going on.

You would be surprised, or maybe you wouldn't, at the squabbles that break out among otherwise reasonable relatives over things like who gets grandma's vegetable peeler.

You might not want to go so far as to leave instructions as to the dispersal of vegetable peelers, but you get my point.

A well-written will obviates that nasty scramble and makes sure that your estate, large or small, gets into the hands of those you want to have it, or not into the hands of those you don't.

One of my mother's favorite cartoons shows an attorney's office with the relatives seated expectantly as the lawyer reads from the will – ". . . and to my nephew Rollo whom I told I would remember in my will, 'Hi, Rollo.'"

In fact, attorneys whom I have consulted tell me that there is no such thing as a will reading anymore, with everybody sitting around waiting to hear what, if anything, they get.

What happens nowadays is that the lawyer who is hired by the executor sends out copies of the will and notices of probate to all concerned; not very dramatic.

Half of living Americans with children do not have a will, either because they must think they are going to live forever, or they figure they really don't need one, or they can't afford one.

I hate to be the one to break it to you, but believe me, you are not going to live forever; *"They"* have never forgotten anybody.

If you die without a will (intestate) the decision of what to do with what you have left is generally decided by a regulated procedure through a probate court in your state.

If you leave a will there's a much better chance that your estate will be disposed of as you intended.

You will be asked to name an executor to make sure that the terms of the will are carried out.

The executor must act in the best interests of the estate and could be personally liable for abusing his or her authority.

Laws effecting last wills vary from state to state so, if you're thinking of creating one, you should consult somebody conversant with the appropriate laws. An attorney wouldn't be a bad idea.

• • •

Some court squabbles over the dispersion of estates have lasted for years – for generations, in fact.

Charles Dickens satirized the lengthy process in *Bleak House* by describing the case of *(Jarndyce v. Jarndyce)* which was only resolved when after decades, the estate's financial resources were absorbed in costs, leaving all the litigants out in the cold after having made a lot of lawyers rich.

Dickens used this as an illustration of the failings of the Chancery Courts which allowed disputes like this to run on and on.

Dickens' example is said to have been inspired by the legal squabbling over the estate of William Jennens who died unmarried and intestate in 1798. His estate worth over £200 million (in today's dough) was fought over in Chancery *(Jennens v. Jennens)* for over 100 years until (you guessed it) the entire estate was eaten up by lawyers' fees.

• • •

Heaven forbid you are ever left in a physical state where you are not conscious and are unable to make any health-care decisions for yourself and your tenuous connection to mortality relies on a series of wires and tubes, machines and medications referred to as "life support."

There are advisories which can come into play if such an unhappy event occurs. They are called "Advance Directives": Living Wills and Health Care Proxies.

Living Wills and Health Care Proxies are not the same things.

A Living Will, at least in New York State, is problematic.

A Living Will generally deals with a patient's wishes as regards artificial life support.

There are no laws regarding a Living Will in New York State, but the courts have decided that a Living Will may be valid as long as it can provide "clear and convincing evidence" of your wishes.

If you are in a condition where you are being kept alive by artificial means and you are unable to make medical decisions for yourself a court may have to decide if you should be removed from life support.

The presentation of a Living Will supported by statements from your family and doctor testifying to the accuracy of the wishes expressed there, could constitute "clear and convincing evidence."

But it's almost impossible to make a Living Will that takes into account everything that could happen in the future, so, circumstances could easily arise that you hadn't thought of.

In complicated medical situations it may be difficult to decide what you would have wanted the doctors to do. That may not be any way to establish "clear and convincing evidence," and there is no one around to speak up for you.

Living Wills are somewhat limited in that they only apply to life-sustaining treatments.

A Health Care Proxy is different; in New York State it is a legally recognized document.

A Health Care Proxy appoints someone you choose to make health care decisions for you in case you are unable to do so.

It covers a much broader range than a Living Will since there are many health care decisions other than whether to pull the plug or not; things like day-to-day care, placement options, and treatment options.

Besides, a Health Care Proxy can include the decision to remove artificial life support if you have authorized your agent to do so.

Remember, these arrangements come into play only if you are unable to make medical decisions for yourself, and they may be revoked at any time.

If you have no living spouse, it is especially important for you to have a Health Care Proxy.

You may also want to choose a backup Proxy in case the original one is unable to perform.

Again, the laws affecting these directives differ from state to state so it is important to have local legal advice in their preparation.

Over two-thirds of the adult population in this country have no Living Will or any advisory explaining what they want done (or not done) with them if they should fall into the state of permanent and irreversible lack of consciousness; a vegetative state.

Mimi and I each are the other's Health Care Proxy.

If you are in your eighties, as we are, a lot of your friends are old friends and a lot of your old friends are really old.

Every year, it seems, some of our friends stop getting older by dying.

Some of them after long stints in a hospital or an assisted living facility.

Long, drawn out terminations do not appeal to me.

As far as I'm concerned, the best was to die is unexpectedly.

CHAPTER 18

• • •

Don't touch that dial! . . .

IN THE LATE fall of 1968, Tim Kiley, who had been Sullivan's director for years, left to go with the Smothers brothers.

By the way, it was Tim who shot the Beatles and Elvis Presley when they appeared on *The Ed Sullivan Show*.

When Tim left, John Moffett, who had been the regular AD on the show for years, was the obvious choice to fill the director slot, but he was in Hawaii shooting a Glen Campbell special. So, since I was the alternate AD, I became the director *pro tem*.

A lot depends on whether you're standing on the right corner when that streetcar named Opportunity pulls up.

This was on a Thursday, and I had to prepare the hour-long show for that Sunday.

It really wasn't that hard. I had been working on the show for years; I had a good feel for camera cutting, plus I knew the crew very well. They were the best; all top-notch pros ready to support any director.

Charlie Grenier, the Technical Director said, "Bob, you've got over a hundred years of experience working for you, they're not going to let you down."

They didn't. Everything went off perfectly.

As I look back, I realize that I probably owe the comparative ease with which I shot my first show to my dyslexia.

When Moffett returned, he was justifiably miffed.

Bob Precht, the producer, realized that John had worked hard for the director's job, and it was only by chance, directing another show for the Sullivan Company, that he had missed the opportunity so, in his wisdom, Precht divided the shows: three for John, two for me.

I'm sure that Precht didn't mind having a backup director just in case.

I was happy; I don't know about John.

And that's the way it went until the show closed in 1971.

• • •

Every time I directed a show, Mimi sat in the audience in the section where the celebrities would be photographed taking their bows. She loved it. The ushers all knew her and treated her like royalty.

After the show, she joined us at the China Song for food, drinks and general revelry. She added some class.

• • •

If you were working on *The Ed Sullivan Show*, it was easy to become blasé and forget what it meant to some performers to appear on that stage.

I remember a moment in 1969 when Janis Joplin was a guest on one of my shows.

One might have thought that, to a rock-and-roll superstar, a spot on *The Ed Sullivan Show* would be just another gig.

But with her, it was not the case.

She wanted to see where she would perform, so we went to the Ed Sullivan Theater on 53rd and Broadway and walked out onto the empty stage.

As a young person, in rural Texas, she must have seen *The Ed Sullivan Show* often. It would have seemed as distant as the moon. Yet here she was.

She stood there for a few moments in silence.

I heard her say, almost to herself: *"The Ed* fucking *Sullivan Show."*

Two years later she was dead.

• • •

I directed about a third of the *Sullivan* shows from Christmas 1968 to the time it was ripped untimely from the air in March of 1971.

The show had been on the air for twenty-three years and we all hoped CBS would let the show run so Ed could celebrate his 25th anniversary.

It didn't.

I knew Ed hardly at all. He never came to the production offices. He did attend the dress rehearsal on Sunday. Then he and Bob Precht would go to Ed's dressing room. There they would re-route the show to make it stronger and change what they felt hadn't played well.

The dress rehearsal would end about 7:00 p.m. The show was going to hit the air, "Live from New York!" at 8:00 p.m. – no messing around with that; and 8:00 p.m. came at precisely 8:00 p.m. but, until we got the new rundown, we had to sit and wait to find out what had changed.

At about 7:30 p.m. the new rundown would be handed out and we would hear: "The show's going to open with the Marine Band, and the rock group is moved to number six. Shirley Bassey isn't going to sing anything she rehearsed: she's going to do something from her new album. We've killed the tape of the juggler, and moved the scenes from *Mame* into that spot," and so on.

The changes involved restacking the scenery, getting dance costumes re-sequenced, changing complicated lighting cues, and rehearsing new music while the director took the lyric sheet and marked the shots on the fly.

It was hectic, and to someone who didn't know how efficient the staff was, it would seem that we couldn't possibly get everything organized in time.

Yet, every week, a minute or two before 8:00 p.m., sometimes a second or two before 8:00 p.m., we'd slide into our chairs and the show would go on.

And there was almost never a hitch.

Shortly before 9:00 p.m. Ed would wave to the audience and bid them good night, tell them to drive carefully.

As the credits rolled, and the network took us off, those of us in the control room felt that once again, we had beaten an avalanche down the hill.

Five minutes later Mimi and the rest of us would all be seated around a table in the China Song, munching the olive from our first martini.

• • •

Nowadays there are very few live shows on the air. When I first started in 1957, everything was live.

There were many live dramatic shows: *Playhouse 90, The United States Steel Hour, The Armstrong Circle Theater*, to name a few that were on CBS.

They all were live, and sometimes it was chancy.

I remember one show in particular; a dramatization of an event that occurred in the Second World War. A submarine sailor had developed appendicitis. He needed immediate surgery, but the submerged sub was under depth-charge attack.

The Pharmacist's Mate was on the radio with the Fleet Surgeon, who was going to talk the mate through the procedure. But the mate was terrified. He had never done anything like this before; he might kill his buddy.

The sound-effect depth charges were booming; the lights were blinking off and on. The set was on rockers and the stagehands were shaking it back and forth to beat the band.

The actors were holding on for dear life.

"Well, son," crackled the Fleet Surgeon's voice through the loudspeaker, "Are you going to proceed?"

Extreme close up of the Pharmacist's Mate: Indecision, indecision, indecision.

Fade to commercial. Sub stops rocking. Makeup artists run onto the set. Artificial sweat is applied to all. Hair is mussed. Tee shirts are sprayed with water. Artificial fog is sprayed into the air.

Everything looks ready as the AD counts 5-4-3-2-1.

The director: "Fade up one, and cue them."

There they stand, four men around the makeshift table on which lies the sailor who is near death.

Boom! Flicker, flicker. The sub is rocking, as the Mate makes the decision on which hangs the fate of his buddy.

He holds out his hand toward his assistant.

"Hypodeemic nerdle."

It was eight minutes to the next commercial.

● ● ●

My stint on *The Ed Sullivan Show* lasted for nearly three years.

Then I was hired then by some friends I knew at CBS to direct a new show being produced by an organization that was then called *The Children's Television Workshop.*

The show was *The Electric Company*; I directed the first season.

The real joy of that hectic year was working with Morgan Freeman.

He was (and I suspect still is) a consummate professional, always prepared, always giving it 110 percent and generally a joy to have around.

Years later when he was on Broadway in *Driving Miss Daisy*, I went backstage to congratulate him. He was the same ebullient fellow, happy to see me and full of expectations for his future. I was so happy for him that I started crying.

When I get emotional I cry; probably not as much as John Boehner, but I do cry.

After that first season of *The Electric Company*, I was fired over the telephone by the same friends who hired me.

The reason was never satisfactorily explained, but it certainly wasn't because my work was not up to snuff.

It took me a long time to get over that trauma.

I was without a steady job for three years, and it was a hard time for Mimi and me. We had just bought a small summer house in East Hampton; the mortgage on that and the rent on our apartment plus living expenses added up quickly. It wasn't long before I was borrowing from my brothers and the few friends I had made at work.

Mimi was sensational during that time, she had faith in me, and even though I was desperate, her support along with Erlo's got me through.

I freelanced for three years.

"Freelance" means that I was unemployed most of the time.

I tried to find work by keeping in touch with show business contacts but, as the saying goes: "A friend in need is a pain in the ass."

Eventually I got a job as AD on the game show *Jeopardy*, which was shooting in New York then. It was enough to keep the wolf from banging the door down, but I could always hear him sniffing around outside.

• • •

In 1975 I got the opportunity to direct a new game show: *Spin-Off*. It was a big chance for me because I had been "at liberty" for some time and those folks at Chase Manhattan wanted the check coming in every month.

By then I had borrowed pretty much all I could and I was nearly tapped out. So it was with high hopes that I embarked on this project.

Game shows are popular with production companies because they are cheap to produce. The expenses are essentially, the set, talent, prize money, the production staff and studio time. The format is always the same, so rehearsal time is minimal.

To make the production as inexpensive as possible, many game shows can record a month's worth of shows in a week, cutting down on studio time.

Shows are recorded at a pace of four or five a day; the way they do that is to record two shows in the morning and two or three in the afternoon. That way they produce twenty shows in four or five days.

A successful game show sells a lot of commercials, which is money in the bank for the network that airs it and the production company that owns it.

Unfortunately, *Spin-Off* turned out to be a big letdown. CBS pulled the plug just a few months after the premier, and *Spin-Off* spun off into oblivion.

Ah, well.

The show's producer was a sweet man named Willie Stein, and during the short lifespan of the show we shared several flights from NYC to LA.

Willie was quite short and, whenever he could, he would book the seats in the front of the section. I would be seated with my legs cramped while Willie had his feet resting comfortably against the bulkhead.

Willie had been involved with TV game shows for a long time and he liked to reminisce.

Here's a story he told me about the old times, and I don't think he was making it up.

It was in the mid-1950s when Willie was working at WNBC-TV in New York. He had a colleague who went by the professional name of Bob Stewart. His original handle was Isadore Steinberg.

One Friday the station manager called the staff together and asked them to come up with ideas for game shows over the weekend.

I tell you now that Mr. Stewart née Steinberg turned out to be an extremely prolific game show creator/producer. He went on to create *To Tell the Truth*, *Password* and the *$10,000 Pyramid* among others. With that resume in his future, you might guess that he came up with something.

You would be right.

The scene is now the staff meeting. Willie, Bob and others are gathered in the Manager's office.

"Anybody come up with anything?"

Bob Stewart raises his hand.

"Whacha got, Bob?"

"Without going over, tell me how much you think that lamp on your desk cost?"

A momentary pause.

"Who gives a fuck?"

Stewart took the idea to Goodson-Todman Productions.

The Price is Right has been on TV, in one permutation or another, for over fifty years, making a lot of money for a lot of people.

● ● ●

Not long after my disappointing experience with *Spin-Off*, I got a call from a friend who was an associate producer on *Search for Tomorrow*. "Would you like to take a shot at directing a soap?"

I wasn't in a position to be choosy or coy. And even though I had never directed a dramatic show before, I had stage-managed and AD'd plenty of them during my years at CBS, so it wasn't a terribly long reach for me.

I told him that I'd give it a try.

Then, when I showed up at the studio, I realized that I had worked previously on the show as a Stage Manager and the cast remembered me. They were extremely helpful in making my debut a success.

At first I thought directing a soap was a step down. It wasn't long before I came to realize just how hard it is.

I was directing *Search for Tomorrow*; three half-hour shows one week, two the next.

There was a lot of preparation.

I had to create the shooting script from floor plans, so there was a lot of staging that had to be done in my mind.

I had no idea that it was my dyslexia that allowed me to accomplish that with comparative ease.

There were six or more sets in each show and, because the shows were live, the three cameras had to be organized so, as one scene ended, a camera had to have been released early to be in position to start the next scene in a different set.

Tricky; it took careful planning. The camera cables had to be laid out so there were no tangles. If a performer was pregnant, I had to take that into account. Most of the time, the writers would help by create a scene in a restaurant so the actress could be seated.

If she made an entrance, she carried a large handbag in both hands, covering her baby bump. As the months passed, she carried a larger handbag, and the shots of her got closer and closer. Until, at last, she decamped to Buffalo to visit Aunt Martha, or some other convenient relative in some other inaccessible place.

There was one actor I worked with who demanded that he be shot only from the left. I would sit him on the right side of the set and he had the uncanny ability to cross the whole set, pour himself a cup of coffee and return to his original seat without once showing his right profile.

My job was to stage and shoot the show in such a way as to get the most out of the material in the time provided.

The real pressure came from the clock. Tick-tock; it marches on.

A typical day would begin at 7:00 a.m. with a "dry" rehearsal in a hall away from the actual shooting stage because, at that time, the stagehands would be finishing the setup and the sets were being roughly lit.

A few chairs and a table or two would represent a particular set.

This sufficed to allow the actors to learn their staging; get their rises and crosses; when they'd pour the coffee, or make a drink.

Tick-tock.

Actors in the first group of scenes would assemble in the rehearsal room.

Most of them had been in make up or hair since 6:00 or 6:30 a.m.

I would talk to the actors and explain the staging.

As the actors rehearsed their parts, I would move into the place where the camera was going to be during each particular speech, so that the actor could adjust his or her performance accordingly.

Sometimes there would be questions, but not often.

All the actors were supposed to have learned their lines. For the most part they knew them, but there were both Broadway and Hollywood veterans who suffered terribly trying to learn speeches; especially if they were having a heavy week.

They developed a healthy respect for the ability of "soap" actors.

Most of the actors had been on the show for a while, and the principal players for decades.

You did not have to explain their character to them. They *were* the character.

We'd run a scene and the Production Assistant would time it.

We would rehearse all the scenes in the Doctor's Office; then all the scenes in the Bus Station, and so on, until we had finished "dry" rehearsing the show.

By then we had a pretty good idea if the show was running long or short, and whether we could make up the difference by having the actors stretch the scenes, or if we had to cut, or if we needed new material to fill the required time.

Actors would rush to finish makeup, hair and wardrobe. Most of them spent what time they shared in make-up or whenever they could get together "running" their lines again and again, so that when the Stage Manager called them they were usually spot-on.

Tick-tock.

I'd hurry to the studio to work with the Stage Manager and the stagehands, setting the furniture and inspecting all the props so that everything would be in place for the camera rehearsal which would begin in a few minutes.

Tick-tock.

The first camera rehearsal was "camera blocking." This was a fast walk-through, without the cast, to show the cameras and booms what their positions were, where the actors moved and which cameras broke to which sets. It gave the techs a chance to know what to expect.

Then the run-through would begin. The whole cast had to be on stage and the show was rehearsed in sequence. Any residual problems that arose were solved then.

The lighting director set his levels; sound effects and music checked their cues.

Tick-tock.

After the run-through, the producer and I would get together; then I'd go out on the set and deliver the notes to the performers.

There'd be a fifteen-minute break and we'd do a non-stop dress rehearsal.

Tick-tock.

Half hour break; then we'd roll tape and do a "live" show. We seldom needed to do any repair work. During the whole procedure, I would try to keep the atmosphere light and positive. My motto, if I had had one, would have been: "You don't have to be grim to be serious."

The studio days usually went smoothly.

• • •

In 1984 – it must have been – I left *Search* and went over to *As the World Turns.*

ATWT was an hour show produced by Mary-Ellis Bunim. I had worked for her on *Search* and she liked how I handled things.

Even though *World* was an hour show, the day went pretty much as it had for a half-hour show, except the day was a little longer and all the scenes that took place in each set were recorded at the same time, to be edited together later.

Weddings and parties were major events.

Organizing forty or more principals and extras was something I was good at, and the cast was happy when I was directing.

Most of these large-cast moments were at the peak of the story line, like the wedding of the two star-crossed lovers who had been yearning to tie the knot for many, many episodes.

The day finally arrives; everybody is there; all the contract players and plenty of extras.

Makeup calls were early; wardrobe calls were early. There was lots of set decoration; swags of flowers were draped wherever there was space; urns were filled to capacity with sprays of white.

The music starts.

Trench Tangler and his best man enter from the back of the church. Everyone looks up the aisle to catch the entrance of Trilby, looking radiant, accompanied by her father.

Close-up of the groom; close-up of the bride; close-up of grandma dabbing her eyes; close-up of a mysterious figure entering from the back.

Wait a minute; a mysterious figure? Who is it???

You may not know who it is, but if you've watched soaps for any length of time, you know it's trouble.

Everything seems to be chugging along smoothly until the moment when the parson asks that question.

The one that goes: "If there is anyone present who knows a reason why this wedding should not proceed let him speak now or forever hold his peace."

The mysterious figure springs to her feet and proclaims, "This wedding cannot go on! Trench Tangler is already married. He is my husband!"

Trench is flabbergasted. "I am not married! My wife was eaten by an alligator five years ago."

"It wasn't an alligator, it was a crocodile; and I wasn't eaten, I was saved by nuns who nursed me back to health and cured me of my amnesia." Ripping off her wig, dark glasses, false nose and prosthetic ears, she reveals herself to be Dagmar who was written out five years ago, but who has been rehired on a two-year contract to cause trouble between Trench and Trilby.

Many astonished gasps – folks turning to one another, "How could—?" "I thought she— . . ."

Plenty of close-ups; Trench, Trilby, Dagmar, Grandma, Trilby, Trench, Trilby . . .

Slow fade to black and sell some soap.

Close-ups and reaction shots were the bread and butter of Daytime; still are.

You can shoot all the action wide, but when that moment comes just before you fade out, the audience wants to see close-ups of Dagmar Triumphant; Trench Bewildered; Trilby Crushed; Grandma wondering what happened to her hearing aids.

I was a Stage Manager on *As the World Turns* in the late '50s. Close-ups at the end of scenes were obligatory then too.

William Redfield was a regular on the show. He was a fine Broadway actor as well as a soap star, and he had a particularly inscrutable expression whenever he got the last close-up.

It conveyed a mixture of things; "You'll never know." "You wouldn't dare." "I haven't the heart to tell you." Maybe all of the above.

I was curious about what technique he was using in order to come up with such an enigmatic expression.

But actors are sometimes reticent about giving away their "fix."

Finally I got up the courage. "What do you use to get that look, Billy?"

"I'm trying to remember if I turned the oven off when I left the apartment."

• • •

At that time the producer of *As the World Turns* was Ted Corday. He went on to create the NBC soap *Days of Our Lives.*

He may have been the life of the party at home, but in the studio it was strictly business.

Ted would watch the dress rehearsals from a room upstairs and then come down to the control room to give his notes.

Tim Kiley was one of the directors and he liked to have a little fun now and then.

On one particular day, the opening scene was in an ICU. During dress rehearsal, Tim had rigged up something he thought would give Ted a laugh.

The camera faded up on a close-up of a blood transfusion bag hanging from an IV stand. Slowly the camera tilted down following the red fluid in the vinyl tube. Then it panned over to where the tube entered the patient's arm. The camera then tilted up to the face of the actor. You could see a thin trickle of blood running down his chin. The camera pulled back to reveal a nurse standing next to the bed.

The actor spoke.

"I guess I'm just not hungry."

Everyone in the control room thought it was hysterical.

When Ted came down to give notes, he didn't even mention it.

• • •

No woman ever had an easy pregnancy on a soap.

Babies were hardly ever born in a hospital. It was not unusual for them to come into the world after a plane crash high on a mountain in the middle of a blizzard. "Oh, my God, here comes an avalanche!"

Nobody just had a nose cold. "I haven't been feeling well lately. I should have seen ol' Doc Crumbly a month ago."

Uh-oh.

You knew it was going to end up in the ICU or the operating room sooner or later.

Soaps did a lot of research on rare diseases; they had file cabinets full of them; always ready when they needed something really exotic.

Most of the diseases that characters came down with had been chronicled only once or twice in the entire annals of medicine.

There was only one doctor who had ever performed a successful double trasnsfabulomectomy, and he was in Uzbekistan. It was a million to one chance that he could make it in time.

The patient was on the operating table.

Dr. Zbrskenskovic was on his way from the airport, but there was an accident and the good doctor was now in a full body cast at the hospital across town.

No help there.

Ol' Doc Crumbly would have to perform the surgery.

He hasn't had a scalpel in his hand for years, but he was the only one available because by now there was a hurricane raging outside and everything in town had ground to a halt.

OK, I'm going a bit overboard, but I'm really not too far off.

We actually had top surgeons, anesthesiologists and OR nurses as extras advising us on proper procedures. Those who knew told us that we simulated the OR scenes pretty well.

Soap opera was a close-up medium and I used to do a lot of low-angle close-ups, shooting up with the surgeon's hands just out of sight. It looked pretty good.

Back to the OR . . .

The beep of the heart monitor is steady . . . beep . . . . beep . . . . . beep.

But things in the OR never went smoothly.

Close-ups of the doctors looking grim behind their surgical masks; glances back and forth.

Suddenly Ol' Doc draws in a sharp breath.

"I don't like this," he mutters through his surgical mask as his hands move just out of sight under the camera lens.

The anesthesiologist begins to make warning comments about the blood pressure, pulse and heart rate.

The beeps get faster until . . .

Beeeeeeeeeeeeeeeeeeeeeeeee . . . .

He's flatlining!

Oh, no.

Close-up, close-up, close-up.

Slow fade to black and sell some soap. After all, that's why we're here.

One time, after dress rehearsal, the producer didn't think that the fade-out was dramatic enough. She wanted the station nurse to call a "code blue" (the signal that there was an emergency and that the crash cart was needed).

So we arranged a microphone for a nurse and had her stand by.

As the patient was flatlining – Beeeeeeeeeeeeeee . . . I cued her.

Strong and clear she called out, "Codah Burrou, Codah Burrou!"

We'd neglected to take into account that the actress playing the nurse was Japanese.

If the patient on the table was Trench Tangler, you didn't need to worry too much, because you knew he was a contract player and he wasn't going to be written out.

A common plot embellishment to a scenario like this was that Trench would end up in a coma for a couple of weeks.

"Now, it's up to him and his will to live."

This allowed Trilby the opportunity to play plenty of tearful scenes sitting by Trench's pale unconscious figure, begging him to come back to her; and having flashbacks about all the wonderful times they had shared.

Contract players like Trench looked forward to being written into a coma.

They didn't have to learn any lines, they were excused from rehearsal, they just had to lie there with a cannula in their nose, and get paid.

● ● ●

There are certain moments in soaps that telegraph a whole new story line.

Right after a wedding is when you are sure to hear something like this.

The happy couple is embracing and the new husband looks adoringly at his wife. "Now that we're married, Sybil, you'll be able to give me the child I have always yearned for." The poor guy obviously doesn't know what transpired in the gynecologist's office a few episodes ago.

The close-up on Sybil's face tells the story.

In those days, amnesia was very big; hardly any of the characters remembered who they really were anymore.

I remember one story line when a character came down with amnesia. After several episodes, the character was discovered working as a waitress in a diner. The original actress had been replaced, so it seemed that she not only forgot who she was, she forgot what she looked like.

As it turned out, almost everybody in town was related to each other.

Birth records had been tampered with; DNA tests and blood samples had been stolen and replaced by scheming scoundrels; babies had been switched; outrageous plot twists like that.

Men had forgotten that they had had an affair years ago.

Women had put their babies up for adoption and never knew what became of them.

So that it came as no great surprise if a character would announce, "I'm not Melissa's sister, I'm really your daughter."

"Oh."

You had to be a pretty good actor to make that stuff believable.

• • •

Writing soaps was no easy matter.

Imagine the logistics involved in the invasion of Normandy.

270

Every six months or so, the head writer, the producers, the sponsors, and probably the network would get together and mess around with the head writer's long-term story line.

How much of it remained intact after the meeting depended on the head writer's clout.

Some writers of top shows simply presented the long-term as a fact, and brooked no changes.

Then the story lines were broken down into weekly chunks.

These chunks were parceled out to breakdown writers, one of whom would take the Monday portion and divide it into scenes describing which characters are in it and what happens in each one.

There were three or four scenes in each act and five acts in an episode. As I recall, there were usually over twenty scenes per show in six or more sets.

Then the breakdowns were handed over to "dialogists," who would actually write the dialogue for the performers.

They had to be able to capture the "voice" of each particular character so it sounded like something that Jethro would say.

The scripts were about forty pages long. The completed script would be sent to the head writer and producer for editing. That was the easy part.

There were fifteen or twenty contract performers. Some had guarantees that they would be used three times a week, others had guarantees of two per, or one. They had to be played or be paid; fitting their stories into a five-day segment called for ingenuity.

Because of the cost, only a certain number of sets could be changed for the next day, the writers had to adapt to which sets were going up and which were coming down.

There were always a couple of crossover sets; bars and res-taurants, where actors from different stories could bump into each other. One of the tables had to be near a door or archway where Frederica could stand, out of sight, and overhear what Tad and Gretchen were planning.

The front burner story got the lion's share of the air time, but the second story had to be kept simmering as well.

There were two or three minor stories that had to be touched on occasionally, so that they didn't get lost.

Each of the twenty or so scenes had to end with a "hook" that would peak the viewer's interest. Each act had to end with a more powerful hook, to keep the viewer wanting to see what happens after the commercial. And, at last, the final scene needed an espe-cially strong hook to make the viewer want to come back tomorrow.

All of the above had to be choreographed so that the front-burner story, or stories, peaked during the ratings sweeps half a year away.

I call that a *tour de force*.

It was hard, nerve-wracking work to put together forty-five minutes of material in eleven hours, and it took a specialized pro-fessional cast and crew to do it. For a director, it was like being shot *into* a cannon from across the arena.

Apparently we directors didn't do our job too badly because we were awarded a Daytime Emmy in 1992.

A former recipient whispered to me that if you put it in your refrigerator, it stops the milk from going sour. I've never tried it.

• • •

I was surprised at how real the shows were to some members of our audience. After an especially foreboding episode, it was not all that unusual for an agitated viewer to phone the office and plead with the secretary to warn Louisa not to go to the school board meeting, because there was a bomb under her car.

No amount of explaining would assuage the anxiety. The secretary would say simply, "I'll be sure to give her the message."

We had to do court trials every once in a while.

It was amazing how often the DA arrested the wrong suspect. Just as amazing was how often the wrong suspect had entered the house after hearing shots and picked up the gun, leaving his or her fingerprints all over it.

You knew in advance there would be a lot of reaction shots in the courtroom.

It wasn't that the trial was not important; it was that the reactions of the concerned parties were just as important.

Most of those shows ended with some sort of revelation by a witness which causes one of the actors to spring to her or his feet and shout, "That's a lie! You're trying to protect Stephanie!" Or Germaine, or Rodney, or Murray.

Then the court would erupt in gasps and shouts and counter shouts, and there would be close-ups of all the principal characters looking mystified, satisfied or stultified, while the judge would be banging his or her gavel calling out ineffectually, "Order, order, or I'll have you all exiled to the Chateau d'If."

Fade to black and sell some soap.

I may not have mentioned it, but I was fast, fast on the draw. I almost always kept to the schedule. That fact went a long way toward keeping me employed as a director in the budget-conscious world of soaps for more than twenty years.

That and my sparkling personality.

During my tenure, folks who eventually made their way to Hollywood and passed through the shows I worked on included; Kevin Bacon, Ellen Barkin, Kevin Kline, Julianne Moore, Meg Ryan and Marisa Tomei.

I directed soaps for P&G until show business and I parted ways in the fall of 1996.

Mimi and I retired to East Hampton where we raised daylilies and continued down the road toward Old Fartdom.

• • •

Mimi has a lot of love to give.

Have any of you ever heard of anybody who kisses her dentist?

Mimi kisses her dentist.

She kisses her other doctors too; she kisses her cardiologist, and she kisses her oncologist.

She kisses Ken Dodge, he's the Physician's Assistant who has been our care provider for over forty years.

She has a lot of doctors and she kisses every one of them.

They all spread their arms and smile as they enter the consultation room.

She makes their day.

And it doesn't stop with the medical profession.

Now that Mimi is in a wheelchair, she still gets hugs and kisses when we go into a restaurant.

It happens all the time.

People love seeing her; she brings a smile and a "Hi, Mimi," wherever she goes.

That's just the way she is.

CHAPTER 19

• • •

The Gorilla in the room . . .

As I'VE BEEN writing this I have come to realize that there has been a 300-pound primate sitting quietly in the corner, and when you reach my age you can't ignore its presence.

Many health problems beset older folks.

But one deserves particular attention: failing memory.

Failing memory can lead to what used to be called senility.

What used to be called senility is now referred to as dementia.

I don't know why, but to me the word "dementia" sounds more ominous than "senility."

Dementia, in itself, is not a specific disease, but rather a broad category of brain diseases that affect a person's ability to think clearly.

Alzheimer's disease (ALZ) is a specific type of dementia that affects your ability to function normally.

Once the symptoms are discovered, ALZ can last anywhere from six or seven years up to twenty; it is always fatal, and currently there is no way to cure it, or slow it down.

One in eight Americans over sixty-five develops ALZ or other dementias.

I was stunned to learn that nearly half the people over eighty-five have it, and two-thirds of them are women.

Women, too, do most of the caring for ALZ sufferers; there are more than twice as many women as men acting as 24/7 caregivers.

As the baby boomers continue to age, the number of those afflicted will continue to rise, and one can only hope that some way to ameliorate this terrible disease will be found.

I am happy to say that I am not an expert on ALZ and you can find all you want to know, maybe a whole lot more than you want to know, by contacting the Alzheimer's Association on the Internet.

There is a condition called Mild Cognitive Impairment (MCI), in which changes in your mental abilities (particularly memory) are generally greater than what is expected at your age, but these changes do not seriously affect your ability to function normally and do not qualify as dementia.

MCI can be thought of as a condition that falls between normal forgetfulness due to age and dementia.

The progression from MCI to dementia is not inevitable; some people remain stable over time and a few actually improve and cease to show symptoms.

Mimi was diagnosed with mild MCI about ten years ago in 2005.

Her memory lapses were noticeable and she often repeated the same question even though I had answered it a few moments before.

This hasn't changed much in the past decade, and she certainly has not descended into the pit of dementia, which can be the result of MCI.

This is where something called "cognitive reserve" comes in.

A high cognitive reserve is a rather nebulous concept that describes the ability of your brain to function at a close to normal level even though it may have suffered damage.

Someone with poor cognitive reserve may not handle the same amount of brain damage as effectively.

Mimi apparently has a good cognitive reserve.

She is not the same woman who taught me to ski in the Austrian Alps.

I'm not the same man she taught, either.

It never rains . . .

Mimi's condition was stable until November, 2013, when things changed.

The circumstances take some explaining and have to do with being old and falling down, and hospitals and heart attacks and Percocet and doctors and time and painful uncertainty and ultimate healing.

I wouldn't even bring it up except it's a good example of what can happen to someone our age.

Everything was fine, until a Friday afternoon in the middle of November in 2013.

Mimi was transferring herself from an easy chair back to her wheelchair when she fell to the floor. She had made this transfer many times previously without a problem.

I know I shouldn't have moved her, but I couldn't just let her sit there, so I struggled her back into the chair.

I was eighty-two; I could do only so much, and if there was something really wrong, I had not the slightest way of helping the situation. I hadn't liked the position of her leg, and when she complained of pain in her hip, I made a decision I hated. The quicker she got to the hospital the better.

Overriding her screams not to, I dialed 911.

I remember the helpless feeling of despair a half hour later, seeing Mimi strapped to a gurney. I remember the kiss goodbye, and I remember watching her being rolled down the driveway into the ambulance.

I went back into the house to make sure everything was closed down and locked up, because I knew it was going to be a long night at the hospital.

It was the beginning of a three-month trial.

I arrived up at the ER in Southampton hospital about fifteen minutes after Mimi. The X-rays came back, showing that she had fractured the neck of her right femur (thigh bone).

The neck of the femur is a thin bridge of bone that connects the head (the round ball at the top) to the main shaft of the thigh bone.

I had done some research on older folks and broken hips; I knew the statistics; I was heartbroken.

By now Mimi was in extreme pain and they administered what I guess was Percocet or another heavy narcotic.

I told them that Mimi reacts badly to heavy narcotics.

Sometime before, she had been hospitalized with a broken collarbone and pancreatitis, and Percocet had really sent her off to Mars.

But here we were, and they had done what they did.

As it turned out, an orthopedic surgeon was making his rounds and, after looking at the X-rays, he said that the next day – Saturday – he would pin the hip.

This is a procedure where the two parts are screwed together and, if everything works out, it should heal back into one piece.

I felt a little better: things were getting somewhat under control.

However, that surgery was never performed.

A normal blood sodium level is 135–145. On Saturday, Mimi's blood tests showed that her sodium level was 120.

Surgery under total anesthetic with such a low sodium level is very dangerous and can lead to brain damage or be fatal. The anesthesiologist refused to participate until her level got up to at least 130.

Raising the sodium level takes time. You can't just give an injection of salt water to ramp it up. They were giving Mimi an IV of a sodium solution that was as potent as they dared.

On Sunday her level was still 120.

Meanwhile, she was in terrible pain and her speech was slurred. The doctors were afraid she had suffered a stroke.

I told them that that was how she reacts to narcotics, and they scaled back the potency until she was on a light regimen of morphine.

She brightened up a bit, but the pain was still awful. Whenever they had to move her, the screams were terrible to hear. I had to leave the room.

By this time I was told that the pinning option was off the table.

Here we were, waiting for the sodium level to rise; it's Monday morning, three days after she fell, and the level is still 120.

A nephrologist was called in and determined that Mimi was severely dehydrated. That was what was causing her low sodium.

I don't know how she became dehydrated. She drank as much liquid as she ever did. Her gall bladder had been removed two-and-a-half months earlier, and her sodium must have been OK or they would not have performed the operation.

How her sodium got that low never was determined.

I was walking around in circles; I hadn't slept much. The empty bed next to me left an empty feeling inside of me.

Mimi was semi-communicative and I was happy when she was asleep.

At around 3:00 on Monday afternoon, an EKG was taken.

A cardiologist said that this EKG didn't match the one they took when Mimi entered the hospital. There had been a rise in the level of some enzyme, and he thought that she might have had a heart attack.

At this point surgery of any kind was out of the question until they found out what was going on, and it might be out of the question after they found out, as well.

They wanted my permission to move her to Stony Brook Hospital, for an emergency angiogram.

Stony Brook is fifty miles farther on.

What do you do; what do you say?

"If you think that's what should be done, of course I agree."

By the time the ambulance crew got there, all the paperwork was completed and they were ready to take her, it was 7:00 p.m. or so. The driver wanted to know it I was going to follow them in my car.

Someone told me once that in a situation like that you must "save yourself first." That makes sense because if you don't take care of yourself you're in no condition to take care of anybody else. It's November, it's dark, I don't like driving at night and I don't know the way, so I have to let Mimi go alone.

I felt guilty as hell kissing her goodbye for the second time in four days, but, I'm not even sure, that with the sedation, she understood what was going on.

I drove the sixteen miles home from Southampton.

At about that time I came up with a new "Old Saying" – "Things are never as bad as they seem – they're worse."

I had a drink and tried to get some sleep.

The next morning I called Stony Brook, and learn that Mimi was in the Cardiac Acute Care Unit.

It's not the place I hoped she'd be.

I drove the sixty-five miles to Stony Brook. They direct me to where Mimi is.

The chain of events becomes a little vague at this point, but they told me, much to my relief, that the angiogram detected nothing wrong with Mimi's heart, and, as far as the doctor who performed it is concerned, she is OK for surgery.

The nurse in charge gave me a thumbs-up.

Mimi's sodium is now 122; they've moved her to the ICU.

You should know that at Southampton, at Stony Brook, and at the Westhampton Care Center, the staffs were professional, compassionate, helpful and forthcoming.

No complaints from me.

I made the 130-mile round trip to Stony Brook every day, arriving at about 10:30 a.m. and leaving by 4:00 in the afternoon so as not to drive too far in the dark.

I believe that my being on the scene for four or five hours a day was helpful to everybody. I kept a low profile and mostly sat beside Mimi's bed.

I handed her tissues when she needed then, I gave her water when it was allowed, I told the nurse when I knew she needed to be changed, and I told the nurse if her IV stopped.

I gave her a lot of kisses and I held her hand and I tried to make jokes.

The staff, seeing me so attentive to Mimi, was appreciative of our relationship.

Mimi was still in terrible pain, and when they had to change her, her screams were terrible.

An oncological orthopedic surgeon had been assigned to her case. One of his assistants sat me down and explained the situation.

X-rays had shown that Mimi's femur was not only broken, but it was very weak – and looked as if it might be cancerous.

The surgery would require an especially long prosthesis to support the femur and that, in itself, presented an added risk.

Mimi was weak and getting weaker; the longer it took to get the sodium up to the required level the more delicate the situation would become.

I thanked him for taking the time to let me know how things stood, but I was devastated. This was the first time cancer had come into the picture. It was awful news.

By Tuesday her sodium had reached 125. They were preparing her for surgery. She was still on an IV and she couldn't have any water.

She was miserable. I was miserable too.

Wednesday came and the sodium was getting up to where it should be. When I left that day, I expected to get a call at home that they were doing the operation.

The call didn't come. Thursday; I was sure that they would operate. They didn't; the surgeon was unavailable. By Friday, I was going bananas.

Everything seemed to be ready; Mimi was 84; she had been sedated, but she was in pain and she had been on intravenous feeding for a week.

Her sodium was fine. What was the problem?

I left the hospital and got home at 6:00 p.m. or so.

The phone rang.

It was the surgeon.

He was very professional; this is how I remember what he said.

"Mr. Schwarz, we are readying your wife for surgery. I want to operate because I believe not to operate would be worse."

I knew what he meant.

I had learned that letting the bone try to heal on its own is a lengthy and agonizing alternative. It means months of immobilization, terrific pain, a lot more sedation, and a good chance of blood clots, infection and pneumonia.

After all that suffering, the chances of a bad outcome are quite high.

I would not put Mimi through that.

The surgeon continued: "Your wife is quite ill and the surgery is risky. We believe she has suffered a heart attack and possibly a stroke. She has a pacemaker and other heart problems. She has had two previous cancers and, after looking at the X-rays I believe she may have cancer in that femur."

"I understand."

Then the anesthesiologist got on the phone.

She told me that Mimi was having difficulty breathing and if, after the surgery, she was unable to breathe on her own and if she (the anesthesiologist) was unable to remove the breathing tube, it could present a severe complication that we would have to discuss at that time.

"OK."

Doctor got back on the phone.

I asked, "If this thing goes well, will we still have some time together?"

"Yes."

"On your famous hospital scale 'from one to ten' how would you rate Mimi's chances?

Pause—"Six."

"Well, do your best, Doctor."

"We will. I'll let you know."

I went to a neighbor's house for dinner; it was a solemn affair, I can tell you.

I was home when around 11:00 p.m. the phone rang.

"Everything went perfectly. The hip socket is in good condition, so I only had to replace the head of the femur. The prosthesis is in place, and, as far as I'm concerned, she can stand on that leg now. She had a lot of hurdles to get over and she still has some to go, but she did very well."

Then the anesthesiologist.

"She is breathing on her own. She's a very strong woman."

I tried to say "Thank you," but I don't know if the words come out.

"Don't thank me; she's the one who did all the work."

I finally recovered enough to say, "I guess I'll stay away tomorrow and let her come out of it."

"She called for you. I think it would help if you came by."

"I'll be there."

That was November 22nd. Two months later, on January 20th, after fourteen days in the hospital and almost two months in rehab, Mimi came home.

In the meantime I learned, much to my relief and delight, that the biopsy specimen from Mimi's femur turned out to be negative; no cancer. Osteoporosis, but no cancer.

She was still not the person she used to be; not as bright, confined to a wheelchair, not as communicative, but she was home.

By the middle of April Mimi had improved greatly; she took her walker to her desk and finished writing the checks to the US Treasury for our income tax. Very much like the old Mimi; not exactly, but close.

This episode taught me a few things. In no particular order:

I learned that when someone is seriously ill in a hospital, it is important, if at all possible, that someone who knows the patient be nearby.

Every day, I would answer questions put to me by a specialist, therapist, technician, or any number of medical personnel who wanted to know about Mimi's eating habits, her speech quality, her memory, how she walked or what she drank.

I think that my being with her every day was helpful in Mimi's recovery. It is comforting and supportive to have a loved one hold your hand and give you a kiss now and then.

When a hospital releases you, after a trial like the one Mimi went through, you are still far from normal. It takes a long time to recover from a serious illness; especially when you are in your eighties.

When Mimi started rehab in December, she was still slurring her speech. She could not stand without the help of two attendants, and she seemed to be far away. But slowly, slowly she improved.

She came home in the middle of December, mostly wheelchair-bound and frail. It is now April and she buzzes around with her walker; she eats better; she wrote the income tax checks; and she laughs at my jokes – some of them.

I expect her to keep improving for some time.

● ● ●

In May of 2014, I wrote about Mimi's fall the previous November that had fractured her femur.

I wrote that she was getting better and had recovered some of the ground she lost in her ordeal.

In June Mimi had another small stroke.

It was a setback, there's no denying it.

She became a lot weaker, and her left leg still won't do what she wants it to do, so she can't get around on her walker; she has to use the wheelchair.

Her mind is still working all right, but her speech is slurred, and it takes her a little time to form her words.

Our neurologist tells us that coming back gets more difficult each time, and there's a ten percent chance she'll have another stroke within a year.

He could have said that there's a ninety percent chance she'll go through the year without another episode, but doctors don't seem to want to quote the statistics that way.

You can get sick and tired of doctors telling you the percentages that apply to your particular malady, but they do it all the time.

It's now nearing the end of July and therapy is helping somewhat.

It may seem like a small thing, but just this morning she was able to button up her blouse.

It's truly amazing how the performance of the simplest sort of everyday function can seem like a milestone.

Well, it is a milestone.

I'm hoping that Mimi will improve, but we just have to see what happens.

Sometimes I'm optimistic and sometimes . . .

There's nothing you can do except keep on keeping on.

● ● ●

It's now November, almost a full year after Mimi broke her hip, and in the past four weeks she has declined precipitously.

She speaks with such a slur that I often cannot understand her, no matter how I try.

She sleeps most of the time and her coordination is quite poor.

The fork slips from her hand; I spoon-feed her.

She can't swallow very well, so it's mostly soups and soft food that I make for her.

When we're having soup, I spoon-feed Mimi, and when I do her appetite is OK.

I am still able to transfer her from the wheelchair to the car, get her out of bed and dress her and transfer her to the lean-back chair where she spends most of the day.

There is a lot of lifting and my heart goes out to the women caregivers who do not have the upper body strength to do the wrestling.

A local home health care group, the Dominican Sisters (I don't think there are any nuns in the local chapter) sends a nurse once or twice week to monitor Mimi's vitals. He's very supportive and has given me a lot of helpful tips.

They also send a physical therapist who is working with Mimi. He is trying to help her to be able to stand up for twenty or thirty seconds so transfers and dressing her would be easier.

I have been told that the sort of descent that Mimi is going through can last for a long time.

Our neurologist calls Mimi's condition the "dwindles." That's a real medical term which describes a situation where the patient fails to thrive; sort of gives up.

It's very disheartening.

I told him that Mimi wasn't eating well and was losing weight. He offered the option of admitting her to the hospital and having her fed through a tube going through her nose down into her stomach.

It was an option I did not consider.

When Mimi had her surgeries previously, they tried feeding her through a tube and she ripped it out. I saw no point in putting her through that.

She has only a few teeth left and chewing is difficult for her; I'm now pureeing her food and hand-feeding her; she is eating a lot better.

As long as I'm around I'm not going to let anybody stick a food pipe up her nose.

A week ago, Mimi's condition took a precipitous downturn. She became even more remote; feeding her and moving her became more and more difficult until on Sunday she refused to eat or take liquids.

She was in no pain and by Monday she was completely unresponsive. I called Ken Dodge, our caregiver. He asked me if I wanted her to be taken to the hospital. I said absolutely not.

Mimi and I had discussed the possibility of such a scenario with Ken, so he knew what my answer would be. He told me to keep her comfortable.

All day Monday and Tuesday she lay on her bed not moving, in what I guess was a coma.

Sometime early Wednesday morning, I was wakened by Mimi slapping her hand on the bed next to me.

I reached for it and she held tight, squeezing. She held my hand for a few seconds and then relaxed.

I thought that she had come out of her coma, and early Wednesday morning I quietly left the darkened room to let her rest.

When I returned to see if she was awake, I realized that she had died during the night.

Later I recalled the hand squeeze.

I cry and I stop, I cry and I stop, I cry and I stop.

I'm grateful that Mimi died in her own home, in her own bed next to someone who loved her and whom she loved and trusted.

I'm especially grateful for the hand squeeze.

● ● ●

I have to tell you that my 56-year marriage to Mimi has been a good thing.

When I asked her father for her hand, he granted my request and said, "You may not always be happy, but you will never be bored." He was right.

Without her urge to travel, I would not have traveled to Europe fifteen or twenty times.

I would not have visited Venice as often as we did.

We traveled all over Europe.

We chartered a sloop for two weeks of sailing in Greece.

When I mentioned this, a jealous friend said, "You don't know how to sail a big boat."

Mimi said, "The crew does."

We visited Turkey, India, China, Japan, Cambodia and Indonesia.

Always living well.

Mimi was a wonderful homemaker, an excellent decorator and, when she was cooking, she was a great cook.

On those occasions when we had fights – and we fought – she taught me to make up quickly and not to sulk; well, not to sulk for too long.

One time after an argument Mimi confessed that I was right and she was wrong.

"But, you'll forgive me."

"Yes, my darling, because you always forgive me."

"I do," she said, "and would you like to know everything I've ever forgiven you for?"

That certainly gave me an insight into a woman's mind.

Yes, we had our ups and downs, but during our marriage Mimi has been incredibly supportive; especially during the dark days when I was broke and unemployed, and I doubted myself and everything looked black.

I don't think it's been entirely one-sided, though.

Not too long ago, out of nowhere, Mimi held her hand out to me and said, "Thank you, for giving me such a good life."

Well . . .

• • •

Two days after Mimi's death, I finished this book.

It's been a month now and I'm able to write about what happened then; it takes a little explaining. In 1986, as a keepsake from Erlo's estate, I was given a small, very primitive, carving of a duck about twelve inches long and three inches in diameter. The body is carved out of a small log. It is crudely painted in blue, green, orange and yellow; its neck and head is a carved twig stuck into the log.

In the bottom of the duck is an indentation half the size of a business card in which was a folded piece of paper. It was a sweet note from Erlo to Ann, his wife. I put the note back and placed the carving on top of a tall bookcase in the guest room. There it has rested for nearly thirty years.

I was polishing what I had just written when I was called away from my desk. On my way back, I had to pass through the guest room and I noticed something lying on the floor near the bookcase. I had just hired a new cleaning lady and she and her helper had gone through the house doing a job of cleaning and straightening up such as I had never seen before.

They dusted everywhere including the top of the ceiling fans, they organized my shoe closet; even arranged all the silverware in the drawers. They vacuumed for nearly an hour.

I'm telling you this because it seems nearly impossible to me that they would have missed something lying on the floor in the guest room.

I pass through the room myself several times a day going from my desk to the kitchen or elsewhere in the house and I had noticed nothing.

There is no way that the cat could have climbed to the top of the bookcase. She is eleven years old and can hardly make it up to my chair.

Nevertheless, there was this thing on the floor and when I reached down, I discovered it was the little branch that was the neck and head of Erlo's duck. It must have fallen off the duck from the top of the bookcase. How? You tell me.

At any rate, I reached up on tiptoe and took the duck down in order to stick the head back on. I saw the note and remembered that it was something Erlo had written, but I had completely forgotten what it was about. I took it out and read it.

"To Ann –

In Korea at great occasions this "totem" is carried as a sign of a *Happy Marriage*.

The great occasion is the Birth of my – our – book.

Love – The Husband"

Mimi and I had been married for 56 years and I had just finished writing this book.

I had to sit down.

That totem had been sitting on top of the bookcase for twenty-eight years; regardless of what caused the head to fall, it fell at that particular moment.

• • •

It's now July 8th, a little over seven months since Mimi died, and I feel obligated to tell you about something that happened just last night.

Mimi's birthday is July 8th, and last night, July 7th, I went to bed without remembering that it would be her birthday today.

To tell you the truth, I never had to remember her birthday because she would always be sure to remind me.

I had been writing checks that afternoon and the date July 7th was fresh in my mind, and as I was drowsing after midnight, I suddenly realized that it was July 8th; Mimi's birthday.

I didn't think much about it.

I don't dream of Mimi often, in fact, only a handful of times since she died. On those occasions she was just another person in what seemed to be an unexceptional dream.

Early this morning, however, this is what I dreamt.

I entered our bedroom and there was Mimi sitting on a bench across the room. She was embroidering on a light-colored fabric. She had not been able to embroider for years due to failing eyesight.

I was pleased to see that she wasn't wearing glasses, glad that her eyesight had improved so much.

I went to her and saw that she was absolutely beautiful. She was happy and pink-cheeked and looking like I remembered her before she became ill.

I wondered how she got to the bench because there was no wheelchair or walker that I could see, and I was happy because I thought that she must have regained her strength.

I held her head in my hands, kissed her on the lips and said, "You are so beautiful."

I started to leave the room, and as I turned back for a last look, she had disappeared and where she had been, was standing a tree with golden foliage.

CHAPTER 20

• • •

The days are getting shorter now . . .

SOMETIMES, IF I wake up at 3:00 or 4:00 in the morning, it's not unusual for me to begin thinking.

For some reason I think about the first snow of the year, and I wonder if climate change will make our winters milder or more severe.

I start thinking about how we're screwing up the world and wonder how the whole thing will end . . . with a bang?

Astrophysicists or cosmologists or whoever they are, say they have figured out how everything started when there was no time and no space, and everything in the universe was packed into an incredibly small package called a "singularity" which, for some unknown reason, began to enlarge, really fast; some say faster than the speed of light.

They say it wasn't an explosion because there wasn't anything for it to explode against, but . . .

Anyway, that started the clock ticking, and space to form, allowing all the pent-up energy inside that singularity to expand into all the stuff that fills the universe today.

That includes everything from galaxies to nebulae; mothballs to toilet paper.

So far, no one has offered an acceptable answer as to how this singularity got there and why it decided to do its thing when it did.

It has also been described as the "Primal Atom."

Thirty-five hundred years ago, the Hindus had a word, "bindu," which applies to an infinitely small entity described as "the point where creation begins"; "the symbol of the cosmos in its un-manifested state."

What were those guys smoking?

The scientists have also figured out how long ago this all happened.

The way they do it is to estimate the diameter of the universe, within a few billion light years; calculate how fast it is expanding within a few parsecs, factor in how quickly the rate of expansion is increasing and figure backwards.

The answer they came up with was that this happened almost fourteen billion years ago; give or take.

I have no argument with that, and if I had a pad and pencil, I could show you.

They say there is no way of knowing about anything that happened before that time, because there was no time before that time, and no space for anything to happen in.

There was nothing.

Then suddenly this – whatever it was – exploded (I don't care, I'm using "exploded"), creating space and time.

That's a very difficult concept for me to wrap my head around; and here's another one.

Did this Bang or Big Expansion just happen to happen to a primal atom that just happened to suddenly appear; or was there a Cause?

No sense beating about the bush. What I say a "Cause," I mean some sort of Intelligence.

If there was a Cause, it changes everything.

You get what I'm driving at. If there's no reason why everything, including us, exists, then what the does anything matter?"

But, if there is a reason, that is, a First Cause, that changes a lot of things.

So, was there a First Cause or wasn't there?

As Hamlet put it in a different context, "That is *the* question" – the most important question of all.

As you may imagine there has been a lot of controversy.

Astrophysicists seem content to say that the Primal Atom simply fabricated itself, or suddenly popped in from another universe.

I find these concepts impossible to imagine, but particle physicists and mathematicians are well known to imagine concepts that seem impossible to me.

I'll bet that one of these days the folks at CERN will come up with a theory about what happened to make that Primal Atom explode or enlarge as fast as or faster than the speed of light.

I predict that when they do develop a theory, probably fewer than three people in the world will understand it, and they couldn't explain it to you.

On the other side of the Primal Atom argument are the religionists who believe that the Singularity was put there by God and was set off by Him – or Her – or It.

I don't practice any religion, and I generally agree with Christopher Hitchens, and those like him, who talk about the problems with organized religions.

Yet, in spite of anything he, or they say, they can't disprove the Causing Impulse.

However, if you believe that God started all this, you have to ask: "Where did God come from?"

Where was He and what was He doing between the time He started the Big Bang almost fourteen billion years ago, and when He created the heavens and the earth four and a half billion years ago?

Somebody suggested that He was creating Hell where He was going to toss people who asked questions like that.

Seems like a joke but it's a real question.

Still, against all logic, a lot of people believe in some kind of Creative Spirit. I do.

Carl Jung, whom I admire greatly, and whose psychology and philosophy has shaped much of my adult life, was once asked if he believed in God.

He responded that he didn't "believe," he "knew."

I don't "know."

Yet, in spite of all the obstacles that present themselves to the rational mind, I find it more comfortable to accept a Deity.

But I am not one who believes that "It" sits around and keeps watch on everything and everybody, and has a big book where "It" writes down all your sins, or decides in the middle of a tornado, who will be saved and who will be blown off to OZ; or when you're dead, sits you on His knee like the Santa at Macy's and asks you what you'd like for eternity.

I do believe, though, that "It" takes a peek from time to time to make an adjustment or two, and the great historical figures who arise and change the course of history are avatars from a cadre of souls who unconsciously affect those adjustments.

We perceive their actions as good or evil but, being only human, we are hopelessly incapable of any true evaluation.

I believe in reincarnation.

Voltaire said: "It is not more surprising to be borne twice than once."

My dear spiritual father and teacher, Erlo believed he had lived several times before.

I have had dreams which I believe told me of lives I have been part of in the past.

I'm not going to tell you what they were, they're none of your business.

But the thought that parts of my soul existed in the past and parts may exist in the future as well, is comforting, even though I'm well aware of the "rational" objections.

• • •

Every once in a while, I do what I call my "Disney pull-back."

That's where I start with an image of me sitting at my desk; the camera pulls back through the roof until I imagine the house getting smaller and smaller. The pull-back continues to reveal the city, the country, the whole world; farther and farther, faster and faster until the earth recedes into the background and the solar system comes into view. The solar system resolves into the Milky Way, then into our galaxy. Other galaxies and nebulae appear until the splendor of the entire universe is revealed in its breathtaking magnificence.

And if you look closely, somewhere in the upper left hand corner, you'll see me sitting at my desk.

Fin

36217058R10176

Made in the USA
Middletown, DE
27 October 2016